T0329622

The Ordinal Society

THE
Ordinal
Society

MARION FOURCADE | KIERAN HEALY

HARVARD UNIVERSITY PRESS

Cambridge, Massachusetts

London, England

2024

Second printing

Library of Congress Cataloging-in-Publication Data
Names: Fourcade, Marion, 1968– author. | Healy, Kieran Joseph, 1973– author.
Title: The ordinal society / Marion Fourcade and Kieran Healy.
Description: Cambridge, Massachusetts ; London, England : Harvard
University Press, 2024. | Includes bibliographical references and index.
Identifiers: LCCN 2023033114 | ISBN 9780674971141 (cloth)
Subjects: LCSH: Information society. | Information technology—Moral
and ethical aspects. | Information technology—Social aspects. |
Information technology—Economic aspects. | Power (Social sciences) |
Social capital (Sociology)
Classification: LCC HM851 .F678 2024 | DDC 303.48/33—dc23/eng/20230902
LC record available at https://lccn.loc.gov/2023033114

Contents

The Ordinal Society

Introduction
Valley Fever

OVER THE PAST FIFTY YEARS, CHANGES IN THE SCOPE OF SOCIAL data collection and analysis have radically reorganized how we experience and make our lives. Much of what we do is now immediately authenticated, recorded, classified, and scored on some sort of scale. We live in an ordinal society, a society oriented toward, justified by, and governed through measurement.

How did this happen? Technology gave us the means to grasp the totality of people's lives in the form of discrete, standardized units of information.[1] It fed on an abundance of personal data emitted by ever smaller and more powerful computing devices that ended up first in the homes, then on the laps, and then in the hands of billions of people. The networked structure of the World Wide Web scaled up and amplified this process. Some of this data was exfiltrated covertly, but much of it was freely and even eagerly given out of hopefulness, convenience, or sociality. Managers and financiers became convinced of its usefulness and started to chase after it.

The increasing capacity to frame and use these data has reorganized markets, the state, and social life in general. Methods for analyzing it are by now everywhere. They streamline and automate processes of risk prediction, resource allocation, communication, and decision-making. Sometimes these methods are plausible and precise; sometimes they are opaque and even absurd. But either way, they group and stratify people in ways that are both highly individualized and flexibly differentiated according to the demands of particular settings. We cannot escape this process; in fact, we count on it. In domain after domain, it is changing the overall distribution of opportunity, the everyday experience of status, and the nature of economic competition. In its wake, our moral intuitions about merit and personal worth are changing too.

Even when the data is bad, or the analytical results are spurious, the outcome is a form of rationalized stratification. It is not that everyone is simply reduced to a faceless number. Rather, the ebb and flow of social and economic life is expressed by and managed through measurement. An ordinal society creates order through automated ranking and matching. The apparent power of its methods justifies the ostensible rightness of its hierarchies and categories. Interaction and exchange are built around a flow of personally tailored, data-driven possibilities. For people who are "well classified," the results are often quite gratifying and carry a sense that what is personally convenient is also somehow morally correct. For those who are not, the outcomes can be more punitive, but are no less moralized.

That is the social form we seek to understand in this book. To grasp the structure of an ordinal society, we must first have a sense of how it emerged, and then try to understand how its component parts work. These components have, of course, more than one source, and detailed histories of their own. Where do we start? We can get our bearings by sweeping across a familiar landscape. The arc to follow is the changing relationship between information technology and power. We begin our history at a moment when the leading edge of the computer revolution seemed as if it might be at odds with the very idea of a well-ordered and carefully measured society. We begin in the home of the 1960s counterculture.

We begin in California.

Homestead Dreams

Until the 1940s, the rolling hills of Santa Clara Valley were best known for their orchards and open fields. The most significant economic activity was canning fruit. At the northern end of the valley, Stanford University was a quiet campus still widely known as The Farm.[2] But change was in the air, quite literally. As early as the 1910s, the Bay Area had been an early hub for ham radio enthusiasts. In the 1920s, entrepreneurs like Bill Eitel, Charles Litton, and Jack McCullough began building vacuum tubes and other components to serve this community. For a time they existed quietly in the long shadow of East Coast giants like General Electric and RCA. The outbreak of the World War II brought a surge in demand for their products from the larger manufacturers, and the attack on Pearl Harbor transformed the importance of their proximity to the Pacific coast.[3] After the war, these tendencies were accelerated by the great surge of US military spending that accompanied the beginning of the Cold War. With science as "the endless frontier,"[4] hard cash from the US Department of Defense started pouring into universities, eventually reaching the West Coast. In 1951 the Stanford Industrial Park opened its doors, encouraging students and faculty to launch businesses. Hewlett-Packard, founded by two Stanford electrical engineering students in the late 1930s, blossomed into a local powerhouse and the darling firm of the era. More established players such as IBM and Lockheed soon followed. They, too, were eager to secure their own slice of the new federal contracts and to capitalize on the local concentration of brainpower. Encouraged by government subsidies, private capital also started to take notice and developed a new form of financing specifically oriented to meet the needs of a high-tech, high-risk sector.

Digital computing was a new and rapidly expanding enterprise. Although born in World War II and raised to adolescence within the military-industrial complex, the culture of computer science in the 1960s was not entirely one of pure secrecy, high seriousness, and Cold War paranoia. To the contrary, it was shot through with thick streaks of both libertarian individualism and communal cooperation. Engineers valued a somewhat cranky form of independence within a context of freely circulating knowledge and a hobbyist ethos of practical tinkering. Perhaps these practices were a cultural sublimation of the "closed world," command-and-control political vision that dominated the era.[5] Perhaps they were responding to the long shadow cast by the earliest computer geeks, working mostly unbothered as "blue sky" researchers with a commitment to the sharing of methods, tricks, and fixes—an approach that later came to be known as a hacker ethic.[6] Or perhaps it was simply a convenient story that allowed each generation of entrepreneurs, especially the very young homebrew startups of the 1970s, to reclaim credit for themselves alone and draw a discreet veil over their sector's deep history of government sponsorship and military applications. It may even have been something of an accident. It took quite a long time for researchers and engineers to fully grasp the distinction between software and hardware, and thus to see the vital importance of software as a thing in itself, over and above the physical computer it was written to run on.[7]

Whatever the reason, as the era of "big iron" in computing gave way to smaller and more personal machines, an influential subset became increasingly vocal about the politics of software and its use. Engineers and programmers tinkered with and extended the operating systems that were licensed to run on their corporate and university mainframes. By the 1980s this tendency had produced a nascent ecology of shared tools. It also gelled into a self-conscious movement committed to the idea that software should be free. Richard Stallman, then at the Massachusetts Institute of Technology, published a license, the GNU General Public License (commonly known as GPL), that permitted the authors of code to distribute their work freely and without any warranty while it also forbade any subsequent proprietary modifications. The practical goal of the Free Software Foundation was to develop a complete alternative to the Unix operating system. The organization wanted software shorn of the burdens of intellectual property, something that could not be reincorporated into any subsequently copyrighted piece of code.

In the end, the free software movement did not succeed in liberating computing from the shackles of copyright. It became somewhat bogged down by internal disagreements about the relative purity of purpose that would be required for the revolution to succeed. Stallman's particular vision was also complemented, or outflanked, by related projects released under less constraining licenses. (These included BSD Unix, which still underpins Apple's operating systems, and the hugely successful Linux kernel, which allowed a Unix-like operating system to run on cheap PC clones.) It did, however, represent the most pointed and uncompromising formulation of a long-standing and more general ethic of sharing of what came to be called open-source software, broadly construed. This way of working persisted and indeed has continued to flourish to a remarkable degree right alongside the cutthroat, patent-ridden world of corporate competition in the technology sector.

In any case, by the late 1980s and early 1990s, advances in computing infrastructure had allowed communities of users to coalesce in a manner enabled by the technology itself, much as radio hobbyists had a half century before.[8] But computing made possible collaboration and participation on a much larger scale than radio ever had. Moreover, its diffusion was much more rapid, and its resistance to centralization—for example, its conversion into simply a new form of broadcasting—ran much deeper. Information technology really did seem to have abolished the constraints of time and space in the manner first predicted by postwar visionaries in the late 1940s and first demonstrated in nascent form by the Silicon Valley innovators of the 1960s.[9] New kinds of communities formed and flourished around these communication networks. They were virtual and global; they had a temporality of their own, emancipated from the demands of synchronicity; most important, the range of choices on offer was enormous, and people could join or leave at will.[10]

Initially they were relatively small in scale. Computers could be remotely accessed via text-based terminals. Discussion communities flourished in the 1980s through various bulletin board systems and on USENET. Files could also be shared over file transfer protocol or, starting in 1991, with a protocol like Gopher.[11] In 1993, the World Wide Web was launched as a protocol running on the internet that specified some seemingly incremental improvements to open document sharing. It might not have seemed particularly transformative, but the consequences were remarkable. Its combination of free-standing sites, simple page-based structure (including images and other media), and the convenience of navigation through hyper-linking enabled its rapid growth. Also, it was free and un-encumbered by licenses. Self-styled virtual communities set up in this new landscape, established their homesteads, and began to figure out how to cultivate and manage set-tlements on their own.[12] Their self-consciously worn social identity was often expressed in this language of pioneer, homesteader, explorer, or frontiersman—people who left the noninitiated in the dust. The hacker myth expanded to offer a path toward a kind of transcendence, toward what Vincent Mosco called "the digital sublime." The computer promised to "lift people out of the banality of everyday life" and the drudgery of history, geography, and politics.[13]

The excitement and often the hubris of this mid-1990s moment can be seen in various manifestos from the pe-riod. America's leading futurist, Alvin Toffler, declared all standardizing and centralizing organizations, including governments, obsolete; he announced the coming "de-massification" of existing institutions and culture.[14] He was echoed by electronic rights advocate John Perry Barlow, who rather grandly proclaimed the internet a realm of pure freedom that anyone could enter "without privilege or prejudice accorded by race, economic power, military force, or station of birth." Within its constantly expanding borders, ideas—of whatever sort—circulated without restraint. Identities were fluid. No one could claim sovereignty, not even the state. In retrospect, this vision seems naive at best and preposterous at worst.[15] To be fair, Barlow did presciently recognize that the global nature of the internet made it hard to govern. But like any good manifesto, his "Declaration of the Independence of Cyberspace" imbued a utopian vision with an air of inevitability. It borrowed its key term, *cyberspace,* from a much darker rendering of the future, William Gibson's *Neuromancer,* but it was an optimistic piece of writing.[16] The expansion of cyberspace would be inexorable but beneficial.

Speculation about new forms of cultural and political organization that technology would enable fused with confidence about the benefits of free and open-source software development.[17] The fantasy of a happy, cooperative anarchy (a bazaar) that also outcompeted the bureaucratized engineering models of IBM or Microsoft was hugely influential, even if the reality of most open-source projects bore little resemblance to the ideal.[18] Beneath the surface, "private corporate networks" still remained "the keystone of the internet arch."[19] Meanwhile, and notwithstanding the assertions of the manifesto writers, the state was very far from withering away. To the contrary, in its role as the regulator of the telecommunications system it did a great deal to encourage the exhilaration surrounding the web. In the debate over the Telecommunications Act of 1996, the doomed effort to regulate obscenity and indecency online received the bulk of the public's (and Barlow's) attention. But most of the act relaxed rules for ownership and market concentration in a way that generally pleased Silicon Valley. "We were all deregulators" remarked Joseph Stiglitz, then chair of the President's Council of Economic Advisers. "By adopting [the language of] deregulation ourselves, we had in fact conceded the battle."[20]

The pace of change had been very high since the personal computer revolution had escaped the bounds of hobbyism in the early 1980s. Computers were now both a consumer good and a business necessity. As fortunes were made and lost through that decade and into the next, the image of Silicon Valley took shape through the repetition of stories that became myths. Giant firms were born in garages and basements. No one wore a tie to work. Corporate hierarchy was passé. College dropouts became chief executives. Self-taught geniuses wrote their own rules. Work, education, and play were tightly connected. Barely out of school themselves, these new executives established their headquarters as "campuses" outfitted with lavish cafeterias and a range of amusements. At the height of the dot-com boom, the workspaces of startups looked like dorms and ran like boiler rooms. In late summer the wider world of hackers and misfit makers met by the thousands in a makeshift city in the Nevada desert, built a gigantic effigy out of wood, and set it ablaze in a paroxysm of expressive frenzy and chaos.[21] It was all very exciting.

Challenges arose as fast as the expansion of the web itself. When the dot-com bubble burst in March 2000, many startups were simply unable to survive, if survival required making a profit. At that point, the importance of hardware design and manufacturing was in steady decline in Silicon Valley. Instead, software ruled, and services offered on the web were at the center of the action. Most of the largest and most recognizable internet startups, such as Google, either sold their services at a loss or simply offered them for free, with no clear view of how they were going to turn what seemed like a novelty, or a useful tool, into an actual business. The ones that did manage the transition were prompted by the valorization of what Shoshana Zuboff has called the "behavioral surplus."[22] In effect, what had previously been a cost of maintaining a service—all the infrastructure of servers and their log files, databases and transaction records, their user actions and their histories—became a source of data that might be turned into revenue. Unprofitable lines of business in search, in chat, in social interactions, and many other places could be repurposed by taking advantage of the digital traces people left behind on their own computers and the servers they connected to. Companies breathed in the exhaust fumes of their own data and found that it smelled of money.

The first, clearest, and largest market was advertising. The search industry rapidly became ad driven. The basis for Google's initial success was a network-based method of ranking searches, analogous to bibliographical measures of influence or sociometric measures of centrality, that allowed the web to speak for itself, as it were, to tell the user where the best answer to their query might be found. Thus, early on, Sergey Brin and Larry Page argued that, by contrast, "advertising-funded search engines will be inherently biased towards the advertisers and away from the needs of the consumers."[23] But they came to realize that what they were in a position to build was the most powerful advertising infrastructure the world had ever seen. The opportunity to learn from the incomprehensible quantity of data passing through Google's servers meant that the needs of consumers might stand a little reconceptualization.

Silicon Valley culture shifted too. It took hardly any time at all for the early frontier mentality of the World Wide Web to become a well-articulated business creed. By the late 1990s the concept of "disruptive innovation" was already taught in business schools as a particular way that markets came to be reconfigured. Rather than something wholly outside or separate from existing markets, the sort of innovation seen on the web could be interpreted as a kind of challenge from below, where a seemingly less useful or poorer-quality product or service cannibalized better-established and more easily understood offerings. The idea was expanded upon and reinterpreted. It came to connote a form of success strongly associated with technological change, and particularly with the displacement of some physical service with an online one. This sort of "disruption" was what the innovator brought, often in the form of a straightforward disregard not just for entrenched convention but also established law.[24] Google held on to its original motto ("Don't be evil") for a while, but Facebook's Mark Zuckerberg chose "Move fast and break things" to represent the culture he was eager to foster. In 2021, former *Wired* magazine editor and flying robots company CEO Chris Anderson asserted on Twitter,

> "Ask forgiveness, not permission" is the guiding motto of Silicon Valley. That means innovating in

the regulatory "gray space" between the obviously allowed (too crowded) and the obviously illegal. Think AirBnB, Uber or even our open source drones, which . . . all found loopholes or ambiguity in existing regs to introduce something new, which then proved too popular to shut down. But once you win with this strategy, you then have to work with regulators to evolve the rules to explicitly cover what you do, so you can scale. That's an unnatural act for tech CEOs, but like it or not, a necessary one.[25]

The shift from the sale of physical computer hardware, first to packaged software and then to web services as the basis for success in Silicon Valley, fostered a firm belief that "code" could and should solve most problems facing society. For the region's "technological solutionists," disregard for legal rules, hierarchies of knowledge, and existing organizational forms was the price of progress.[26] There were echoes of Karl Marx and Friedrich Engels, who also acknowledged capitalism's astonishing power to rip up the world and replace it with something new and almost incomprehensibly dynamic. "All that is solid melts into air": capital discards obsolete technologies and fills up junkyards; it sheds the chrysalides of antiquated social structures, leaving a trail of destruction in its wake; it mocks ideas whose time has passed and incites the laity to pray to new idols. The metamorphosis is painful for everyone, even capitalists. To survive, they too must undermine their own production base. Joseph Schumpeter, himself a fine reader of Marx, termed the process "creative destruction": the opening of new markets, the creation of new capacities, and product innovations, which "incessantly revolutionize the economic structure from within, forever destroying the old one, incessantly creating a new one."[27] While the new revolution was made of code rather than coal, scripts rather than steam, its language and imagery was curiously and inescapably industrial. Code was made, it seemed, in forges, with engines, through pipelines, by foundries—an entire metaphorical world of intensely physical production was conjured up to represent the activities of people who spent their days in front of screens, typing. They were not *writing;* they were *building.* Soon they would be mining also.

Wild fortunes were amassed out of this Schumpeterian ferment. In the Bay Area, several batches of twentysomethings became millionaires, and a few turned billionaires. The associated mythos was also economic, luring the hopeful and the skilled, year after year. In the physical setting for all of this—in the actual place—property values soared, rents became astronomical, and homeless encampments sprung up as neighborhoods transitioned to accommodate the new class of coders.[28] By 2018 San Mateo had the most interpersonal inequality of any county in California.[29] Local politics remained firmly Californian, combining a lofty progressivism in principle with a fierce conservatism when it came to one's own property. As more and more people lived and died in the streets of San Francisco and Oakland, Silicon Valley continued to cheerfully trumpet its ambition to "make the world a better place" through dataism, artificial intelligence (AI), and biogenetics.[30]

It was all a long way from the dream of cyberspace (though perhaps not that far from the original vision of cyberpunk). And yet, long after its arguments appeared quaint to the point of embarrassment, there were moments when Barlow's optimism seemed on the verge of bursting forth once more. In the early 2010s, around the world, these new communication technologies were at the center of a momentous wave of political upheaval, briefly reviving the old dream of the web as a democratic force. In the early 2020s, decentralized finance and cryptocurrencies seemed to revitalize and once again radicalize the promise of digital homesteading. But the Arab Spring failed to deliver the expected transformation. Social networks turned alarmingly divisive.[31] Crypto markets descended into fraud.[32]

Crabgrass Frontier

Why did technolibertarian ideas about freedom and the internet seem initially plausible? By the same token, why did they become dated so quickly? Part of the answer is simply the speed with which the World Wide Web expanded and diffused after it was established. Once a new technology is incorporated into everyday life, and once there are enough people who not only use it routinely but also have grown up with it, it will simply be taken for granted. "Real power," Mosco reminds us, is achieved when a technology "[leaves] mythology and [enters] banality."[33] The diffusion of the personal computer and, later, the internet, the web, the search engine, and social media, enabled and amplified a culture of connection, personal growth, and individual fact-finding right across people's lives. That sort of process will reliably strip the sheen off any revolution, even if the new arrangements have ongoing effects that really are properly revolutionary. This is not the whole answer, however. Looking back on the expansion of the web, we can see why its initial architecture was so appealing to a broadly countercultural and moderately anarchic constituency, but also how its foundations gradually came to support layers of additional organization that resulted in a very different outcome from what these optimists had imagined.

The first wave of speculation and generalization about the web was able to emphasize the twin themes of freedom and community because the protocols that ran the internet and the web were open. The specifications for network transportation, for applications like email and later hypertext-based web connections, were all decentralized and accommodating. The "P" at the end of abbreviations like TCP/IP, SMTP, and HTTP is for "Protocol."[34] Like a standard or a specification, a protocol organizes a task and allows for it to be controlled.[35] Despite the military sponsorship of much of the early research into distributed communications networks, the specification of the internet's suite of protocols had an intrinsic openness to it that carried through to the hypertext transfer protocol (HTTP) written down by Tim Berners-Lee and Robert Cailliau around 1990. Combined with hypertext markup language (HTML) for documents and a system of unique identifiers for locating them—universal resource locators (URLs)—the web rapidly established itself as a means for making material of all kinds available.

In principle, anyone could write a piece of software that implemented the protocol for serving up web pages. And in principle anyone could use that software to set up a server and use it to make text and images available to the world, or host discussions, or establish communities, or do any number of other things. Once the pages were public, anyone with a browser could just grab them from the server with a minimum of fuss. Earlier tools had done similar things. But there had been nothing quite like the web. Its relative lack of centralization and ease of use was tremendously attractive to early users and prognosticators.

The protocols that carry the web's information have been greatly expanded and refined since their origination, but their core remains stable. The very oldest web pages still render in modern browsers. Protocols are slow to change. As it turned out, however, making direct and relatively unmediated use of them was not what most people wanted. Although the most enthusiastic writing in the early days of the web was filled with images of the frontier, of homesteading, and of unfettered, free-form exploration in "cyberspace," it quickly became apparent that the overwhelming majority of people were not in a position to run their own servers or actively manage their own virtual homesteads in any kind of regular, self-sufficient manner. Even the small minority who *were* equipped for that sort of task generally preferred not to if they could pay someone else to do the job instead. Administering a server turned out to be frustrating when it was not merely boring. Certainly people wanted some means of connecting to what was on offer online. Many also wanted a way to actively contribute. It was just that, if they were in the business of producing what later came to be called "content," they wanted that process to be easy and quick. That meant having someone else do the work of serving it up. And finally, when it came to *finding* interesting things (or just locating people they knew about), they wanted some effective means of search and navigation to make that task easy also. This became all the more pressing as the web very quickly expanded far beyond any individual's ability to keep track of its content.

These fundamentally demand-side forces propelled the rise of so-called Web 2.0 technologies. This newer wave of places on the web offered sites and services that did something useful or fun but also made it relatively easy to be their client. These services were not, as a rule, part of the utopian world envisaged by early enthusiasts. Commentary around this transition sometimes recalls the disappointment verging on contempt that revolutionaries can have for the preferences of the peasants they have liberated. Repeatedly, the opportunity to build a little online homestead from the ground up was rejected in favor of services that did that work and facilitated the interactions and experiences people wanted to have, or the services

they wanted to consume, or the tasks they wanted to perform. The values of self-sufficiency, autonomy, and privacy
seemed to give way easily before the desires for convenience,
ease of use, and practicality. Like Silicon Valley, the web
steadily became more suburban.[36]
Even today, there is nothing intrinsic to the architecture
of the web, nothing in its underlying protocols, that prevents the kind of widely distributed, robustly local, essentially decentralized network of free communicators—both
cultural producers and consumers—that the likes of Barlow
imagined.[37] But that is not what the overwhelming majority have chosen to do with it. Putting this point in the
language of choice may seem like a mistake given the sheer
social power of the organizations and institutions that constitute the digital economy. And indeed, we shall explore
and critique the character of that power throughout much
of the rest of this book. But the growth of these services
and the digital economy in general was not simply imposed
on people. The tech landscape is littered with the wreckage
of huge investments that were catastrophic failures, rusted
hulks of grand schemes that were a gigantic waste of money
because people simply did not care to use them.[38]
The concentration of power on the web is not at the
level of protocol but rather of infrastructure, of the servers
that deal with billions of requests for content and services.
This is not just a matter of the relationship between dominant large firms and atomized individuals. When it comes
to their presence on the web, even the largest firms are
themselves usually in some client-like relationship with a
very small number of core service providers. Amazon's

Web Services division or, in a different way, content distribution networks like Akamai or Cloudflare sit behind all manner of different sites. Today the hyping of blockchain and AI technology might reenact something like the earlier transition that gave rise to these giants.[39] Excitement about newer, unproven tools strongly recalls the early phases of the web's expansion and its first major wave of consolidation. In crypto, a practical layer of relatively focused, centralized service provision once again has emerged on top of a decentralized protocol that has many different applications in principle. Just as with the first wave of dot-com expansion and subsequent Web 2.0 reconfiguration, there is a great deal of money to be made. And again, as before, enthusiast investors (such as venture capital firm Andreessen Horowitz) and tech evangelists, as the industry calls its product marketers, tend to focus on the liberating possibilities of the protocol rather than the centralizing tendencies of the server / service layer being built on top of it. In the interim, half-baked ideas, ill-advised enterprises, and outright scams have proliferated. They have drawn in new participants eager not to miss the moneymaking moment. The evangelists insist that this is simply a temporary phase, the regrettable but inevitable birth pangs of a new era. Once things settle down, the benefits of the new way of doing things will be transparently, reliably, and equally accessible to all. The difficulty is that reaching this point tends to bring just the sort of concentration in infrastructure and elaboration of administrative control that the evangelists insist we are about to transcend.

In the dream of a transition to "cyberspace" it was the "weary giants of flesh and steel" (Barlow's metaphor for state agencies) that were about to be surpassed. The bureaucracies of the industrial age were to be displaced by the pure flow of "transactions, relationships, and thought itself." The freedom to create and consume would be available to all and "anyone, anywhere may express his or her beliefs, no matter how singular, without fear of being coerced into silence or conformity."[40] Thirty years on, as another round of this dialectic plays out with a new set of protocols, the residuum of the earlier vision can be seen littered across the social web. A stew of intimate convictions and personal "research" underpins the process of knowledge production and belief formation. Its outputs are shared across gigantic commercial platforms with unprecedented reach, enabling a thriving ecology of self-broadcasters, streamers, and influencers.

Soft City

The tools made to help people navigate the rapidly expanding web exemplify both the early importance of autonomy and the subsequent shift toward more powerful models of organization and control. The social mechanism that bridged from one to the other was the notion of reputation, and in particular the way that a measurable system of reputational assessment and ranking could act as a means of asserting individual value and also be a method for matching people with what they were looking for. One of the earliest cases of this process in action can be seen in the initial struggles and subsequent growth of eBay, the auction and trading site.[41] Selling items online or brokering transactions for real money was a challenging proposition in 1995. Early sales immediately gave rise to problems of trust and social order as people were scammed or otherwise ripped off. The solution eBay came up with was a feedback system that allowed the parties to a transaction to rate one another and publicly assess their satisfaction with the transaction. The ability of users to contribute to and be judged on public reputation was what propelled eBay's imperfect but viable expansion. Reputation allowed buyers and sellers to more confidently assess listings and successfully match with exchange partners.

As eBay became a national and later a global marketplace, this system was repeatedly tweaked and adjusted, almost always in the direction of imposing more thoroughgoing structure and more detailed policy on what had initially been a quite open flea market. In the end, a reputational system could not by itself sustain a market at this scale. Feedback itself became a target for gamesmanship and exploitation. But as an initial mechanism it was extremely powerful. Feedback was formalized into measures of reputation, which facilitated ranking and matching, and helped create groups of recognizably better and worse participants. As we shall see, this process of producing groups or categories through a rank-and-match process, and of habituating people to think in terms of that process, was repeatedly adopted as a solution to all kinds of problems.

Something similar happened in the world of web search, just at one level removed from individuals seeking to connect with one another to transact. Here the problem was not finding the right exchange partner but surfacing the right piece of information. The first properly successful search tool was a web directory run by two Stanford graduate students. It was called Jerry and David's guide to the World Wide Web. Renamed Yahoo! in 1995, the guide offered a top-down approach to the search process. The name stood for "Yet Another Hierarchically Officious Oracle." Not everything was worthy of inclusion. People who wanted to list web pages had to submit to a review process run by a small army of human editors known as "surfers." The websites were selected and categorized by hand. As a search engine, Yahoo! originally sent queries to this directory and encouraged users to browse it. In structure and spirit, searching its listings was the last gasp of the sort of comprehensive index of interesting stuff that had been pursued by the *Whole Earth Catalog.*[42]

The Yahoo! directory survived until 2014. By the time it was at last retired, a different model of search had long since supplanted it and, in the process, completely reorganized public and professional understandings of what using the web was about. The PageRank algorithm, developed by another pair of Stanford graduate students in 1998, didn't just search *through* the network; it searched *with* it. That is, rather than simply sifting through a topic index, or looking for the needle of a specific bit of text in a haystack of pages, Google's search understood that the network structure of the web encoded information about the reputation and reliability of its content. Links between pages formed a de facto structure of judgments about the quality and relevance of those pages. That structure could be extracted and turned into a ranking. Google ordered its search results based on a calculation of the reputation of pages it indexed, where reputation was roughly the number of other places linking to that page, but with the importance of each incoming link itself weighted by the reputation of the page it came from.

Someone with a good reputation enjoys the high regard of highly regarded others. In their early papers (and the patent) defining the PageRank method, Google's founders explicitly linked their approach to network-based methods used in library science to rank the influence of articles, and also to tools for the calculation of centrality developed by social network analysts.[43] PageRank began life as a method of (in effect) treating web pages as a giant adjacency matrix and calculating centrality scores from it.[44] As Google's scale and scope increased, the methods it used and the way they were implemented became substantially more complicated and ever more secret. But the general idea of leveraging the global structure of a network of links to generate an indicator of the quality of its individual nodes remained central to Google's success. The efficient implementation of that model of search is the reason Google far outperformed every other search engine in the early days of its life, from hierarchical directories such as Yahoo! to fast but indiscriminate textual indexes such as AltaVista. An appealing side effect was that it also promised to be much more economical to run. There was no need to independently validate the content of pages. The structure implicit in the network of links itself was the best and most reliable kind of external validation. Or so it seemed.

PageRank boiled the complexity of search on the network down to an algebraic expression, on the one hand, and a large but tractable implementation problem, on the other. It began life as an academic exercise in discovering a better method for finding what you wanted online. When released into the wild it was fantastically successful on its merits. It was rapidly incorporated into the understanding and practice of a majority of internet users, and it became the focus of professional efforts to further assess its quality, and indeed to probe and exploit its weaknesses.[45]

In one way, Google's search model brought the freedom of the homestead vividly back to life within the rapidly suburbanizing web. It made the now much larger online world come alive again by making it navigable and useful to people looking for things on it. But it also precipitated a move to a third form of organization—not a homestead or a suburb, but something more like a self-monitoring network, a kind of "soft city."[46] Its inhabitants were still independent and remarkably free, but also much more observable. Once it became common knowledge that Google's results were also effectively a measure of reputation, other uses for these results quickly suggested themselves. So did generalizations of the idea that rich information about individual entities on a network had tremendous potential value. Why, after all, stop with web pages? Why not also think of networks of page visits (tracked through persistent browser cookies) as carrying a similar metric? Or, for that matter, why not imagine networks of consumers linked by shared purchases as implicitly providing information about the structure and value of market segments? Why not further leverage all of this knowledge to make services more useful to individual users, personalizing results and recommendations to the known or predicted tastes of individual users? Doing this sort of thing accurately, reliably, and at speed was no easy task. But the prospects it opened up were breathtaking—and irresistible. They captured the public imagination and filled the business literature. Tech companies' affiliation engines proposed lists of "people you may know" or "people you may want to follow." People heeded the suggestions. Network effects worked their expansive magic: the more people joined in, the more useful and powerful these platforms became. They shaped everyday interactions and propelled the emergence of new kinds of collective actors. Social media technologies performed and produced the social reality that engineers had claimed simply to describe.[47]

As companies like Facebook grew to reach billions of people, they found themselves with direct access to both very large quantities of data about individual users and the ability to produce a detailed, "network's-eye" view of the social whole. In a prophetic text, Gilles Deleuze has argued that this kind of infrastructure expresses a distinctive conception of power. Unlike institutionalized "spaces of enclosure" such as prisons, schools, or factories, "spaces of control" are distributed and connected through technical gateways and standards. Movement from one space to another may require some kind of authentication, so they are not entirely open. But people move through them smoothly. The kind of power deployed in such spaces, Deleuze suggests, is not about directly "molding" people but about "modulating" action at a finely detailed level through continuous adaptation and feedback loops. That is to say, control is accomplished cybernetically rather than mechanically.[48] Rather than governing by directly disciplining populations, these systems sense and react to the actions of individuals going about their day. We can also see this is an extension of the liberal injunction to exert power *through freedom,* and specifically through "the mechanisms of the market and the imperatives of self-realization."[49]

It might seem as though all this talk of power exerting itself through freedom is a little abstruse, not to say slightly paranoid. For one thing, technical systems exert control quite directly, through processes of authentication and validation, or by way of methods for balancing demand or processing queues. But the more diffuse sense of power as a kind of collective capacity flowing in part through sequences of choice is also perfectly familiar to us. We experience it in quite mundane ways. For example, if you want an image of cybernetically modulated control via continuous adaptation to the flow of free decisions, consider all the drivers who get where they want to be each day with the assistance of Apple or Google Maps. Each individual has a particular destination in mind. Each person's phone helps them look for the most effective route, monitoring the position of their car, receiving information about the general flow of traffic, the state of the weather, the presence of accidents or speed traps, and so on as they make their way.

In navigating this flow, drivers also constitute it. As transportation planners like to say, these commuters are not *in* traffic, they *are* traffic. Their phones track them individually while also aggregating information about the global state using data from thousands of beacons just like theirs. Some information from the resulting network's-eye view is fed back to the user. This aids individual drivers, helping them choose the right route. But this information also modulates the overall system by prompting drivers as they make their individual decisions. Would you like to accept a faster route, or stay on your present course? A speed trap is reported ahead. The next off-ramp is temporarily closed. Sometimes this mode of control takes the form of reassurance: There is a twenty-minute delay ahead, but you are still on the fastest route. (Please do not do anything rash, like believing you know a shortcut.) Whether navigating a network of roads or a network of pages, the individual user relies on the information flowing through the space of control in order to make their choices, and the flow of choices updates and enhances the system's global view of its own state.

The process is remarkable, all things considered. A substrate of networked hardware and software produces the flow of information that makes all of this possible. At the level of hardware, the most important phenomenon by far has been the global diffusion of the modern smartphone, to the point where almost everyone in a position to afford an internet-enabled device actually owns one. The software running on these phones, along with every other networked sensor, locator, and transmitter, produces data in order to act on it. Software was "eating the world."[50] The superpower of software—and, by implication, of software developers—seemed to be its ability to absorb and represent all manner of tasks, functions, and knowledge previously confined to specialized devices, tools, or occupations. If a method or technique could be specified, then it could be implemented as a software application. As it turned out, software development itself was not immune from this tendency. The circle was closed just a few years later, in 2017, with the parallel claim that, thanks to the computing power of modern graphics processors leveraged for more general uses, AI was now eating software.[51] The methods of machine learning threatened to consume and replace expert, professional knowledge in all its forms, including the expertise of software engineers. Commentators who heralded the rise of "knowledge workers" in the 1980s and the "creative class" in the 1990s went on to see those occupations become a target for algorithmic absorption a few decades later.[52]

Once trained, the software appeared to have the ability to far surpass its teachers in precision, reliability, honesty, and speed. Markets that were well guarded by powerful corporations, state-sponsored concessions, or legally backed licensing schemes stood ready to be automated away. So did tasks that were once protected by legal privilege and organized action. The certified expert, the salaried worker, the licensed operator, and the small shop owner all faced the threat of displacement, shrinkage, or de-skilling due to the rise of "coder-kings."[53] But increasingly, even the developers were in danger of being automated out of existence themselves.[54] Like the Greek god Kronos, the new capitalists were eating their own children.

The idea that artificially intelligent machines might end up doing all the work, and taking all the jobs, is, of course, an illusion. The computers seem indefatigable, but turn out to need round-the-clock human assistance—often in the form of cheap labor located beyond sight, preferably in the Global South.[55] Algorithms feel ethereal and intangible, but their operation consumes colossal amounts of energy and raw materials.[56] They seem rational and objective, but are only as objective as the data that trained them.[57] They appear less prone to corruption, ill will, or incompetence, but system gaming, corner cases, and deliberate misuse are common.[58] They are not supposed to notice political pressure, even as those who produce them routinely accede to the demands of authoritarian governments. And they are, of course, vulnerable to the whims and tantrums of Silicon Valley tycoons. As Nick Seaver puts it, "if you cannot see a human in the loop, you just need to look for a bigger loop."[59] Still, the real advances in information technology have been economically transformational, and the idea of automation remains culturally compelling. As they project into the future, the thought leaders of capitalism need more than numbers. They demand stories, fiction, narratives—in other words, belief.[60]

The cultural beliefs that underpin digital capitalism are characteristically modern. The main claim is that it works more efficiently than previous economic systems. In a way that strongly recalls Friedrich Hayek's argument about the superiority of market competition, methods for search and other algorithms have come to be seen as the most efficient way of processing a society's naturally dispersed stock of information.[61] The sort of automation that user-facing software revolutionized had less to do with robots assembling things in factories and more to do with people quickly figuring out how to get something done, make a connection, or come to a decision. A second, more normative claim is that all of this data-based intelligence can be deployed to support people's self-realization as individuals. The web allows them to access the world from their keyboards and to rely on automated tools and analytics to make educated choices about everything in their lives. If early excitement about the internet imagined it to be a foundation for negative freedoms (*freedom from* any kind of interference, and from the government in particular), the heralds of the mature web insisted that it offered people the means to achieve positive freedom, the *freedom to* choose, to express themselves, and generally to direct their lives as they see fit.[62]

The broader historical context was a change in the nature of capitalism itself. After the top-down standardization of the Fordist era, network technologies seemed to offer a means to fulfill a yearning for personal authenticity and emancipation.[63] The sociologist Daniel Bell commented on the new cultural aspirations back in the 1970s, noting their apparent incompatibility with the sort of discipline demanded by the capitalist enterprise.[64] But the internet supercharged them, and harnessed them to reconfigure capitalist discipline anew. These changes have been overwhelming and strange. In a few decades we moved from a quirky protocol for sharing documents to a system of organization, evaluation, and control that is remarkably convenient, often delightful, and at times frightening. It is on the point of encompassing our lives. Understanding the structure of this new society is the task of this book.

1

The Box of Delights

> Kay had the box of delights in his inner pocket and
> sometimes poked his hand inside to be sure it was
> still there.
>
> —John Masefield, *The Box of Delights*

CONSIDER TWO BASIC EXPERIENCES OF THE WORLD OF COMPUTER-driven smart devices and internet-enabled things. The first sort of experience is the bad one. It is caused by the malfunctioning, misconceived, or badly designed pieces of software and allegedly "smart" pieces of hardware you have encountered over the years, or indeed over the course of this week. You visit a website that promises to make it easy to do something, but it will not allow you to perform some simple and obvious action. You buy a smart light bulb, but it will not turn on when it is supposed to. You try to sign up for a service, but it insists that the kind of name you have is invalid. You stick your hand under the automatic soap dispenser and nothing happens. You talk to a virtual assistant that has the voice of a reassuringly competent and compliant woman; it pretends to understand what you say, yet from experience you know that it is in fact operating on the narrowest of syntactic gauges. Stray just a little from the expected path of instruction and the illusion of interactivity and competence will be destroyed.

The second kind of experience is more pleasing. It is the feeling that some piece of technology "just works," the feeling that a computer or device *knows* what you want it to do. It properly anticipates your needs and acts on them appropriately. This is a feeling of *magic* and *delight,* or at least a sense of ease and convenience. While this experience of delight is often pitched in terms of increasing one's productivity or enhancing some convenience in life, it need not have any useful purpose at all. It can be an end in itself.

In the early 1990s, for example, if you were among the small group of people with access to the nascent World Wide Web you might have gotten that feeling from being able to fetch photographs of Mars from a computer located at the Jet Propulsion Laboratory in Pasadena, California, despite being a continent away. There was no particular reason you *needed* to see photographs of Mars, but the simple fact of being able to do so was a marvel. Toward the end of the first decade of the 2000s you might have gotten that feeling from watching the full-color screen on your new phone slowly but accurately produce your location on a street map. Perhaps there was something useful you could do with that information; perhaps not. In the late 2010s the scope of what you could do had expanded to the point where you might have experienced this kind of delight the first time you stepped out of a building, touched your phone a few times, and saw a car appear to take you where you wanted to go. Just as easily, it might have come from watching fifteen seconds of video that made you laugh by giving you a window to some aspect of the sheer variety of joyful, pointless creativity there is in the world. At present, an AI that can produce detailed images at your behest seems wondrous. Soon, something else—something you don't yet anticipate, something that does not yet exist as a piece of technology people can easily use, something new—will give you that same feeling.

Social theorists underestimate the power of delight. When a technology can deliver that experience—again, whether in the service of something "useful" or simply for its own sake—people really *love* it. They will seek it out. They will show and tell it to their friends. The instinct of the critic is to say that this delight is misleading or illusory. If it is associated with something useful to you, such as the wish to be a little more physically active, this is because (the critic may insist) your Apple Watch or Fitbit is exercising a subtle form of control by encouraging you to meet your step count for the day. Not only that (the argument continues), it is also nudging you to value the act of meeting your step count for the day. Most perniciously (the conclusion arrives), you experience all of this as a satisfying personal choice rather than the symptom of neoliberal governmentality it really is. Critique in this vein urges us to examine the structures and forces producing these illusions. The network sending you pictures of Mars is the product of massive state investment; the infrastructure supplying the directions to nearby cafés began life as a network of military satellites; the system providing you with a ride across town is built on the back of a minutely surveilled and relentlessly casualized labor pool. Compared to these forces, focusing on the role of individual delight in technology and its affordances is surely trivial, or even vaguely obscene.

These points are not without merit. But by the same token, social theory in this vein tends to *overestimate* how often technology works properly. Theorists don't usually make this mistake in their own lives. This is because their lives are filled with malfunctioning laptops, broken insurance company websites, and stupid pieces of learning management software. But in their theories, algorithms rule. The algorithms embed bias, reexpress structural power, and congeal into a massive, inescapable system of social reproduction. In this way, social-scientific critiques of information technology can end up as mirror images of the happy talk that comes out of the mouths of pitch-deck purveyors. Like a mirror, they reverse left and right, so that Panglossian hype becomes a blanket critique of technology. The world is always being made a worse place, not a better one. But—also like a mirror—these critiques do not reverse up and down. The technology is still assumed to work as claimed, even though in practice it may be buggy or broken most of the time. Thus, while the temperament of theory is critical, a fundamental belief in the propulsive power of technological change still lives in its marrow. The algorithms and the science behind them are assumed to *work*. It is just that their effects are, in truth, malign. The task of theory from this perspective is to expose that malignancy.

Theories about the relationship between information technology and society reflect this ongoing tension between delight and discontent, between benefaction and dispossession, between being given things and having them taken away. Even the vocabulary used by social scientists suggests a deep ambivalence. Writing in 1952, the sociologist Howard Becker noted that we use the word *datum* rather than *captum* for the elemental unit of evidence. The former is the Latin past participle of *dare,* "to give"; the latter, the past participle of *capere,* "to take." Becker thought this an "unfortunate accident of history" because "all data are in some sense capta, for nothing is given unless it is simultaneously taken." He was writing about academic science. But as Rob Kitchin notes, the idea could hardly fit better within the context of commercial data science, where the sense of capture, even theft, is uncomfortably present.[1] At its heart big data is "big capta." There have been occasional efforts to express this idea more explicitly, if uncritically. For example, in the early years of this century, a line of work at Stanford University proceeded under the label "captology." The idea was to develop a practical program of research devoted to discovering the product design and psychosocial strategies that are best at directing and manipulating how people interact with computer software and hardware.[2]

The object of interest there was habit formation and behavioral change. The implicit focus on addictive techniques at the level of individuals, often similar to those used in the gambling industry, encouraged an obvious set of objections. A more critical line of thought frames the expanding scope of data collection in general, and its transformation into a source of value and profit, in terms reminiscent of Karl Marx's analysis of the emergence of modern capitalism. In this story, the problem is the way people are dispossessed of a valuable, intimate resource, or at least their rights to it. This is a process of enclosure akin to the primitive accumulation of more tangible forms of property. Preexisting practices, social norms, and the law are shoved aside in a predatory scramble for control. A blunt disregard for existing states of affairs is an essential part of the process. Convinced of the transformative potential of their technology, firms capture the commons, disregard the legal rules that structure industries, automate workers away, and commodify everything in their path. Google digitizes entire libraries or sends a fleet of cars out to drive and photograph every road in the world; Uber upends and re-constructs the market for taxis; OpenAI ingests the whole of the web; every major organization tries to collect as much information as it can about anyone who wanders into view, the better to transform them into bundles of compa-rable, valuable data. During this expansionary phase, the best strategy is simply to see how much you can get away with. In Shoshana Zuboff's terms, a firm like Google launches "incursions into undefended space," presses until "resistance is encountered," and then "seduces, ignores, overwhelms, or simply exhausts its adversaries."[3] Often, data extraction is presented as the natural, desirable, and legally acceptable order of things. Such a quasi-colonial grab for the new ter-ritories of intimacy requires some justification.[4]

For those enrolling in digital systems, however, the ex-perience is generally benign, and often even delightful. Moreover, software now almost always enters people's lives as a freebie, initially available at no cost. Gone is the time when it was physically packaged and expensive.

Like the web itself, the success of almost all major software services depends on their reach, and this in turn depends on them being given away for free or sold at a loss to begin with. The process works through a mixture of sociality, reciprocity, and self-interest. Those early observers who optimistically celebrated the wealth of networks and the independence of "cyberspace" were onto something. They saw that the social logic of digital life has a strongly participatory, effervescent, even emancipatory streak. Indeed, on its face it is about widening the circle of inclusion, so much so that policymakers and advocates have come to frame access to digital technologies as a fundamental human right. If this is robbery, it is less like being held up at gunpoint on the street and more like having your pocket picked at a party. This is the "political tragedy of interactivity," where willing, often enthusiastic participation in digital media ends in "universal capture."[5]

If these services expand through freebies, where does the profit come from? Strategies for cross-subsidization in the digital economy come in various forms. Finding a way to convert users on the free tier into monthly subscribers is the most straightforward strategy. The largest services keep things free to end users. By doing so they hope to create a network or, better, an entire platform that provides third parties with opportunities to extend the service and owners with a steady flow of data that can be mined and sold.

We are left with a field of oppositions that, even if they do not rise to the level of true paradox, remain at least puzzling. In everyday use, software makes previously impossible things easy but remains riddled with irritations and failures. The industry that produces it is intensely competitive, but large parts of it rest on a foundation of open-source tools. Platforms accumulate users and profits but seem to give away many of their products for free. Surveillance and tracking in the service of monetization is pervasive, but people irrepressibly share things with one another and with the platforms. How can so much be taken through the process of giving?

The Gift of Everything

In a classic essay on gift exchange, Marcel Mauss argued that sharing what one has is a primordial feature of social life.[6] Acts of generosity that ostensibly need not be repaid, and from which the pursuit of profit appears to be absent, are common and spontaneous. Gifts stitch together the social fabric. This does not mean that sharing is easy. The recipient of a gift is, de facto, in a kind of debt. They feel morally obligated to reciprocate. Giving back, properly timed and framed, offers a way out. The surest way to erase an obligation one has incurred is to repay it exactly and in full. Calculation and money arise out of the desire to escape the inequality and moral entanglements created by gifts. Historically, though, these are late-arriving innovations. Far more of social life is caught up in the ongoing back-and-forth of gifts that never quite balance to a point where neither party owes anything to the other.

The strange power of the gift lies in the "initiating" or creative character of the first "free" act of giving and in the instability and intrinsic ambiguity of subsequent exchanges.[7] Mauss emphasizes the structural and ritualistic element of gifts as a means of establishing and continually affirming alliances. The give-and-get of this sort of exchange has several features that distinguish it from the buy-and-sell of the market or the pure quid pro quo of a direct exchange that leaves nothing more to be accounted for. Gift exchange has an intrinsically hazy or fuzzy character that allows both for clear calculation and a kind of plausible obfuscation.[8] Its continuity through time puts it at the core of ordinary social relations. Meeting the obligation to return or reciprocate what one has received, in some appropriate form and at some appropriate moment, is what makes gift giving a social relationship. Indeed, that sort of activity is what an actually existing, ongoing social relationship *is*. There is nothing more to it.

The deliberate lack of clarity about what, precisely, one must do to discharge an obligation allows for cycles of gift exchange to remain slightly out of balance. This is just another way of saying that social relations and the expectations that come with them are sustained through time. A combination of awareness and denial, of interest and disinterest, tends to obfuscate or decenter the economic aspect of gift exchanges. Pierre Bourdieu calls this "misrecognition."[9] It is tempting to see these tendencies and jump to the conclusion that gift exchange is inimical to the calculation of material benefits or intrinsically opposed to counting up credits and debits. But the long history of

scholarship on gift exchange in anthropology and sociology makes it clear that gifts and reciprocity create social
and economic dependency just as surely as market exchanges. Indeed, pure market transactions mediated by
money can be thought of as an effort to make exchanges
happen in a way that *escapes* the tendrils of the gift, that
avoids the tendency of gift giving to draw transactors into
ongoing cycles of obligatory transfers with all their attendant spillovers and duties.

By the same token, having discovered the economic or
calculative aspects of gift exchange, it is also an error to interpret these instrumental elements as the only important part of the process.[10] This leads to the view that the
calculative actions and payoffs are what is "real" or "rational" in exchange. The attendant elements of gift giving
are then seen as merely window dressing, a kind of pointless waste of time and energy that could be dispensed with
if only people were honest with themselves about their true
purpose. But particular gift exchanges express and encom-
pass social relationships as a whole, making the elements
of politeness, deference, honor, and obligation far more
than simply empty ceremony. Instead they are, in Mauss's
phrase, a "total prestation" that in any particular case met-
onymically expresses the existence of the social order it
forms a part of, and whose ongoing reality it helps sustain.

Of course, the digital economy is not straightforwardly
Maussian. We cannot simply graft a framework for understanding ceremonial exchange across a range of small-
scale societies onto the world we now see around us. Nevertheless, we can take seriously the idea that, even in

contemporary economies, some sort of "Maussian bargain" is being made over and over.[11] Relationships and exchanges in digital capitalism are routinely framed as gift-like. But these are, to quote Dave Elder Vass, "loaded gifts."[12] They imply some form of stealth reciprocation. Often, and in a very Maussian fashion, what ends up being given away in return—your personal data, for instance, or information about your social network—is not something that had any materiality before the relationship was initiated. It only comes into existence through the relationship itself, through the act of enrolling into the nominally free service that facilitates voluntary, lateral interactions between users. That is why such exchanges are often misrecognized and their economic dimension is so underappreciated—or at least it was at first. But it is very real. Just as traditional gifts often involve the exchange of materially valuable goods, the immaterial goods of the Maussian bargain go on to be appropriated, traded, sold, valued as assets, or "shared" again.

Economists typically treat the issue as one of cost-benefit analysis. By one estimate, the median user in the late 2010s would have had to be paid over $17,530 to give up search for a year, $1,173 to give up YouTube, and $576 to give up Facebook.[13] If each person, individually, gets a lot more value out of Facebook or Google than Facebook or Google gets out of them, then it is not worth sweating over. But this kind of calculation misses the fundamental reason why people cannot really dispense with these services. Thanks to network effects (the self-reinforcing dynamic between the number of users in the network and the usefulness of the network to each user), the infrastructure they provide has become integral to people's social lives. Most could not even work without them. From the point of view of the distribution of social power, the advantage is entirely on the corporate side when it comes to any particular choice to opt in. The idea that the Maussian bargain is a voluntarily agreed-upon contract is a mystification, a kind of corporate will "sublimated" through the legal magic of terms of service.[14] That myth not only masks but naturalizes the structurally asymmetrical relationship between giver and recipient. It overlooks the imposition of an unsought gift. It creates an object whose value is deemed uncertain and trivial. It produces the fiction that this object existed, lying there for the picking, before the relationship was initiated. And it organizes its immediate trade under the pretense of a self-conscious, rational exchange whose legal terms the user understands and agrees to.

This may all seem a little mysterious or obfuscated in itself. People sign up for free services all the time. In what sense is something being created out of nothing? By way of analogy, it is helpful to think of how much clearer and more obvious things seem when the process runs in reverse. Consider intangible things that we perceive as being *taken* from people rather than being given away. If something already has a socially real and economically defined existence, if it already is seen as a species of property, then its unilateral transfer back into the world of gift exchange by way of some new technological tool will look like simple theft, at least to its legal owners.

For example, one such moment of reabsorption was the explosive growth of music (and later movie) sharing services. In the late 1990s, LimeWire, Napster, and later various torrent sites appeared on the scene. They were embraced with such gleeful avidity and spread with such astonishing rapidity that they quite terrified the recording and production companies that held the rights to the songs and films that were being exchanged. The gift-based structure of these networked tools was built right into their architecture. At the bottom, small-time users were encouraged to participate by making their own little media collections available to others rather than simply "leeching" from larger sources. At the top, the really large repositories of files, or pointers to them, presented themselves to the world with an extravagant and sometimes outrageous profligacy that was reminiscent of a kind of massive potlatch. All of this was, of course, obviously illegal. From the point of view of entertainment companies and many creative artists it was simply copyright infringement on a massive scale. For them, this sudden reconversion of their intellectual property, of things they had the rights to, back into "things given" represented the annihilation of real value and the elimination of profit opportunities guaranteed by law. But reining in the easily exchangeable and generally nonexcludable character of digital copies of musical, cinematic, literary, or other sorts of creative goods was not easy. It necessitated the development of a huge infrastructure of administration, monitoring, and enforcement—of "digital rights management"—in order to defend the viability of revenue and profit flowing from these materially di-aphanous but legally real goods.

Thirty years on, the efforts of media companies to put the lid back on have largely succeeded. Control over music rights is once again securely in their hands thanks to the consolidation of streaming services such as Spotify (for music) and the successful implementation, by platforms like YouTube, of bot-driven "copystrike" methods that con-tinuously monitor uploads for copyright violations and automatically remove unauthorized material. The former make it easy to participate (and pay) legally; the latter make it more difficult to distribute copyrighted material on a wide scale. Recording artists may justifiably complain that the revenue they receive per stream is miniscule, but rights holders capture the available value by streaming their libraries to users for a monthly fee. Much as with the value of any particular user to Facebook or Google, the profitability of the modal recording artist to Spotify is very low. What matters is the presence of their work, the availability of their catalog alongside thousands of others in the broader network of the streaming service. Conversely, Spotify's (or YouTube's) service is very much more important to the modal artist in search of an audi-ence than vice versa.

In the ordinary course of things, musicians and audi-ences form an extensive "art world," the output of which is experienced live and in person.[15] People make music and sing songs together. The ability to capture and reproduce recordings, to isolate and freeze a piece of this practice, made possible the now familiar world of intellectual property in musical compositions and performances. While music is something people just make, and a song or a tune is something people can learn, a recording is something someone can own. The character and scope of that ownership is intrinsically strange for reasons explored in any analysis of the paradoxes of intellectual "property."[16] It is a kind of enforceable fiction. The partial escape of recorded music back into the commons, and its subsequent recapture by rights holders, illuminates the relationship between the social practice of music and the infrastructure of ownership enabled by technology.

In a similar way, the constant flux of social life, the flow of things given in everyday reciprocation, does not naturally exist in the form of bundles of enforceable rights, in legal claims over tangible goods or services, or in measured and analyzable datasets. It is simply what people do, as easy as breathing. The idea that one could in some sense capture and represent this flow—not just every song, but every greeting, every friendly chat, every disagreement, every joke, every frown or smile, every small bit of social existence—seemed, until recently, like a fantasy. And not just fantastical, but also pointless in most cases. Certainly, highly specialized institutional environments measured and managed in this sort of way did exist. Most obviously, some firms and some kinds of financial markets produced, and were required to produce, streams of quantitative data, sometimes in real time, documenting their activities in a very high degree of detail. But no such data-generating substrate existed in most social settings or for most kinds of interaction. Nor did one seem required.

Digital technology, leveraged by the power of the gift, has changed all of this. Far more of our everyday activities now leave some digital trace in their wake, and we have seen a huge scramble to profit from the creation and capture of this information. Within markets, firms are driven to expand as rapidly as possible, to become platforms rather than simply service providers. In the language of economic theory, they tend toward two-sided or multi-sided markets that rely on users' freely provided "content" to meet the commercial demand coming from third parties, such as advertisers and developers.[17] The flow—the overflow, really—of what comes out of ongoing creative social existence is what stands to be corralled and made valuable. Its mainspring, the give-and-get of ordinary reciprocity in all its forms, drives the expansion of these platforms through gift exchange, and the gift's marketized simulacrum, the freebie.

The Social Substrate

Business analysts and investors conventionally acknowledge that one of the critical advantages of information and communication technologies is their ability to *scale*— that is, to rapidly expand their scope without significantly increasing costs. This gives first movers the potential to capture and then enclose the activities of some large number of people within a short time span, and then to control the rules of the game once the boundaries are established.[18] In the somewhat hyped-up words of Linke-

dIn's founder Reid Hoffman, "software has a natural affinity with blitzscaling, because the marginal costs of
serving any size market are virtually zero. The more that
software becomes integral to all industries, the faster
things will move. Throw in AI [artificial intelligence] machine learning, and the loops get even faster."[19] This sounds
quite exciting, although companies and tech leaders rarely
acknowledge that this kind of progress generally involves
using a great deal of cheap labor, natural resources, and
energy.[20]

The value of many digital services to each user increases as more people participate in them, triggering self-
propelled growth. The importance of scale, and of network effects more generally, came to be recognized as
computers entered workplaces in the 1970s and homes in
the 1980s. The entrepreneur Robert Metcalfe, for instance,
gave his name to the idea that the utility of a network to its
users was proportional to the square of the number of
users on the network. Subsequently, in academic economics, the theory of network externalities was developed in more detail as was, later, a general account of how
intermediary platforms provide frameworks that connect distinct groups that stand to benefit from exchange
with one another. This is the theory of two-sided markets.[21] Yet a focus on the formal benefits of platforms and
markets tends to obscure the process through which
these new intermediaries were assembled. As the real
power of networked computing started to become clear,
observers and participants began to grasp its ability to be
a kind of "social substrate"—that is, a means of fostering,

capturing, and also "programming" sociality in a measurable, analytically tractable form.[22] People started to see that theory, technique, and society might coevolve in an accelerating sequence.

The importance of network ties and imagery to market exchange was already recognized by what, thirty-five years ago, was beginning to be called the New Economic Sociology. Sociologists like Mark Granovetter conceived of the circulation of people and goods in society as flow in a dynamically evolving structure of real network relations.[23] Social network analysis grew from an academically peripheral position in the early 1970s—or, more charitably, from its niche as a respected but specialized subfield of sociology—into a central project within contemporary social science and beyond. As network analysis proliferated and diffused across the intellectual landscape (becoming "network science" in the process), its ability to cash out some of its most important theoretical concepts and images in formal methods and usable tools was a vital part of its success.[24]

To begin with, the applicability of these new methods and tools was highly constrained by the scarcity of usable data. The physicist-turned-sociologist Harrison White's research group at Harvard University, for example, was directly concerned in principle with the theory of large-scale social structure. White and his students explicitly differentiated their approach from a previous generation of sociometric studies of small groups, the sort of semiformal probing of the length of social network chains made famous by Stanley Milgram's discussion and subsequent study of the "small world" problem.[25] They also were committed to developing formal tools—"satisfactory methods for aggregating networks among individuals"—that could be applied to real data.[26] But their analytical breakthroughs far outran their computational resources and, crucially, the data available to apply them. While they kept the macrostructure of societies squarely in view theoretically, four of the five applications of the models they developed in a classic early paper on blockmodeling techniques had fewer than twenty-five cases each.

They were well aware of this problem. They argued, following Émile Durkheim, that "the organic solidarity of a social system rests . . . on the interlock and interaction of objectively definable social relationships." But they acknowledged that their reach exceeded their grasp: "We see at present no intelligent way to develop role interlock for open networks extending through large populations, even though this topic is much closer to the heart of sociology than is small-group structure."[27] Early efforts by network scholars tended to be dogged by the criticism that they rained an unreasonable amount of mathematical firepower down on the heads of, variously, a small group of monks who did not get along very well, or eighteen debutantes attending a series of dances, or a persistent conflict within a single karate club.[28]

Despite these initial difficulties, time was on the side of the network analysts. The scale of computing power and data collection started to catch up, and fast. New tools allowed for the accumulation of large databases and the potential to analyze their contents. It also revealed the prospects for surveillance by those in control of information collection and storage. These implications began to be articulated by the end of the 1970s. By the early 1980s a series of well-publicized breaches of government and corporate computer systems by youthful hackers introduced the public to the idea that confidential data was reachable over the phone, possibly by anyone. Commentators saw that computerization presented opportunities for new kinds of data analysis and that this would have broader social effects. A *Washington Post* article from 1984, for example, discusses the effects on privacy of "a world in which employers are monitoring workers" and "friends and neighbors are prying into one another's private affairs," especially "the young computer generation."[29] Scott Boorman, a key member of the research group led by Harrison White that helped catalyze interest in social networks at Harvard in the early 1970s, is quoted in the article. His comments are of interest for the two dimensions of the issue he identifies. The first is the prospect of managers being able to identify "patterns of association between individuals" by way of electronic records. He describes a hypothetical situation in which a manager is concerned that some of his "bright young engineers" might be planning to quit and form a rival firm. "What kind of early warning can one have for that kind of split-off?" Boorman asked. "That can be picked up by phone patterns . . . the phone calls are flying. Electronic mail is flying."[30]

At around the time that network analysis was becoming more common as a consulting product to be used in this way, in the business literature network imagery and "networking" metaphors became increasingly prominent also. People were aware that large electronic databases containing detailed personal information—including network information—were held in both public and private hands, and that this data might be accessible to enterprising hackers over the phone. But although the business side emphasized network imagery (connections, payoffs, brokerage, and so on), discussion on the computing side still tended to be framed in "information society" terms. In that way of thinking, the revolutionary potential of computers and information technology was acknowledged, but its encapsulation within existing organizational and institutional forms tended to be taken for granted. Boorman's comments in 1984 are again of interest:

> "I would say that the concept of privacy is profoundly changing," Boorman said. "In the old days, 10 or 15 years ago, an invasion of privacy meant that someone had somehow gotten at some personal secret of yours and had revealed it to some third party or to the world at large."
>
> But large new databases of "very mundane information" about individuals . . . make it "possible to characterize one's life history on an almost minute-to-minute basis" on and off the job and to use this information for "something much more interesting than ferreting out particular secrets."
>
> "I think that this goes well beyond the immediate, classic problem of government agencies exceeding their statutory mandate . . . In a funny way, the people we are most vulnerable to is [sic] our own immediate employer."[31]

The discussion here represents a point when the social possibilities of networked information technologies were beginning to come into focus. They foreshadow a shift from a concern with the effects of "computers" as such to an emphasis on the connections between repositories of information, and beyond that to the prospect of detailed personal data being used in more interesting ways than just exposing secrets. The growth of data collection is acknowledged, and the implications for the concept of privacy are picked out sharply. But the social units involved are still the individual, the organization, and the state. Data repositories are seen as allowing for the ex post reconstruction of preexisting social structure through formal analysis. The networked dimension *of the data itself* is conceived in much more limited terms, essentially as a problem of unauthorized users hacking their way into systems. What is missing is the idea of a network flow of quantified but "very mundane information" that might constitute rather than merely characterize one's life history and which might be actively constructed by users themselves rather than simply collected by some supervisory entity.

The core infrastructure of the internet was already in place by the 1980s, though the internet itself was not especially large in terms of the number of computers attached to it. The development of the World Wide Web protocol and browsing software in the early 1990s gave people the basic tools to connect across it and pushed its growth out beyond government and educational institutions. In the early days of the web (before 1995–1996 or so), the marvel was the simple fact of connectivity, the ability to follow threads through a huge network, like a speeded-up version of Milgram's "small world" experiment. The fact that a network of this sort even existed, was more or less freely navigable, contained a motley assortment of content made available by all manner of people and organizations, and was a network that one could contribute to easily was remarkable in itself. The dominant metaphors of the period emphasized the flow of information across the network ("the information superhighway") and its abstracted, ethereal quality ("cyberspace").[32] The first wave of investment in dot-com startups, however, funded all manner of ill-advised efforts to get people to buy various products online or provided unwanted alternatives to things already available elsewhere.

Otherwise, though, few websites did anything useful. Retail sites were catalogs. The most widely used navigational tools were catalogs, too, and early search engines did not perform well. Although the majority of websites were reachable from one another, and the existence of links between them made the network imagery more than just metaphor, the structure of the web had no semantic content built into itself. Prognosticators envisioned a world of much richer information flow and connection, but the web during its first boom period did not exemplify it.

So-called Web 2.0 services came closer to the forecasters' ideal. The key innovation in these technologies was not the network infrastructure or basic protocols for data transmission but the ability to encode, extract, and make useful much of the semantic content of data that had previously been untapped. This was sometimes characterized as a transition from "information silos," or networks of sites that are formally connected but substantively isolated, to "architectures of participation."[33] The wave of what later came to be called social media began in earnest.

The growth of the web was greeted with understandable excitement by social network analysts. Here was an amazing demonstration of the reality of their subject matter, unfolding before everyone's eyes in real time and on a very large scale. And here also, at last, was the potential to collect, visualize, and analyze absolutely vast amounts of data on truly gigantic network structures. That potential had remained a distant possibility for a long time. Within the space of a few years, though, the size of actually existing networks that were in principle accessible to quantitative analysis jumped by several orders of magnitude. The upper limit surged from perhaps a few hundred nodes inside a company to millions or tens of millions, as in the case of something like the AOL Instant Messenger network or, later, into the billions with Facebook.

It is at this point that the more sociological aspects of network effects and scale become more salient. The economics of platforms and platform dependence were clear quite early in the expansion of computing, where they took the form of arguments about the importance of compatibility and first-mover advantage in physical computing devices and protocols. But the rapid growth of community-focused websites in the 1990s made the potential economic value of a network of users very clear. While the economic returns to widespread compatibility could be immediately realized in terms of profits per unit of physical computer hardware sold, however, the value hidden inside online communities or social networking websites was much harder to extract. The problem was how to make money. Having constructed a substrate for the generation of quantifiable data on a new sphere of social interaction, companies found that turning a profit from people's willingness to engage with websites and one another online was quite hard. Outside of some very narrow professional settings, attempting to charge up front for membership in a social network was a guarantee of failure. While it was fashionable to insist that "information wants to be free," or to argue that the marginal cost of one extra user, or one more reader or viewer, was zero, in practice someone had to pay for all that bandwidth and all those servers. In the early days of the internet and the World Wide Web, the basic human tendency to connect and exchange was a delightful experience, but once it got moving at any sort of scale it became a huge commercial liability, a puzzle that led straight to insolvency. The first dot-com boom brought forth firms that could not find a way to profitably sell physical goods to customers and startups that acquired huge numbers of users that they did not know what to do with. Propelled by the new infrastructure of networked hardware and software, the power of sociability helped platforms grow to a previously inconceivable size but in many cases also helped them burn a proportionately inconceivable quantity of venture capital before they failed.

The Exfiltration of Sociality

Scalability, then, is not a purely technical problem. It depends on sociability in order to expand, at which point the problem becomes how to canalize all that activity in a way that turns "users" or "eyeballs" into profits. Firms and platform owners repeatedly try to harness basic human propensities to form social relationships, to creatively make things, and to communicate with one another.[34] The motives and purposes underlying this sociality are incorrigibly plural. People connect with one another—or come into conflict with one another—for innumerable reasons. From an economic point of view, this flow of human interaction and creative activity is a little like the energy of the sun: it floods across the earth continuously and in vast quantities. Only a tiny fraction of it is captured in a way that is both formally measurable as economic activity and transformed into something financially profitable.

Writing in the middle of the nineteenth century, Karl Marx cast a cold eye on the process of "primitive accumulation," whereby an initial capital stock had to come from somewhere in order to get the cycle of capitalist growth off the ground. Marx saw this as a kind of highway robbery where "the social means of subsistence and production are turned into capital, and the immediate producers are turned into wage-labourers," and which tended to be glossed over by the political economists of his own time. ("This primitive accumulation plays approximately the same role in political economy as original sin does in theology," he drily remarked.)[35] Marx's account focused on the land and the means of agricultural production. It was the means of subsistence that was expropriated, detached from its prior form of existence and converted into capital stock. In our own time, in a different domain, digital entrepreneurs sought to do something similar with social interaction. To borrow a term from the world of information security, they set out to *exfiltrate* the flow of sociality. That is, they wanted to bleed it off, corral and convert it into something tangible, tractable, and profitable.

During the first phase of the World Wide Web's expansion, culminating in the dot-com boom and bust of the late 1990s and early 2000s, firms repeatedly found themselves with very large numbers of users happily connecting with one another while producing what would later generically be called "content." But they had no effective way to turn a profit from these users. A recurrent phenomenon was the tendency for activity on these platforms to exceed or overflow its original bounds as users sought to expand the range of activities and interactions that were possible on the platforms. The problem was how to "monetize" what users were doing, saying, or making on one's site. In the 2000s, firms began to find new and unexpected ways to exfiltrate a greater proportion of this flow of social energy. They began to take advantage of the digital traces users left behind in log files and other records of activity. Then they began to realize they could actively create as well as retrospectively analyze traces like this. In order to benefit from network effects, digital firms had to find ways to tap the flow of social interaction without drowning in it.

It is important to understand the reciprocal character of this process. In the language of gift exchange, these "things given" do not give themselves, since they have no materiality outside the physical bodies that "produce" them. Instead, human activities must be reconfigured so they become an abstract, information- (and money-) producing process, what McKenzie Wark calls a "hack."[36] The hack is relational and participatory, using design infrastructures to exploit various aspects of human desperation and spontaneity: the critical need to make money, the desire to belong, the ambition to compare favorably. The world of social media, for instance, has been a particularly fertile ground for the deployment of psychosocial techniques that fuel sociality.[37] From the endlessly flowing experience of a website or application with an infinite scroll to the dark patterns of opt-out defaults, from the use of recommendation algorithms on streaming platforms to the gamification of user interfaces, from bottom-up advertising campaigns to the promotion of organic viral content, everything is built so that people may indulge in the affirmative pleasures of social connectedness and of leaving their mark online.

These efforts extend far beyond the particular market of self-consciously social media. It would also be a mistake to think that these features are simply the result of deliberate, top-down efforts to design exploitative or extractive features into a platform. Quite often—for good and bad— changes are driven by or originate in user innovations that either increase frequency or intensity of social interaction or widen the scope of what people can do in a particular setting. Platform owners and application developers repeatedly find enthusiastic users "overflowing" the application, pushing the product to do *this* rather than *that*, changing its character and purpose in the process. Again, this is not by definition some blandly positive affair. These kinds of activities can, according to taste, range from reconnecting with old friends to relentlessly trolling strangers. As people explore these "off-label" uses, platform owners face the question of whether to accommodate some or all of these activities, at the risk of having their service eaten alive by them.

The feedback process is not a matter of being responsive to the demands of users in a way that always gives them what they want. Managing the flood, so to speak, must ideally be done in a way that allows the firm to take advantage of all of this effervescent interaction in a measurable, profitable way. Take something as simple and mundane as Facebook's Like button, invented to simplify the comments feedback process from a verbal form to something that could be counted. As Leah Perlman, the Facebook employee who is credited with designing the button, explains, "I was trying to solve what we called the redundant problem. So for example, if you write 'We're getting married!' all the comments used to say 'Congratulations' over and over again. I found that really aesthetically ugly, plus, every time someone did say something heartfelt, the post was hard to find among all the other redundant ones. So I wanted to solve both problems at once."[38] Initially the company's innovation was to include *only* a Like button and not a complementary Dislike or Downvote button of the sort found on other sites. Eventually users demanded to be able to iconographically express a wider range of emotional reactions, and Facebook had to explore the number and character of the responses it chose to add. Each reaction emoji provides an additional bit of information about the user and the post they are responding to. Or, to take another example, in 2015 and in response to audience demands for representation and inclusiveness, the Unicode consortium, which manages emojis, introduced skin-tone modifiers to the iconographic pictograms widely used for brief communications, jokes, and reactions. These recommendations were subsequently incorporated into operating systems and some apps, such as Slack or Discord.[39] A step forward for diversity, to be sure, but also a marvelously compact means of unobtrusively generating data on the race or ethnicity of users who choose to react to things.

Similarly, if it turns out that Facebook users are—to your surprise—using the platform to say little prayers for themselves or on behalf of their friends, why not formalize that use-case with a feature that allows a prayer to be requested or sent? Why not allow them to directly send prayers to one another, or "privately" just to themselves, their God—and you, in your capacity as platform owner? That Facebook might now know what people are literally praying for seems like something from a ham-fisted dystopian novel. But it is not that people are "forced" to tell Facebook their prayers, or that it "colonized" or "appropriated" those activities. Often, users introduce wider aspects of sociality and social practice into this world, and then the company realizes this is a behavior that might be fashioned into something more delimited, organized, data-generating, and ultimately profitable: something that can generate a manageable order, fit for an algorithm to digest, analyze, and sell to advertisers.

Finally, these decisions by Facebook have a kind of performative effect. They normalize the use of cartoonish buttons as an expression of care, adjusting people's sense of social propriety and obligation, or their yearning for validation, or their desire to be liked not only privately but publicly through the new interface.[40] Perlman recalls that the like button "was successful immediately.... The stats went up so fast—all the stats we thought would be affected, but 50 comments became 150 likes, almost immediately. Those people would start making more status updates, so there was way more content and it all just worked."[41] In other words, likes (or views, or retweets) became a form of social currency by which people managed their own social position and assessed the position of others. The resulting psychological obsessions and competitive frenzy fueled the development of what Tim Wu calls "attention markets" and the rise of the ad-driven platform.[42]

Facebook's success as a company was initially predicated on making it easy for users to find people they knew and, subsequently, on the way it made it routine to observe the ebb and flow of activity on one's personal social network one or two degrees out. Controversies over the degree of information that Facebook made available to users about what it saw and stored go back to the very beginning of the company. As it grew, Facebook's leadership became increasingly eager to discover what, if anything, might define the upper limit of users' willingness to feed large quantities of mundane but intrinsically relational data to it. More than any of the present-day giants of information technology, Facebook accommodated and then egged on people's social and creative impulses—their willingness to freely give, freely connect, freely produce, and freely exchange with one another—while also converting that tendency into profit.[43] When they have come to light publicly, its discussions of internal strategy repeatedly emphasize this push to have people "share, share, share" as much as possible—with one another and, by implication, with Facebook itself.[44] Facebook's user interface and relationships with third parties (that is, developers and advertisers) were and still are oriented to meet this basic goal.[45]

This process of exfiltration is not limited to what we might call first-order or first-person levels of data collection. With the passage of time, strategies for exfiltration have tended to extend a degree or two out along people's real-world networks. In particular, we can see the rise of what might be called "secondary enrollment" through gift exchange. Consider, for example, a grade school teacher looking to efficiently track their students' behavior and progress in the classroom or with their homework. A software company offers an app that allows students to do their work. The teacher encourages or requires the students to use the app. This provides a beachhead to the devices and the households of the students. Often there is a companion (perhaps fee-based) application for parents to see how their child is doing, which also collects data on engagement and interaction. Having successfully recruited the teacher by providing a useful classroom tool, the application developers now also secondarily enroll students and their parents. Families are the most basic structure of sociality, and thus the most natural one for companies to tap into. What goes for schools also goes for day care centers, hospitals, and prisons. Any institutionalized community provides an opening for drawing in a child's, or a patient's, or an inmate's immediate social network.

If a site or service can ride the flood tide of sociality, it massively accelerates the process of data generation. So companies are eager to foster "engagement," which in practice means reciprocity, response, tagging, uploading, and virality. These tactics easily backfire. Unanticipated adaptations, gaming the system, voyeurism, and subversive content are rife. Agreements and contracts are worthless. Basic decency and civility are hard to maintain. The more a firm succeeds in increasing the amount of time people spend within its ecology of services, the more those people bring *all* of social life in there with them. Then firms have to deal with the general problems that come with controlling any large population of people, at the limit facing the problems of government itself. The thrill of engagement becomes the madness of crowds. And yet, people keep coming back. Sociality is hard to live with but impossible to leave altogether. As Michel Callon remarks in a different context, "Overflowing is the rule. . . . Instead of regarding framing as something that happens of itself, and overflows as a kind of accident which must be put right, overflows are the rule and framing is a fragile, artificial result based upon substantial investments. . . . In addition to requiring expensive physical and symbolic devices, [framing] is always incomplete and . . . without this incompleteness would in fact be wholly ineffectual."[46] Even when organizations manage to keep their users under control and measure what they are doing, a great deal of work remains to be done. Having successfully exfiltrated some volume of material, organizations must still find a way to make use of it, without triggering all kinds of alarm bells. The digital residue of interactions, exchange, and encounters seem like they must, surely, be a source of tremendous knowledge and therefore value. Again, this is not something confined to the world of social media or even the consumer economy more generally. Although the ends are different, much the same idea applies across institutional spheres, from the detailed internal data a company can collect about its employees, to the efforts of an education system to monitor the performance and behavior of its students, to a criminal justice system's ability to check on the people it processes, to a state agency tracking the recipients of its welfare programs. Yet in practice this sort of information is hard to store, awkward to manage, difficult to integrate, tricky to analyze, and risky to exploit. Organizations know they are supposed to collect it. But what are they to do with it all?

2

The Data Imperative

As we "make things work," what kind of world
are we making?

—Langdon Winner, *The Whale and the Reactor*

THE PROBLEM IS THAT THERE IS JUST TOO MUCH DATA.[1] FROM A
conventional point of view, *too much* is not the problem we
usually face when analyzing data, or indeed when living
our lives. Instead the problem is that there is not enough.
In Lionel Robbins's classic definition, economics is "the
science which studies human behavior as a relationship
between ends and scarce means which have alternative
uses."[2] A scarcity of means in the face of potentially bound-
less human wants is the natural state of affairs—that is,
until we remember a somewhat different perspective on
this question, one shared both by economic insiders, like
John Maynard Keynes and Thorstein Veblen, and anthropological outsiders, like Georges Bataille and Marcel
Mauss.[3] While a concern for scarce resources and the rational weighing of costs and benefits is all very well, in
some ways social life is anything but scarce and people are
anything but reasonable. From this point of view, human
societies are driven by reckless profligacy, impulse, and
rivalry rather than prudent saving, coolheadedness, and

self-interest. People routinely find ways to squander whatever riches or surplus they have managed to accumulate, no matter how small. Thus, capitalism should be understood as, in Bataille's words, an "afflux of energy," an "accumulation of available forces" that depends on a continuous pressure to *expend* wealth rather than simply amass it.

Bataille called this pressure, and the often catastrophic exertions it inspires, "the accursed share."[4] Excess wealth is accursed, in Bataille's view, because once it exists it must be expended, often as extravagantly as possible and sometimes in quite gruesome and violent ways. While this perspective is quite alien to a modern economic point of view, it is tempting to see our present moment in its terms. After all, once vast quantities of data have been exfiltrated, once the share has been amassed, then what is to be done with it? It can hardly be allowed to simply sit there. As Maciej Cegłowski notes, the imagery of data accumulation and storage—in particular the notion of a "data lake"—carries connotations of a disaster waiting to happen.[5] A huge volume of information presses outward against its vessel. It threatens to overflow its bounds, to burst upon the world in a flood, or be released over it invisibly and ominously, like some mass of radioactive material. When gathering and then storing data in huge volumes is routine, it becomes impossible to imagine such a resource remaining untouched or fully encapsulated indefinitely.

Just as users tend to overflow their platforms, data tends to overflow its containers. Security failures, breaches, leaks, and gross misuses are not rare exceptions but routine events. Collecting more and more data means having more and more secrets to guard. Firms, even those that market themselves as data-safety operators, are systematically incapable of securing it all. Their failures feed an increasingly large criminal enterprise of industrial espionage and ransomware. As Karl Marx's expropriators ended up becoming the expropriated, so the exfiltrators become the exfiltrated. Even as these problems cripple systems, from school districts to health networks and energy grids, simply refraining from collecting data on a large scale is not really an option. Instead the accumulation of excess continues, and with it the expectation that it will be in some way expended.

Thou Shalt Count

This tendency to systematically collect and attempt to use structured data has deep roots. Organizations have always sought to gather information about themselves and about their environments. While present-day digital tools are novel, the application of "algorithms," in the most general sense, to the production and marshaling of knowledge is nothing new.[6] Indeed, the practice of data collection and recordkeeping reaches back to the origins of literacy and the emergence of the state itself.[7] It is almost coextensive with what is formal about formal organization. We can certainly find plenty of early examples of recordkeeping and accounting across the earliest settled societies. But the systematization of numerical thinking as a technology of truth and administration is more recent. William Deringer, for instance, sees a critical shift in the British seventeenth century. This is when, he argues, numbers "were gradually recognized to have special virtues," to be seen as a privileged medium for political knowledge.[8] The nineteenth-century statistical revolution further elaborated on this moral promise by turning numbers into what Theodore Porter called "technologies of distance," to be deployed in heavily politicized contexts to create an aura of impartiality, certainty, and finality.[9] No context was more heavily politicized than the modern states that were being built during this period. In this narrative, the rise of quantification is almost consubstantial with the ascent and legitimation of public administration.

The materiality of modern information processing is also distinctive. It relies on specific technological advances in communication and transportation, and the concomitant expansion of bureaucracy. Between 1840 and 1920, the rising complexity, scale and speed of production, distribution and trade precipitated what James Beniger called the "control revolution"—a "complex of rapid changes in the technological and economic arrangements by which information is collected, stored, processed and communicated."[10] Writing at the tail end of this transformation, Max Weber discussed the step-by-step, distributed, nominally objective procedures for selection and sorting that characterized decision-making in modern bureaucracies, whether commercial or administrative.[11] Even seemingly humble innovations such as the filing cabinet were, in their time, quietly revolutionary.[12]

One of Weber's key insights was that capitalist markets and bureaucratic organizations shared an affinity for the systematic application of rules and measures. Whether they fell under the eye of the state, the factory, or the commercial enterprise, people and things had to be visible if they were to be managed. The rise of statistics, popularized through counts, charts and atlases, structured new social imaginaries around such conceptual abstractions as sex, race, region, or occupation.[13] It is also in the nineteenth century that organizations started paying close attention to the individual persons behind the records. In the American credit market, business guides developed methods to identify good credit prospects. They collected various bits of information about the economic reliability of individuals and corporations.[14] Arbitrary as it often was, the use of this data to "place firms in a clear set of ordinal categories" created the impression of precision and order.[15] They got better at it as time went on.[16] The information used to produce the evaluations was gradually standardized. The ordinal scheme on the output side was steadily refined, allowing for more categories of creditworthiness. Around the country, dedicated organizations compiled and circulated local lists of businesses or individuals to subscribers, providing addresses and occupations, along with numerically or pictographically coded information about their qualities as potential debtors. Classes of people, scores, and prices became closely connected.

The same thing happened in other domains too. Life insurance companies "ranked among the first companies to seek profit from data processing: New York Life . . . adopted about 1903 the nation's first numerical insurance rating system, with values assigned to various factors affecting the insurability of patients."[17] In the 1920s, as head of Ives & Myrick, one of New York's largest life insurance agencies, the composer Charles Ives made it his business to turn life insurance scoring into an objective, scientific operation. Because of the difficulty of storing and circulating individual records, it was often used in aggregated form, as broad, population-wide summaries. Regional maps and statistical graphs allowed for the development of ideas about demographic aggregates, as well as facilitating control over them.[18] Meanwhile, measurement scales of all sorts were getting increasingly popular, so the next step was slotting individuals into statistical distributions.[19] By the end of the twentieth century, the ambition for more precise measures and more fine-grained classifications continued to proceed unabated in the insurance industry and elsewhere.[20] As systematic data collection about populations advanced along with the expansion of formal organizations, the subjects of data collection efforts also increasingly came to see themselves in terms of the classifications applied to them, whether economic, political, or sociological.[21]

Control efforts were internal as well as external to organizations. The fantasy of mechanizing labor by breaking it down into quantifiable parts arguably began on slave plantations. Later, the birth of social-scientific studies of business organization systematized managerial efforts to measure and control first the most literal physical movements, and subsequently also the mental states, moral characters, and private lives, of factory populations. (At the Ford Motor Company, the name of the division responsible for internal security and the surveillance of workers was the Sociological Department.)[22] By the turn of the twentieth century, time-and-motion studies sought to disaggregate the industrial work process in the most detailed way possible. Frederick Taylor held a stopwatch to time workers as they performed tasks. Frank and Lillian Gilbreth used the best technology then available— film cameras—to observe and record the work process in order to understand and reorganize its component parts.[23] Their ambitions ran well ahead of the technical capabilities they had at their disposal, but their work pointed firmly toward the future. That future was one of ever greater *granularity* in observation, data collection, and analysis. Measurement was not just precise, it was as focused as possible. In principle, every relevant detail should be captured and subject to investigation and optimization.

The increasing powers of computing in data collection and analysis complemented these trends very well. Prior to the end of the nineteenth century, counting people and things depended on an elaborate human infrastructure of manual sorters. This started to change when, in 1884, a German American statistician named Herman Hollerith developed an electromagnetic tabulating machine for the 1890 US Census that worked with punched cards made of stiff paper. The tabulator mechanized and dramatically lowered the cost of processing records. "Young, unmarried women" were brought into government offices in large numbers to "ensure that the monotonous labor of punching holes was performed conscientiously, quickly, and inexpensively."[24] Compared with manual ledgers, punched cards also enabled the recording and storage of a larger amount of information about individuals, allowing census statisticians to quickly generate aggregated figures about various population characteristics. Hollerith would soon found the Tabulating Machine Company and go on to win contracts with census operations outside the United States, including the United Kingdom and, infamously, Germany.[25] The technology quickly spread to the business sector, and the company was renamed International Business Machines—or IBM—in 1911. Precious company data such as paper-based customer and staff records; purchasing, billing, and accounting ledgers; and more were all moved over to punch cards with the assistance of temporary workers who were the original "coders" and "calculators."[26]

The Hollerith card "would become an essential tool for making the world legible to governments and corporations."[27] But it also expanded what was possible, as it dramatically increased the volume and detail of data that *could* be collected on anything and anyone. It did not simply act as a means of recording what was already there. It allowed new things to be done. It was an engine, not a camera.

The arrival of the digital computer supercharged these control ambitions.[28] The move to digital information en-

coding dramatically expanded the possibilities for computation and recordkeeping applications. It seemed like
these technologies would not just give organizations the
ability to count but the ability to count *everything.* Computers were versatile. Their powers could be applied anywhere. Every industry, every business should want them.[29]
Not only did they vastly increase the scale and scope of
feasible data collection, they also hugely enhanced its
resolution. It became possible not just to collect detailed
individual-level data but also to represent and analyze it at
that level. Indeed, there was no requirement to stop there.
Even more fine-grained scales—transactions, spells of activity, tasks, subtasks, procedures, events, and beyond—came
into focus. The combination of organizational enthusiasm
for data collection, growing analytical capacity and anemic
privacy protections meant that digital files about employees,
consumers, or (non)citizens could be assembled in many
settings. Depending on an organization's purpose and
reach, its data might consist of cases or records containing
just a few, a few hundred, a few thousand, or tens of thousands of measures, tracked in a continuous manner over
time. Individuals themselves were representable not as some
fundamental unit but as entities aggregated from records
of more detailed decisions or activities tagged with the appropriate database key or identifier. This is what Kevin
Haggerty and Richard Ericson call "the data double."[30] The
promise was of a system of information that could be
as informative in its details as it was comprehensive in
its scope.

Thou Shalt Gather

Digital traces logged on servers are the resource that powers some of the most potent prediction and discovery activities in history—in both corporate and noncorporate settings. But they were not always seen as valuable. Search engine companies, including Google, initially dismissed the metadata that people leave behind when they search the World Wide Web as digital "waste." Shoshana Zuboff describes the realization, by one of Google's earliest employees, of their possible usefulness as a sort of "accident" and explains how this "discovery" of what she calls "the behavioral surplus" in the early 2000s radically transformed Google's business model (or, rather, it gave Google the economic rationale that it did not previously have).[31] The crystallization came in a patent filed in 2003 in which residual user information was repurposed for targeted advertising. From then on, everybody wanted to pick up the trash—and not only their own. Companies could analyze their own confidential data. Later, they could also absorb volumes of material from the open or commodified web. Later again, they could use either or both to train customized AI models.

One may argue that this shift was no accident. All firms depend on making profits and seek to exploit whatever wealth that has been created.[32] But competitive pressures are not the only reason why *this* particular way of seeking profits came to institutionalize itself. The real achievement was naturalizing the idea that the long-term profitability of organizations depends on the collection and exploitation of data. This notion, which we call "the data imperative," was a cultural and political accomplishment, beyond the economically driven search for efficiency. As sociologists have shown, people inside and outside an organization have beliefs about the legitimacy of its modus operandi, and they engage in repeated patterns of interaction that structure everyday life within and around it.[33] In the 1970s John Meyer and Brian Rowan further argued that such beliefs and routines tend to be institutionalized at a supraorganizational level, in a diffuse but culturally imperious sort of way. In other words, the broader environment within which organizations operate emits powerful injunctions about what they should look like and what they should be doing. Maintaining an allegiance to institutionalized norms takes a lot of effort. This elaboration has a ritualistic character that often becomes detached from the immediate technical demands of work. But the cultural imperative to comply is strong. Any organization that fails to signal conformity with the rationalized myths in its field exposes itself to being regarded as illegitimate. This explains why organizations in the same domain tend to formally look similar, but also why their formal structure is not always aligned with their actual activities, which are subject to different constraints.

These prevailing beliefs about what rational organizational structures and practices should look like may have various sources. Meyer and Rowan mention *professions, programs,* and *techniques.* The injunction coming from professions is normative and moral: "We do these things because we must." Professionals and experts, sometimes self-proclaimed, standardize organizational expectations by articulating a rationale for them. They define and enunciate rules, circulate knowledge, and control certification processes that are designed to ensure compliance to best practices. Legal experts are the most important formalizers of such activities. For instance, Julie Cohen and Margaret Radin show that platforms rely heavily on legal logics and legal documents to naturalize their rights to data and their lack of public accountability.[34]

The injunction coming from programs, by contrast, is mimetic. It is based on firms looking around their wider environment. "We do these things because that's what leaders in our field do—and so they must be good." A surprising amount of organizational practice bears this imitative character, even when justifications have long been forgotten and disillusion about their effectiveness has taken hold.[35] Like people, institutions observe each other, fear missing out on the hype, and strive to enact the scripts available in their field.

The institutional command coming from technology is voluntaristic: "We do these things because we *can*." Science and technology, Max Weber remarked, are "chained to the course of progress."[36] They contain within themselves the principle of their own inexorable movement forward. That principle, or the notion that everything can be mastered by calculation, Weber calls "intellectualization" and "disenchantment." Economic constraint is the main thing that stands temporarily against it. But as the cost of technology's deployment in the world plummets, there is little that can prevent the products of scientific

progress from taking hold everywhere and wholly transforming our relationship to the world and to one another.
A careless observer might attribute the practice of collecting personal data to the simple wish to make money,
the unhealthy desire to pry into people's lives, or the grand
ambition to surveil and control a population. But in practice, data collection often has a ceremonial character, just
as Meyer and Rowan predicted. Professional exhortations;
conventional wisdom; falling computing and storage costs;
and most recently the gigantic training demands of large
language models for content production—all of these
forces have pushed organizations to sweep up increasingly
large quantities of bits about whatever crosses their path.
"Thou shalt gather data" has become second nature for
private and public institutions alike. It does not matter that
the volume and character of what gets collected may vastly
exceed the imaginative reach or analytic grasp of the
organization at the moment of acquisition. The assumption is that it will, somehow, eventually be useful or valuable at some economically justifiable cost.

There are many types of data to be gathered, and some
are more important than others. At the center of any data
infrastructure is what Robert Kitchin calls "indexical
data"—data that "enable identification and linking across
files . . . unique identifiers, such as passport and social security numbers, credit card numbers, manufacturer serial
numbers, digital object identifiers, IP [network node] and
MAC [hardware device] addresses, order and shipping numbers, as well as names, addresses, zip codes."[37] Though private and nonprofit systems have become heavily involved

in efforts to stabilize the identification of individuals across time and space, the roots of the "identificatory revolution" go back to the state.[38] The development of states' power of taxation, security, administration, conscription, and redistribution have all depended on the institutionalization of systems of citizen registration and control, whose uses and affordances often far exceeded their original purpose. One example is the Social Security number (SSN), launched during the New Deal in the United States. Originally intended only as a means of allowing the Social Security Board to track the earnings of people who worked in jobs covered by the Social Security program, SSNs gradually became a de facto national identification number for American citizens and residents.

The process took about sixty years. At every stage, the government insisted it was not interested in developing a national ID system. But it was, in effect, doing something more ambitious: maintaining a longitudinal file—a "data double"—on every American. The Internal Revenue Service began using SSNs for tax reporting in the early 1960s. Various state agencies followed: Medicare in 1965 and the military in 1969; by 1970, banks, savings and loan associations, credit unions, and securities dealers were required by law to collect the SSNs of their customers. Expansion of the scope of SSNs continued through the 1980s, eventually connecting to all interest-bearing accounts and most government programs, as well as extending to new classes of person, such as temporary and permanent resident aliens. By the early 2000s, the SSN was ubiquitous. It provided a crucial means of tracking individuals in a consistent fashion across institutional settings and their associated data-bases, and it was vital to the practical construction of a credit reporting system that could go beyond the scope of data collection by individual banks about their account holders.[39]

Quite separately, and later, the state invested in the creation of the internet. Initially spurred by concerns about the robustness of command and control structures in the wake of a nuclear attack, the US federal government supported the development of a network infrastructure for computer communication and directly funded or coordinated the establishment of robust core communications protocols such as packet-switching networks, and a system to manage the allocation of server and client identifiers and addresses on a large scale. While these initiatives had military roots, the government subsequently promoted the open standardization through which the technology was able to flourish at first: "At its heart, the internet is just a system of protocols and information exchange rules that all computers involved recognize. . . . The federal government encouraged a stream of free, quickly shared software that promoted continual innovation on the network."[40]

The conjunction of these two distinct developments helped create the possibility of reliably tracking individual activity across open networks in a way that could be connected to both private financial circumstances and interactions with the state. The internet's infrastructure is fundamentally about the identifiability of bits of information traveling to and from particular devices rather than individual users. But with that in place, subsequent developments allowed for the creation and monitoring of all kinds of more or less stable identities over time, from unnamed but reliable patterns of activity originating with particular devices to known, named users and their accounts. The facticity of "the user" varies widely. An account may be backed by nothing at all, or by an email address (which could mean anything); but perhaps also by a name, an address, a phone number, an associated credit card, an official government identity, a persistent numerical ID, or some biometric tag (one's face, fingers, eyes, voice), which are altogether more identifiable. Unique identifiers such as these serve as anchors for personal data that might be collected from or matched to other sources. What matters is having a system whereby individuals can be reliably identified and their status rapidly queried, keyed, or merged as needed. The state played a key role in establishing the conditions for the rapid institutionalization of individual identification in this way, and the adoption of this idea by private firms.[41]

The piecemeal development of traceable markers of identity and the open character of the internet's evolving infrastructure created persistent ambiguity about the character of "online identity" and its connection to individual selves. But whether we think "being online" is a distinct form of sociality or simply continuous with the rest of everyday life, it means leaving digital traces of our actions. That allows for data to be collected about an awful lot of particular, mostly unsuspicious individuals. Initially, the potential of log files to yield useful data on users was not fully grasped by firms. But they came to see every click or eyeball as having possible economic value. Keeping track of who visited, how they arrived, and where they went afterward was useful enough in itself. But the additional possibility of tracking users across different settings (with the now almost phased out cross-site cookies managed by third parties or simply by fusing data from various sources) and profiling them based on that activity was very appealing. In addition to silently collecting fine-grained data, there was also the prospect of extracting richer information from deliberately contributing individuals. Ratings, comments, recommendations, connections to peers: all are cheerfully fed to companies, perhaps to your benefit, perhaps to theirs. This is by now such a well-established niche that a quite lucrative economy of advice intermediaries flourishes, dependent on the reliably provided collective feedback and pro bono work of the crowd.

Information collected in this way is valuable. Organizations believe it is useful for them to engage in the data collection business, even when they do not yet know what to do with the records they have collected. That is the normative, ceremonial part of the data imperative. But the economic dimension of this imperative also looms large. By now all organizations, including brick-and-mortar shops or public agencies, have learned to see the data they have collected as an asset, which they can hold on to and process, sell, or leverage in their interactions with subjects and with third parties.[42] If they are not sure how to transform it, there are other organizations that know, or claim to know, how to extract value, how to unpack the data to enhance prediction, contextualization, and the personalization of services. And these third parties are willing to pay to access this data.

At the core of this process in the United States are data brokers. Their rise largely predates the advent of the web and of the large data monopolists such as Amazon, Facebook. and Google.[43] Some of these organizations, like LiveRamp (formerly Axciom), are traditional marketers who built their wealth in an earlier era, often by digitizing public documents held in analog form and assembling enormous consumer intelligence databases from a wide range of offline sources. Others, like Oracle or Salesforce, developed their data brokerage business from a core expertise in computer software. Yet others, originally specialized in risk analytics (notably, credit risk) or fraud detection, have expanded outward, repurposing their own data troves for marketing purposes. Since then, the sector has become a free-for-all. Dating websites, insurance companies, and health care organizations have branched out into data brokerage. Meanwhile, acquisitive strategies have multiplied and diversified. These may include scraping posts, comments, photos, and "likes" from social media websites; purchasing databases from private corporations and public administrations; entering into data-sharing agreements with other vendors; and, last but not least, buying up companies in other sectors of the digital economy (e.g., identity verification, personnel management, and payment systems). The purpose is to clean, merge, and match data across sources. The result is usually lists of digital identities that sell for pennies and can be purchased by anyone with very little oversight (at least at the time of this writing).[44] To

prove the point, in May 2017 Spanish artist Joana Moll
and the activist group Tactical Tech purchased one million
online dating profiles for €136 from the US-based company
USDate. The batch of dating profiles, which came from
across the globe, "included pictures (almost 5 million of
them), usernames, e-mail addresses, nationality, gender,
age and detailed personal information about all of the
people who had created the profiles, such as their sexual
orientation, interests, profession, thorough physical characteristics and personality traits."[45] At least in the United
States, business has been brisk for the data brokerage industry. According to a Vermont law that requires data brokers to register in the state, there were no fewer than 120
data brokers operating there in 2019. Unsurprisingly, these
companies are particularly active in the domains of security,
border control, and fraud and risk assessment. In February 2021, for instance, a leaked contract between the
"risk industry" firm LexisNexis and US Immigration and
Customs Enforcement (ICE) showed that the firm was to
"provide Homeland Security investigators access to billions of different records containing personal data aggregated from a wide array of public and private sources, including credit history, bankruptcy records, license plate
images, and cellular subscriber information. The company will also provide analytical tools that can help police
connect these vast stores of data to the right person."
   Barely a year after publishing this story, the same jour-
nalist reported that ICE had "searched Lexis-Nexis over
1 million times in seven months."[46] A subsidiary of the
firm, ThreatMetrix, operates globally.

And yet, despite the level of activity in this sector and the demand for the service that brokers provide, it also has the feel of a secondary or even bottom-feeding segment of the ecology of the world of data processing as a whole. The resources available to brokers pale in comparison to the sort of information that the biggest players have accumulated within their own platforms. In principle, and in the aggregate, what the largest contemporary organizations have at hand is the immense yield of the social substrate in the broadest sense, a source of data about what people are doing, writing, or saying (or thinking of saying, as in unsent draft messages) that exists in a form that can be parsed, saved, and mined for information. But "in principle, and in the aggregate" is sloughing over a lot of detail here. Formal organizations have long felt the demand of the data imperative. From time to time, technical advances have transformed either the quantity of information that can be collected or its substantive nature. With data in their possession, in some form or another, the task facing organizations is to find a way to manage and learn from it. This is not as easy as it might seem.

Thou Shalt Learn

Getting hold of a really large amount of data is one sort of challenge. Learning from it is another. Data needs to be properly stored and cleaned before anything can be done with it. Journalistic accounts and depictions in cinema—not to mention discussions by social theorists—frequently

gloss over the boring, frustrating, and often disquieting realities of building a dataset, properly securing it, and extracting any kind of meaningful results from it. In the movies,
one simply needs to type a natural-language search query
or tell the computer to "zoom and enhance" for the desired
results to appear. Anyone who has done original analysis
on quantitative data of their own, however, will be well
aware of just how much work is needed before anything
useful can be accomplished with even modest quantities
of data—and how problematic much of what is routinely
accomplished can be. Even worse, confusion and failure
only multiply if there is a need for analyses to be repeat-
able, or comparable with past efforts, or easily transpos-
able to new settings. At the sort of scale we have been dis-
cussing, these issues become serious technical challenges
and potentially severe managerial or security problems.
An entire body of semiformalized practical lore focuses
on what will routinely go wrong in such circumstances.[47]
Thus, to grasp the changing character of the data imperative, we must understand how the bureaucratic logic of
organizations interacts with the computational logic of
machines.

Some of the challenges are chronic to any kind of formal
organization. Those have been the bread and butter of
organizational sociology for decades. For example, upper-
level managers or administrators may demand that subordinates build the material infrastructure that will supply
a flow of actionable information. Yet the further they are
from the organizational site of the actual collection and
analysis of whatever information they think is relevant, the

less able they will be to really grasp what it means. Meanwhile, subordinates working to set up these systems will need to make practical decisions about how to proceed. Perhaps their choices will have unpredictable or hard-to-see effects later on. These gaps and tears in the seams of organizations are the source of decoupling between nominal procedures and what is happening in practice. This, too, is the focus of much science and technology scholarship. A substantial tradition of research has shown that the gaps tend to be filled in, if at all, by local politics and negotiation, tacit knowledge, and adaptive strategies—including expediency and approximation.

These familiar tendencies take on new forms in modern data collection and analysis. It is easy for data pipelines to interact badly with organizational routines and managerial demands. Data collection tools are complex and often brittle. Even when large in size, data sources themselves may nevertheless be incomplete, unrepresentative, internally incomparable, or subject to various forms of "drift" over time.[48] Managerial understanding of them may be weak, especially the farther away from the front line the results are carried. In sum, learning from data at any scale and scope is easy to do badly. Even when applied successfully, analytical tools can be opaque or simply difficult to understand due to "interlocking technical and legal prohibitions" that prevent outsiders from "understanding fundamental facts about them."[49] Malfunction, misuse, and misinterpretation is not only possible but likely. According to the best specialists, much of it is no better than "snake oil."[50]

The first computers to analyze data calculated statistics that were meant, at a minimum, to establish descriptive patterns and, ideally, to adduce some evidence for causal relationships. The world of "classical" programming and data analysis as one where some combination of rules and data are algorithmically combined to produce informative answers. Many modern machine learning (ML) methods, by contrast, can be thought of as taking a large batch of data and a smaller set of known correct answers and then computationally combining them to produce rules that can, for instance, be used to accurately classify new batches of data as they are produced.[51] That is, computers are programmed to use statistics to identify patterns directly in the data. The computer "learns" from the data and, in the process, optimizes how it performs this task. Computers can also learn to classify data on their own, as it were, and thereby predict how new observations should be classified.

In contrast to the classical case, where decision rules are directly written down by a programmer, the precise rationale for why a modern classifier behaves the way it does is not always obvious. We know what the procedure is in general, of course, because that must still be specified by the software developers. And it is clear what quantity is being optimized by the model because a particular loss function is also specified in advance. But the thing itself, the operation of the classifier in detail, is often opaque to the point of being uninterpretable. Again, it is important to remember that this is always true to some degree for statistical models of any sort of complexity. Even boring old "shallow learning" methods are subject to something like this tendency. After all, with just a few multifaceted interactions or a couple of nonlinear terms, an ordinary regression model quickly becomes quite tricky to properly interpret. But the properties of this sort of model are, on the whole, analytically well understood. The structure of any particular such model can be investigated in a relatively manageable way. Deep-learning models, by comparison, are much more like true black boxes. Their overall properties are harder to understand, or are not yet established analytically. Their internal structure is much less amenable to piecemeal decomposition and investigation. Instead, by their fruits shall ye know them.[52]

Methods for layered neural networks have been around for some time. Initially developed in the 1960s, they came into more widespread use in applied statistics in the 1980s and 1990s. At that point they were seen as "a flexible nonlinear extension of multiple logistic regression."[53] Their usefulness seemed relatively limited. In comparison to more familiar methods they were both analytically less transparent and computationally more trouble than they were worth. While they had some notable successes, they also tended to come off poorly in comparison to their main competitors in the sphere of classification problems.[54] But continuing research; the rapid expansion of cheap, large-scale computing power; and the concomitant availability of enormous datasets for analysis and cheap, platformized labor to annotate them resulted in a sea change in the usefulness of these methods.[55] Their application began to

yield rapid progress in notoriously intractable problems
such as speech recognition, image classification, and natural
language processing. Today these approaches drive experimentation across a huge range of areas.

Modern ML methods extended the simpler neural networks of the 1990s to many more processing layers—
sometimes thousands them. In these models, each layer
produces its own representation of an aspect of the data
and relays what it has learned to the next layer, all the way
to the final one, which uses all the information passed
along to generate the resulting classification. Notably, this
way of doing things is not like repeatedly applying some
more conventional kind of model over and over again. Sup-
pose we have measured some quantity that can be either
one of two things, like yes or no, positive or negative, black
or white. If we have also measured some other things about
our data, we can use a logistic regression to model the
probability of any particular case falling into one or other
category, conditional on those other things. A social scientist might say logistic regression models the predictors of
some binary outcome in order to show the degree to which
each predictor is associated with the outcome and how different predictors perform in comparison to one another.
A data scientist might say the same model is a form of supervised learning that can be used to make a classifier
based on the features we have measured. A deep-learning
model is in some very broad sense a much more complex
descendant of this way of doing things, with much larger
datasets and many more intermediate steps. But its results are
not equivalent to iteratively updating a logistic regression

hundreds of times. A deep-learning model is optimized jointly across layers. The weighting applied to each layer is efficiently adjusted in response to information from the loss function about how well things are going in the estimation process. This is the crucial backpropagation step. Finding a way to efficiently implement this for large datasets was at the heart of the success of deep-learning methods. It is this global optimization that yields the superb empirical performance that the models are known for. But it is also what produces their characteristic lack of transparency.[56]

The combination of large amounts of data, high levels of accuracy, and a general lack of interpretability has several organizational consequences. Convolutional neural networks and other deep-learning methods hunger for as many cases as possible. They thrive on ever larger volumes of data in a way that their chief competitors tend not to. This appetite for data requires a pipeline to provide it in the right form and in sufficient quantities. On the input side, an organization employing such a model will be pushed to rethink its operations and digital interfaces in order to facilitate a continuous flow of data. Meanwhile, on the output side, the relative opacity of the method tends to encourage a kind of magical orientation to the results. At their best, these approaches really do perform astonishingly well. But their scale and complexity invites a kind of deference to the oracle, both in terms of its care and feeding, on the one hand, and its pronouncements, on the other. Once more, even well-understood modeling techniques will often tend to be treated in this way in practice by their users. Anyone who has seen statistical results misused in a business context will be aware of this. But the temptation is all the stronger in the case of deep learning methods, perhaps especially when—as in the case of large language models—the model's outputs take the form of paragraphs of text. This makes it easy to pretend (or even believe) that it is rather like a properly knowledgeable assistant.

The process looks both inward and outward. The public character of identities and the general digitization of public life have lowered the cost of collecting data on all kinds of information about people and their networks, from their exercise habits and their diet to their good character in the community or their tendency to take risks. The assumption that this kind of information will, naturally, be sought out and collected also seems to be diffusing. Commentators often speak blandly of "digital natives" as if they had a natural technical facility with computing. The reality of the idea may lie more in the tendency to accept a social ecology where everything is indexed, tracked, and measured. One is not born, rather one becomes a digital native. Organizations share this attitude, too, as advances in ML have solidified "the unnerving belief that everything is data and is there for the taking."[57] Realizing this belief demands a collective, sustained overhauling of the sociomaterial environment. It means adjusting the rules of human exchange to circumvent normal expectations about privacy, drawing on an infrastructure of logins and passwords, unique device identifiers, and biometrics; routinizing the use of trackers and sensors in virtual and physical spaces; socializing people to volunteer inputs and respond to machine feedback through addictive designs; nudging them into frequent check-ins and assessments. With its algorithmically produced feed, endless scroll, automated data collection and learning, its quantified metrics and modulated interventions, the social media app exemplifies this regime more than any other mode of computer interaction. Is it surprising that social media apps increasingly resemble shopping, transportation, streaming, payment, educational, and cooking apps, which in turn all resemble social media apps?[58]

The application of ML to real problems has seen some spectacular successes, of the sort where performance verges on the magical. Areas such as automated translation, image classification, voice recognition, and automated text extraction and transcription have been transformed by ML approaches in general and deep-learning methods in particular. Even more impressive, the world is now being populated with synthetic objects that blur the boundaries between the fake and the real: machine-generated text, speech, images, video, and more. In these areas, ML methods have rapidly entrenched themselves in everyday use. Other areas, especially when directly applied to decision-making about groups of people, feel rather more hazardous. This is true for both fashionable deep-learning approaches and technically less novel but still widely used methods that depend more on "feature engineering," or what social scientists would call model-fitting and variable selection. In that case, features—that is, independent variables, or predictors—are directly evaluated by modelers and chosen purely for their predictive performance.[59]

In social-scientific applications, statistical methods are generally used in an effort to establish causal relationships and thus are typically deployed in conjunction with some sort of experimental or plausibly quasi-experimental research design. In principle, an awareness of the difficulty of identifying causal pathways is at the forefront of the researcher's concerns. This leads to a focus on eliminating spurious associations.[60] With the sort of purely predictive ML more typical of industry applications, analysts want, of course, to understand the structure of their model but they care most about whether a feature is predictive, even if the causal structure is less clear. Sometimes the measures or features that work best as predictors perform well because they short-circuit causal pathways. For example, it might be that some measure of poverty or race reliably predicts whether it is cost-efficient to give a patient medical treatment. Or some aggregate measure, such as the demographic makeup of a neighborhood, may be a more powerful predictor of loan defaults than an individual's credit history. From a social-scientific point of view, the main issue with empirical associations like these is figuring out what the causal pathways underlying them really are. This requires a theory of those pathways, and some sort of method capable of distinguishing in principle between properly causal and merely associational patterns. From a regulatory standpoint, the lack of a logical connection between the data collected and the outcome of interest is problematic too. As Barbara Kiviat has shown in the case of the (well-established) statistical relationship between credit scores and insurance claims, these kinds of associations offend the moral intuitions of both legislators and the public.[61] On both theoretical and methodological grounds, some features of the data will thus be deemed unacceptable—and dismissed—regardless of how well they predict outcomes.

The problem is, very few algorithms are scrutinized that way. Standard methods for benchmarking their performance may be of questionable validity.[62] Meanwhile, in many applied settings, prediction trumps everything else, with causal attribution or explanation following along some way behind. It is in these settings that the feedback between effective prediction and presumptive causality can start to loop in ways that are counterproductive. Perhaps a service provider automates a procedure for identifying which children are at risk of domestic abuse, thereby triggering organizational actions—typically "increased surveillance and strict behavioral compliance requirements"— with consequences for the labels attached to parents and children.[63] Or perhaps a system for disseminating information or political advertising turns out to push people toward more radical positions and identities because this makes their behavior more predictable later on and thus easier to work with.[64] Or a third-party recruitment and hiring platform is unable to explain how its automated video interview software picks job candidates, prompting fears that the old disciplines of phrenology and physiognomy are being revived underneath the technological hype.[65] In the words of a Silicon Valley insider, it is in these sorts of settings that predictive analytics come dangerously close to alchemy.[66] Some uses go beyond even alchemy and cross over to the absurd. Perhaps substantively meaningless correlations are taken at face value to determine important decisions, or overfitted models are used in ways that would embarrass any well-trained analyst, or a method requiring any number of careful assumptions is put to work on terrible data.[67] The kind of learning that takes place when the aim is to accurately predict is different from the kind of learning focused on the real structure of social processes. The kinds of knowledge generated are correspondingly different also.

Some of these concerns are as old as the formal statistical analysis of data itself, and cautions about them can be found throughout the history of the literature on data analysis, from introductory textbooks to valedictory lectures.[68] Moreover, as is well known, the enthusiastic application of statistical methods to questions of social classification is not merely a curious sidelight in the history of statistics but rather a mainspring of its modern development and early influence on public policy.[69] The new methods for learning from data promised to avoid past pitfalls and stigma. It seemed that, with information available in unprecedented volume, analysis would no longer be constrained by unrealistic assumptions or inaccurate generalizations. An implicit assumption here was that the deep-seated desire of organizations to always know more— about themselves, their employees, or their clients—would be enhanced in a way that would remain comprehensible in its results. The output of all this learning would be like the kind of knowledge we had before, only better in every respect. But the sort of knowledge these systems actually yield may turn out not to be like this. It may be that all we are left with is a pattern of associations, with little understanding of the intelligence or method that produces them.

Arthur C. Clarke's third law of prediction is, famously, "Any sufficiently advanced technology is indistinguishable from magic." The kind of technology Clarke had in mind was one that truly works, but in such a sophisticated way that it is entirely opaque to the ordinary people who use it. The optimistic reading is that Clarke pictured our descendants in the role of the makers of such technologies as people who actually understood it. But perhaps not. Magical technologies work . . . mostly. When they fail and you ask for an explanation, they present you with a blank face. When you try to intervene to fix them, they offer you no purchase on their surface of smooth glass. Instead of controlling technology as a wise wizard might wield a staff, you are forced to fall back on magic's traditional social function—namely, the ritual performance of specific but obscurely relevant steps meant to compel the gods to do the thing you want. Yet the gods care nothing for ordinary people; their ways are mostly unfathomable, and our means of control over them are obscure and unreliable. Instead of *elevating* us to a world of magic, the world of artificial intelligence and machine learning *reduces* us to it. A final wrinkle is that, as it advances, this process tends to shrink and ultimately undermine the caste of priests. In simpler technological worlds, the gods may communicate more directly to supplicants. They speak cryptically, but the initiated understand what is being said. Beyond a certain point, though, there is both less room for understanding and fewer means of intervention. With few exceptions, technology's priesthood may find itself degraded to the unhappy state of the laity. It, too, must confront what it means to live in an age where a sufficiently advanced technology really has become indistinguishable from magic.

3

Classification Situations

OUR MACHINES CLASSIFY BECAUSE PEOPLE DO. WE COME TO KNOW and relate to the world by way of categories. To be human is to be able to recognize patterns and distinguish things according to type. Ordinary communication is the most immediate expression of this faculty. We refer to things through sounds and words, and we attach ideas to them that we call concepts. Some of our categories remain tacit; others are explicitly governed by custom, law, politics, or science. The application of category systems for the same things varies by context and in use. The notion of an animal species, for instance, might in one setting best be thought of as described by folklore and myth, in another as a detailed legal construct, and in another as a system of scientific classification.[1]

The way we divide up human populations into groups and classes has this quality too. Independent of whether they "carve nature at the joints," as philosophers like to say, what gives categories their authority—what makes them appear natural to us—is the fact that they are collectively crafted, sustained, and enforced. This is not a deliberately collaborative process, of course. The most basic insight of sociology is that the joint action of human beings produces a social world that has the character of objective fact. The intersubjective, mutually reinforcing character of our expectations is the basis of the strange facticity, or quasi-objectivity, possessed by socially constructed things. Institutions flicker into existence in the light of mutual expectations and are sustained by them.[2] They are highly scripted, chronically available, repeatedly enacted, and presumptively real. They can also be obligatory and coercive, as in the case of classifications of caste, or gender, or race.

Social classifications are entrenched in people's emotions, in their bodies, and in their everyday practices. This makes them hard to change. But change happens anyway. It has to. Intersubjective expectations must be constantly re-created and revalidated in practice. This process is neither error free nor uncontestable.[3] While the most important categories and classifications are deeply entrenched and have a "systemic" character, it is not the sort of system that is necessarily coherent or perfectly self-replicating. Social life is messy. Since some social categories are advantageous and others detrimental, people struggle over their definition. They press to be fitted into one type rather than another.[4] They come up with new categories. In Ian Hacking's felicitous phrase, people are "made up" and remade all the time that way. New concepts come along to identify with and be identified by.

Certain kinds of classifications, typically those applying to human or social collectives, are "interactive" in that "when known by people or those around them, and put to work in institutions, [they] change the ways in which individuals experience themselves—and may even lead people to evolve their feelings and behavior in part because they are so classified."[5] These "looping effects," in turn, may further transform how institutions intervene in people's lives, perhaps even upending the classification system itself. Human societies are forever being destructured and restructured by the continuous interactions between classifying institutions and the people and groups they sort. This is especially the case when categories are public, visible, or legally recognized. A public or official status is a mark of objectivity that also makes it easier for collective action to find a focal point. More deeply, present-day liberal democracies tend to have a "politics of recognition" that accords moral importance to ideas of self-categorization, personal authenticity, and dignity. This makes it easier for many formerly primordial categories and classes to be contested.[6] It also makes possible the sort of entrenchment and sacralization that is distinctively modern, centered on the individual.

The abundance of rich, multidimensional, digital data and the means to analyze it has profoundly affected how social categories are made and how people sort themselves or are sorted. Relative to their analog predecessors, classifications produced by computer code sifting through digital data are more likely to be anchored in direct measures of behavior. They also tend to be more fine-grained, inductive, and flexible. And they are often more opaque, in the sense that they may depart from established categories and fail to be readily interpretable in terms of them.

An engine of social differentiation sits on top of this evolving—but increasingly precise and routinized—infrastructure. As people move through the world, reams of data are assembled about them. Analytics tools begin the work of arranging longitudinal and cross-sectional profiles and disaggregating and sorting these "data doubles" into predicted categories.[7] While you exist as a physical person in the world, your data double is the representation of you, your tastes, and your actions that can be reconstructed in whole or in part from the records and traces you leave behind. The categorical systems themselves may vary depending on the purpose at hand—people may be sorted into types of person, market segments, risk brackets, expected value targets, and more. But what unites these systems is that they are actionable. Writing about market research in the early 1990s, Oscar Gandy Jr. called this now ubiquitous process "the panoptic sort":

> The panoptic sort is a system of disciplinary surveillance that is widespread but continues to expand its reach. The panoptic sort is a difference machine that sorts individuals into categories and classes on the basis of routine measurements. It is a discriminatory technology that allocates options and opportunities on the basis of those measures and the administrative models that they inform. The panoptic sort has been institutionalized. It

is standard operating procedure. It is expected. It has its place. Its operation is even required by law. Where it is not, people call out for its installation. Its work is never done. Each use generates new uses. Each application justifies another. It is efficient, having largely been automated. . . . The panoptic sort is a system of actions that governs other actions. The panoptic sort is a system of power.[8]

As this "cybernetic triage" unfolds,[9] the analysis of tracked and classified behaviors forms the basis of differential treatment, thus affecting social stratification through the allocation of similar sets of opportunities to similarly situated people—what sociologists since Max Weber have called "life chances." Organizations apply labeling and scoring methods to slice people into groups and ranks suited to their particular ends. People find themselves more or less comfortably fitting into these categories. Often these categories are not—or sometimes, as a matter of law, cannot be—constructed from standard demographic classifications such as race and gender. Instead they tend to be behavioral and probabilistic, predicting the likelihood that people will do or like certain kinds of things, or the position they may reach on a particular scale. In that sense these methods construct a "postdemographic" classificatory infrastructure.[10]

We call these outcomes *classification situations*.[11] These are positions in a generated system of categories that are consequential for one's life chances. Classification situations are not merely approximations of commonly identified social groups and identities—though, of course, they may overlap substantially in specific cases. Rather, they are independently generated taxonomies that can come to have distinctive and consequential effects on the "outcomes" people experience in life.

Naming and Ordering

Social order, like computational order, comes in many varieties. To begin, we can distinguish between different ways to classify and measure things in the world. *Nominal* judgments are oriented toward essence. They define what something is. They are judgments of type, labels that describe some intrinsic quality, perhaps in relation to other sorts of things. Think of the efforts by Carl Linnaeus to classify the flora and fauna of the world in his *Systema naturae* early in the eighteenth century. Specimens from all over the world were compared and carefully organized in relation to each other, following rules of resemblance and difference. Later, nonbiological aspects of human life were subject to the same process of collection and classification. By the end of the nineteenth century, the accumulation of human artifacts and knowledge of exotic languages and rituals allowed for the ostensibly scientific definition of cultural differences between human groups.

Nominal judgments require decisions about the criteria for resemblance and then some sort of interpretive assessment of where something belongs. Resemblance legitimates lumping together, but the basis for establishing

proper resemblance is always difficult and often contested. Moreover, nominal categorizations tend to work
with ideas about ideal or typical members of a class, on
the one hand, and departures from some default or standard, on the other. Even though nominal classifications
are in principle just names or labels, not numbers or positions, they may still express priority and hierarchy.
This can be explicit, as in terms of relations in a tree of
categories and subcategories. Or it can be implicit, as
when default orderings lead to marked and unmarked
categories, with the unmarked case—the one you don't
have to point out or specially label—being intuitively prior
to the marked.

Nominalization may also be informal or formal. Bottom-
up processes driven by homophily and more top-down
institutional rules for naming both create categories. In the
former case, when left to their own devices people have a
tendency to associate with others who are similar to them
in various salient ways: birds of a feather flock together.[12] In
the latter case, organizations or institutions group like
with like, too, in the light of their own goals. While informal
sorting might arise from local actions and choices, nominalization finds its formal representation in clustering
and classification methods. A recommendation algorithm
might find each person's "nearest neighbors" in terms of
positions in an abstract space defined by patterns of consumption or purchasing or voting or any such quality. People
with similar tastes or other characteristics in common can
be lumped together into more or less internally homogeneous groups.

Ordinal classifications, meanwhile, are explicitly organized by measures of position, priority, or value along some countable dimension. Something is ordered, rather than simply named, and distinctions are expressed in terms of scores or ranks on that scale of measurement. In everyday society, ordinal measurements can be found in graded examinations, standardized tests, competitive sports rankings, occupational pay scales, and so on. Almost any repeated activity can be converted into some sort of score, even if only in terms of a count of frequencies.

In both social and technical practice, distinctions between different schemes of measurement are potentially fluid depending on the goals of the measurement. Conversion pathways are common. A continuous measure may be simplified to a numerical rank, or binned into some number of ordered categories, or dichotomized into a binary classification. Nominal clusters or categories will often be created on the basis of calculating continuous distances in some multidimensional space of relative similarities or dissimilarities in conjunction with the application of some criterion for determining when things are similar enough to be placed in the same class.

From the point of view of social order, the most basic kinds of processes are those of *nominalization* and *ordinalization*: the naming of kinds and the designation of ranks. They are not, to repeat, inimical to one another. In practice, ranks can be collapsed into types. Similarly, those in search of social examples of purely nominal classifications will have a hard time finding cases that have not, somewhere, been treated as explicitly or implicitly ordered.

It is tempting to think that it is the act of numerical measurement as such, just the sheer fact of quantification, that makes ordinalization pernicious. This is a mistake. As social phenomena, naming and ranking are much more general than quantification. Catechisms, shibboleths, purity regimes, ritual compliance, degradation ceremonies—in short, symbolically infused distinction making in all its forms—can serve in the place of numerical measures of position. Insofar as they are about distinguishing better from worse, as opposed to simply affirming the uniqueness of every single thing in the world, qualitative modes of classification can be as powerfully disciplining as quantitative ones. What is of real interest is the fusion of socially fundamental processes of naming and ranking with novel tools and data for carrying out those tasks. Large-scale measurement allows for thinking about scores and ranks through the lens of small differences and high dimensionality. What does it mean for computers to intervene in the business of seeing and organizing society?

Testing and Matching

For one thing, machines, like people, are prone to error. A machine learning (ML) classifier is a function or procedure that assigns a class label to a case. Classifiers are not foolproof. They can be tricked into misclassifying objects in photographs, or elements of speech, or kinds of person. These failures can be consequential. Out in the world, false arrests have been made on the basis of false predictions.[13]

A large literature in computer science, law, and social science finds that the social machinery sustaining the deployment of algorithms might contribute to the reproduction of categorical inequalities around gender and race.[14] A key source of trouble is the need, in many methods, for some baseline or "ground truth" of correctly classified items or training data that the model must be built with. It can be hard to find datasets of sufficient size or quality to train models on, and the circumstances of their production are often opaque.[15] Even if they are large and varied, training data is often lacking in ways developers are unaware of or do not think to consider. The result is poor or (to use the most common euphemism) problematic performance in real-world applications. For instance, early commercial facial recognition programs were prone to misgender Black women. Similarly, Amazon had to scrap a much-vaunted ML recruitment tool after the software "learned" from the company's practice of hiring almost exclusively men in technical positions and systematically weeded out the résumés of women applying for these jobs.[16] US law disallows such behavior—though it does not prohibit the use of algorithms to manage hiring and firing.[17]

There are no easy technical fixes to what is at root a sociological problem. Training data, almost necessarily, comes from a social world already structured by deeply entrenched categories and classifications, with various degrees of formality and normativity. Linguistic corpora used to train text classifiers, for instance, are often sourced from a core network of related sources, such as Wikipedia. This can have knock-on effects when the data is subsequently used to prepare models of all kinds.[18] Predictive methods used to determine who will make a good employee, a lousy parent, or a dangerous recidivist are, in the end, built on top of histories of discriminatory practice and asymmetrical surveillance. People who frequently encounter the police, the criminal justice system, social services, or other institutions of social control are likely to be overrepresented in training data drawn from these agencies. These organizations may share data with one another in an effort to enhance the accuracy of their data-hungry methods, which only tends to make things worse. And, of course, the outcome of interest, the thing "the algorithm" is trying to optimize on, matters a great deal too. When Virginia Eubanks studied a method for assessing a child's risk of being abused in Pennsylvania's Allegheny County, she found that cases of child maltreatment-related fatalities and near fatalities, which are of greatest concern to the state, are extremely rare.[19] To produce useful results, the county's predictive model had to optimize on more common outcomes. In the end, two proxies for child harm were used: the likelihood that another call will be made about the child to the abuse and neglect hotline, and the likelihood that the child will be placed in foster care.

The problem is that what motivates both referrals and foster care placements in practice is difficult to disentangle from a general condition of poverty. For instance, malnutrition, lack of decent housing, or lack of health care are considered neglect. As a result, poor and minority families were overrepresented in the outcome variables. The urban poor also interacted frequently with public services, and so they, too, supplied a disproportionate number of the available data points for the predictive variables. Suburban middle-class families, by contrast, were nowhere to be seen in the data. This is not surprising: they live in places that are out of the reach of social services and deal with problems through private insurance and experts, whose interventions, in the name of privacy, are not recorded in public databases or shared with public institutions. And so the system returned few red flags for them. In sum, oversampling, data redundancy, and an ill-defined objective function created a predictive instrument of great power to profile those who have the least to get by, in effect stigmatizing their social condition as an immoral and dangerous one—and adding yet another layer to the seemingly incomprehensible moral logic of a system that will financially support a child's foster parents, but not their parents, to raise them.[20]

The world is patterned, and the social world is no exception. Nothing, no matter how mundane or tacit or confidential, is a priori irrelevant as a basis for honing a classification scheme. But what sort of structure will be found by a classifier? One danger is that unnoticed but strictly irrelevant features of the data will end up becoming the basis for identification and labeling. In the field of medical image classification, for example, a widely pursued research goal is to develop classifiers able to correctly identify pathologies from images at a level of accuracy better than trained doctors or technicians. In one study, researchers sought to train a deep-learning network to reliably identify cases of pneumonia from chest X-rays. The training data consisted of about 160,000 images sourced from three different locations: a network of hospitals associated with Indiana University, Mount Sinai Hospital in New York City, and the National Institutes of Health Clinical Center in Bethesda, Maryland. While the system performed quite well, it turned out that a key reason for its success was that, based on consistent similarities in the production quality of the images, the model was able to detect which hospital an X-ray originated with and adjust its predictions accordingly. Different hospitals had different rates of pneumonia, and they also had subtle differences in the look of their X-ray images. The model effectively exploited the latter feature to predict the former. It learned, but not in the intended way.[21]

The general problem of spurious correlation plagues data analysts everywhere. Its manifestation in settings like this is distinctive and interesting, however. Across many different kinds of classification and prediction tasks, the likelihood of specious associations producing "shortcut learning" is high.[22] It happens because while these methods are astonishingly good at pattern detection, their mode of establishing similarity and difference is quite different from the way people recognize and classify things. For example, it can be possible to carefully craft an "adversarial" image that breaks the classifier by exploiting the way some internal layer works. The image may look nothing like the items being classified, or the change might be invisible to the human eye, or indistinguishable from noise. But the classifier does not look at things the way we do, and so it breaks in unexpected ways.

A second and more comprehensible mode of failure is the sort that tripped up the pneumonia classifier. In this case, real structure—that is to say, features that users can see in the data and whose predictive relevance they can understand—is used in an illegitimate way. In the pneumonia case, the classifier learned what hospitals looked like when it was supposed to be learning about what pneumonia looked like. Because the character of the hospitals was correlated with the distribution of pneumonia, taking it into account improved the model given the data it learned on.

Even boring, run-of-the-mill methods of the old-fashioned kind are bedeviled by problems of poor model specification, unwarranted inference, and spurious associations. But the new methods make things even more tricky. In the case of the pneumonia classifier, we can straightforwardly say what went wrong in the training of the model and easily see the reason why it would not do to have it implemented that way in practice. But the implications for more purely social data are not so clear. By inciting organizations to treat all data as useful, and by developing tools with a hitherto unmatched ability to find patterns, software engineers have created tools endowed with new and somewhat alien powers. Together the social origins of training data and the unblinking eye of a deep-learning classifier combine first to translate the social world into a model and then, potentially, to recombine and reconfigure categories based on what it sees. The particular features that these systems detect and act on are likely to reflect social realities of *some* sort. But how exactly they do this, which features are selected, and whether the result is fair or just is another matter.

One of the chief motives for using these tools in the first place is their ability to take large volumes of data and see things that a human user or even a traditional statistical analysis cannot. But when the model is opaque, the question of its performance is intrinsically tricky. If we are attempting to accurately identify handwritten numbers or things that are cats, then at least validation is straightforward on the basis of spot checks and comparisons to labeled sets we are confident about. In the case of more challenging classifications—kinds of employee; species of credit risk; varieties of recidivist; terrorist or not—the process is much more murky. Deep-learning models might classify based on weighted combinations and transformations of hundreds or thousands of features, leaving users with little idea which conventionally identifiable features are really important. Worse, deciding whether the result is fair or unfair to any particular person classified is even more difficult.

If we trust the model, we should go along with its output even if the results seem surprising. Again, there is already a tendency to treat the output of conceptually much simpler approaches, such as those used to estimate credit scores, in a somewhat Delphic manner. Because the fine details of credit score estimation are trade secrets, information about how to manage and improve one's score tends to take on the aspect of lore. This or that behavior is supposed to help; perhaps you could try doing it. When properly "deep" methods are applied in circumstances like this, not just the methods but also the resulting classifications may appear strange and uninterpretable. People find themselves in a system of categories where their own location is determined by difficult-to-understand methods, and the label they end up with might not even be recognizable or known to them. A steady income or a bank balance is replaced by a synthetic risk score. A passport or visa is trumped by membership on some watchlist or other. Generally, placement on such lists depends on people, organizations, objects, events being identified through patterns in the data pertaining to them.

Rule-based "algorithms" and "clusters of attributes" have always served to draw boundaries between kinds of people and things.[23] But modern methods may be especially unnerving—not only because they are difficult to audit or contest, because so much of the data is ad hoc, or because they pry so deep into people's lives, but because they reconfigure the meaning of categories people took for granted and reorganize what can be done with them. For instance, the significance of what John Cheney-Lippold calls the "right of the algorithm" and what Amoore calls the "deep border" of ML, may supplement and even supersede national citizenship and the physical border.[24] The analogically derived certainty of belonging somewhere may be shattered by one's place in a dataset and the inferences made from it. The risk score associated with a recognized face's cluster of attributes may determine the movement of the turnstile at the airport. One's data double crosses the border first.

We have already mentioned some consequences of the partially achieved, partially assigned categories emerging from algorithmic methods. Sorting and slotting procedures of various kinds shape access to goods, services and opportunities across many institutional spheres, from employment, health care, insurance, and education to housing, citizenship, credit, social welfare, and more. They are also busily reformatting the structure of ordinary sociability, from opportunities for friendship and dating to getting around town at the weekend. But we often fail to appreciate the extent to which these technologies now mediate the whole social process itself. They identify new classes of people, reformat identities, help control social action, and produce new criteria for truth telling and ethical judgment.[25] These classification situations are created across different settings—in markets of all sorts, as well as under the eye of the state. In market settings, as we explore in Chapters 4 and 5, their main purpose is to assist in extracting value. In connection with the state, as we shall argue in more detail in Chapter 7, they are used to establish qualification standards for social inclusion and appropriate levels of merit and desert. This tendency to better score and rank users on multiple dimensions, and the subsequent linking and integration of measured profiles across domains, conjures up images of individuals positioned in a vast multidimensional space of personal and behavioral characteristics, each one a vector of characteristics with an associated set of possibilities, prices, and experiences.

Eigenvalues and Eigencapital

Think of the totality of your interactions where behavioral and interactional data is recorded and collected. All of those traces represent a kind of resource. It is accumulated over the long history of your recorded actions and choices, built up from traces left on everything from social media to credit bureaus, shopping websites and fidelity programs, courthouses, social welfare agencies, pharmacies, and the content of emails and chats. It incorporates whatever value is in your social network, along with synthetic measures of your trustworthiness or accountability in the world. It is heterogeneous and multidimensional and, of course, it is not all gathered into a single place or condensed down to a single quantity. But in principle it might be. It might take the form of some vector of information that summarizes your situation and value across many features—something that compactly represents your position in the multidimensional space of classification situations. It would, in short, characterize your social location. In data analysis, this procedure often involves the decomposition of matrices of data into orthogonal eigenvectors, the better to characterize them. (One of the more old-fashioned translations of *eigen* in the terms *eigenvector* or *eigenvalue* is "characteristic.") From an individual's point of view, these quantities and their representations would be a kind of resource. Call it *eigencapital*.[26]

Following the work of Pierre Bourdieu, social theorists and researchers have named many forms of "capital" over the past forty years—absurdly many, perhaps. Do we really need another sort? There is human capital, economic capital, cultural capital, social capital, bodily capital, and more besides. Each type begins with the same initial idea. People may possess some quality or capacity that directly or indirectly benefits their prospects in life, over and above a direct measure of income or wealth, class position, or membership in some demographic category. These qualities or properties might be a little harder to measure, but they are quite real and they can, in some more than metaphorical sense, be cashed out or converted into more conventionally material benefits. An admirable skill, a network of helpful friends in desirable places, the right sense of good taste, or even an appealing face: all can be "capital" of a kind, because each is defined in some context where what is "admirable," "desirable," "right," "good," and "appealing" reflects whatever the entrenched distribution of assets, opportunities, and status happens to be.

On this view, higher-status people tend to think of and present their tastes, abilities, and achievements as the unforced outcome of their natural talents. Even if they are not always acting in consciously strategic terms, this is one of the main means through which they legitimize their social position and, in the process, stay ahead of the competition. A sense of good taste and the right "feel" for what works and what doesn't in particular social settings can be a valuable kind of resource. That is cultural capital. Bourdieu was fascinated by the conveniently natural fit between people's backgrounds and their tastes and ambitions. His theory of practice tried to get a grip on how people's class position organized or structured their tendency to speak or act in particular ways, to develop some tastes rather than others, and to think they were "cut out" for some kinds of work while not even considering some alternatives as possibilities. Bourdieu's concept for the individual's experience of this process is a notoriously slippery one: the "habitus." This is the "feel for the game" or "sense of the rules" that you carry around with you. It emerges from your experience. It structures your dispositions and your actions. When a situation feels comfortable or a decision feels like the right thing to do, the habitus is the feeling in your gut that grounds that experience.

In *England in the Age of the American Revolution* the historian Lewis Namier remarks that "A man's status in English society has always depended primarily on his own consciousness. . . . Whatever is apt to raise a man's self-consciousness—be it birth, rank, wealth, intellect, daring or achievements—will add to his stature; but it has to be translated into the truest expression of his sub-conscious self-valuation: uncontending ease, the unbought grace of life."[27] It is the process of generating the apparently "unbought grace of life" that fascinated Bourdieu. Direct efforts to acquire, display, and demand deference to one's taste and learning tend to fail. Transparent use of one's wealth to buy status is effective but crass. Better to put it to work in a less blunt fashion and allow it to express itself more indirectly. Best of all would be to be able to put in the time to gradually acquire the accoutrements of good taste and right thinking, and then "forget" they were acquired at all. Like wine left to mature in its cask, what begins as deliberate cultivation eventually manifests itself as the wholly natural expression of authentic inner qualities.

In Bourdieu's picture, this process mostly happens during the long period of formal education. It takes money and, above all, time—two resources that not everyone has in equal measure. One kind of capital, the straightforward monetary kind, is slowly converted into another, the cultural kind. Education gives you public credentials, certainly. In Bourdieu's terms, this is the "institutionalized" form that cultural capital takes. But it also gives you "embodied" cultural capital that you express without needing to show people your college diploma. In the best cases, your habitus lets you comfortably fit into an already-structured social world, one that in the limit case smoothly meshes with your talents and skills in a seemingly natural, spontaneous, effortless manner. On the other side, and of equal interest to Bourdieu, are the times when things do not mesh and you are left feeling out of place or awkward, knowing—and painfully feeling—that you do not really belong.

Bourdieu insisted, and critics have often complained, that cultural and symbolic capital are not easily measurable. In his view they are primarily "known by their effects"—that is, by the extent to which they allow actors to accrue specific material and symbolic profits, such as money, power, or authority. This lends the Bourdieuian approach a flexibility of application that skeptics feel makes a virtue of endogeneity. But there is also something deeply true about the insight that the organization of the outside world, with all its unequally distributed resources and often obscure rules, gets inside people in a way that makes life go more smoothly for some than for others. This tends to encourage us to see our experiences as manifestations of a natural order and to see our actions as expressions of natural talent or innate goodness rather than as a kind of side benefit of lucking into the right background. In this respect, Bourdieu's analysis of the forms of capital and their role in social reproduction can be seen as an effort, well before its time, to theorize the now ubiquitous concept of "privilege."

Eigencapital is a little different. It has its origins in particulars—in the totality of one's interactions with the digital economy—but it has a generalized, relational character that is not found in the usual list of novel forms of capital. Its specificity is retained in the variable way that it is applied or expressed in specific contexts. The meaning of one's "score" or "stock,"[28] so to speak, depends on the specific setting one is in at the time. More than just an image or metaphor, it is also a contingently realized empirical phenomenon. Estimating and using something like it in practice is not a fantasy but a genuinely huge engineering problem subject to failure or incomplete realization. But in principle an individual's eigencapital is calculable from all of the digital information available about them, encapsulating the totality of their relations as expressed through digital traces, ordered and characterized through numerical methods. In the Bourdieuian manner, it, too, is visible through its effects. Advantages accrue to those who accumulate it. At present it exists mainly *in potentia*. For it to come closer to what we have in mind, present-day tendencies might fuse into a more encompassing system of measurement.

Like cultural capital, we can think of eigencapital as taking *embodied, objectified,* and *institutionalized* forms.[29] In its *embodied* form, eigencapital is expressed in durable dispositions. This is the "habitus," incarnated directly in the body and the mind, and expressed in the overall presentation of self. The well-situated individual naturally inhabits their data double. They feel the benefits of eigencapital directly, automatically. Reputation is no longer confined to a local community of peers. The trust the individual feels confident extending is no longer circumscribed by a concrete social network. Instead, they carry it with them in their bag or on their phone. Moreover, to the extent that the practical expression of such a resource works successfully—and as we have been emphasizing, getting it to work is a huge technical challenge—the process fades into the background. The ideal, in fact, is much like the National Security Agency's defense of its methods of ubiquitous but invisible surveillance. You do not see the bad actors who tried to use your card but were automatically denied. You do not have your integrity questioned by a salesclerk. The camera takes a quick look at you, and you can board a plane or cross a border.

When things go wrong with systems like this, their automated decision-making will seem stupid, rigid, or rule bound. Why doesn't my card know I am simply in a different city, trying to buy a meal? How come my online transaction was flagged just because I am buying something a little unusual as a gift? But when these systems work properly, instead of throwing up a roadblock they smooth the way for us in a pleasant, barely detectable manner. They allow transactions to happen in the blink of an eye; they prevent fraud; they enable good matches; they help us make good choices. The fortunate consumer experiences this as a well-deserved, delightful form of ease. In a way, the infrastructure of eigencapital revives an old kind of privilege. It promises the portable, universally recognized trustworthiness and good reputation of the gentleman abroad, sustained by his word and letter of introduction. It is the "unbought grace of life," but in a newly quantified and nominally egalitarian form. It takes an aspect of life long familiar to the very rich, a specifically personal attention to one's needs, and spreads it just a little further down the social hierarchy, providing a still-small minority with the pleasingly exclusive experience of recognition and authorization.

The varying amount of time different people must spend to access various services offers a good example of the embodied dimension of eigencapital. Sociologists have long studied queues and lines as structures that allow for both control and status. Who can be made to wait, for how long, and for whom? These simple questions are surprisingly robust indices of the structure of interpersonal relations. "The distribution of waiting time," Barry Schwartz remarks, "coincides with the distribution of power."[30] Organizations that serve the poor have a low staff-to-client ratio, so people wait to obtain service. They line up to get food or to climb on the bus. The mark of being rich, on the other hand, is the ability to spend the time of others.[31] In that case it is the staff who wait upon the client, literally and figuratively. It is no surprise that this most basic of social dynamics has been amplified by the availability of data on who exactly is in the queue. With the rise of predictive analytics, the social differentiation of wait times has been automated. For corporate call centers, a first and easy step away from a first-call, first-served basis was by means of some nominal approach. Premium members might get a special number to call. But there is no need to stop there. By modeling various salient features of a customer's account, a financial, telecom, or airline company might easily produce a "customer importance score" expressing the current and likely future value of the person on the line. This can be used to determine response speed and quality of service. It will likely be positively correlated with their wealth, but predictive models may also include variables such as the urgency of the problem, some measure of the person's importance to the company, or their estimated likelihood of dumping it.[32] Whatever the prediction method, it is typically opaque, so the outcome tends to be experienced as fate.

In its more tangible, *objectified* form, eigencapital is realized in transmissible property. Over and above making ordinary experiences run more smoothly, it helps provide access to goods and services, at better prices, and with better social consideration. The well-informed parent carefully manages their child's credit so that the child, too, will appear trustworthy, even if they are not. The hopeful driver installs monitoring software on their phone to lower their car insurance premium. The objectified form is a reminder that eigencapital must be produced in specific ways. For those who have not been trained that way, its accumulation takes effort, discipline, and often money. This form is all about legibility: You can work toward a better position by paying attention to producing "good data" for yourself. But you need to know what good data is in the first place. This recalls modern debates about the auditability of algorithms—the right of people to know the rules by which they are judged, and the right of experts to inspect these rules. Many algorithms embrace this semi-objective character. Credit scoring companies publicize their evaluation criteria, even if the final formula remains a trade secret. Your banking app will helpfully dispense advice on how you can do better. So does your health and fitness app. Eigencapital in the objectified form is prescriptive, and it feels like work. But eventually this labor does pay off, and assiduous effort fades into the background and becomes second nature. This is when the objectified form folds into the embodied form and the benefits of eigencapital—the shortened wait on the phone, or at the airport counter—are experienced as ordinary, well-deserved and effortless.

The simplest eigenstatus of all is an indicator of mere presence or absence, observed or unobserved, on some dimension. If you are not included, you cannot be measured or assessed. And so, at the most elementary level, platforms and other systems strive to include everyone under their purview. Being outside carries an increasingly high cost, as economists have long noted in the context of network effects, and sociologists in the context of the digital divide in access to the internet. But as data collection becomes ubiquitous, so do the expectations of being seen. As the physical world fills with sensors, and people live increasingly hybrid lives, resisting these expectations is hard in practice. Furthermore, it is not necessarily desirable: being invisible to digital infrastructures is suspicious, and organizations code it negatively. The failure to engage and properly care for one's data double is a moral fault at best, a sure sign of illicit behavior at worst.[33] Invisibility is as much a trap as visibility. Simply avoiding debt will not do: you'll just end up with a bad score, which you can only hope to improve by subjecting yourself to more intrusive data inquiries. Likewise, a user's failure to like, share, comment, and message others on a social media platform will prompt a demotion of their contributions relative to others who are more involved. In Chapters 6 and 7 we will look more closely at why this is the case. For now we can say that people who are inactive are of little value to organizations. They are expensive to know and unprofitable to manage. By the systems' standards, they perform poorly. And so they get punished for it. Likewise, public institutions also increasingly operate according to a logic that privileges electronic visibility: the extension of rights depends on digital incorporation and the steady production of data about oneself.

To a first approximation, the acquisition of eigencapital depends on being seen by, and making oneself visible to, digital architectures—with a credit card, an email account, a smartphone, a smart speaker. As personal data of various kinds is pumped throughout the internet, the moral injunction shifts from obligatory incorporation to proper data management. People are taught, often from a young age, that they must "build credit." In the United States, twenty-one states require schools to teach financial literacy. Banks and credit reporting companies helpfully supply educational resources about financial probity. Educators share their preferred pedagogical strategies on blogs and specialized websites, while tech entrepreneurs have designed credit apps specifically for children.[34] These materials generally emphasize not only the benefits of early financial incorporation and visibility but also what it means to work toward a scored position in the world. A generic knowledge of relevant algorithmic categories, constant monitoring of outcomes, and quick intervention in times of crisis are part of the expected posture of the datafied citizen. People's relationship to their personal data exists in a moral universe shaped by both the direction provided by institutions and their own personal conjectures about how to do well in life. Far from being passive, they are emotionally involved in systems of data production and management and sometimes take great pains to develop strategies that "feel right"—or properly balance the need to be visible with the desire, however hopeless, to safeguard their privacy.[35]

Training a population to embrace its own ordinalization can sometimes take the form of a bold exercise of political will. In 2014, the Chinese government declared its intention to deploy a national "social credit" system anchored in general measures of "honesty." The project spearheaded a myriad of experiments by municipal governments harvesting information from dozens of subunits and dedicated local committees on a broad array of punishable and honorable behaviors. Legal judgments against one's person, politically sensitive behaviors, incivility, or moral turpitude can downgrade one's score, while volunteering, government work, or making a donation contribute bonus points.[36] The criteria are generally public, so people know, on the whole, what they are supposed to do (or not do). The specific implementation logics vary a great deal from city to city, but the core principle across various systems and locales is that citizens or organizations whose score does not reach a certain mark face practical hurdles (such as travel restrictions, and exclusion from certain occupations, markets, and services), and, sometimes, public shaming. Those with good scores might experience public praise and faster processing across institutions. Some of these systems rely on an infrastructure of paper pushers, while others use digitally sourced data supplied through partnerships with technology corporations, such as ride operators.[37]

A single summary number is the most minimal form of eigencapital: only one value matters. But when formally connected to a set of rewards and punishments, it can be quite powerful as a governance tool. Indeed, a broader ambition in the Chinese case is to link data and scores across systems in an effort to regulate the behavior of entire populations in the name of collective harmony.[38] This is the theory. The reality is more mundane. Despite the headlines, many of these systems still lack in both capacity and authority.[39] For now, it seems people's ability to live their lives is stymied by more mundane roadblocks that quite ordinary methods of monitoring throw up—or alternatively by darker, and much more opaque, deployments of digital surveillance.[40]

This brings us to the third state of eigencapital. In its *institutionalized* form, eigencapital may exist as a measured quantity that may be widely used and circulated. Here, what matters is the general recognition of the measure across institutions. A single measure condensed from a collection of noisy data sources is obviously a rougher and more approximate token of one's "true" eigencapital. To produce it, differences must be flattened, equivalences must be made between incommensurable qualities.[41] The resulting one-dimensional measure will contain much less information than its multidimensional parent. In the same way that, for Bourdieu, a diploma is a highly reduced and unsatisfying way of apprehending the concept of cultural capital, any particular score or rating will be only a rough approximation of a person's general eigencapital. The benefit is that it makes decisions easy to automate. In the United States and a number of other countries, credit scores have attained this generic status and social significance. They can be bought and sold as such, and combined with other measures to produce superscores. They are, for instance, routinely used as an input for "off label" risk prediction in other markets, such as insurance, housing (tenant screening), or dating.[42] China's experiments in social credit have a similar ambition, though they have yet to attain this kind of generality.

Though the particular conceptualizations vary, the quest for the one score that will bind them all is quite universal.

A search for "trustworthiness" through the patents database maintained by Google shows hundreds of applications related to the algorithmic scoring of individuals and entities going back to the early 2010s. The earliest were filed by the behemoths of e-commerce, such as Amazon and eBay. In the same way that the widespread diffusion of credit scoring—a risk prediction tool—enabled the massive expansion of credit,[43] a platform's success depends on its ability to guarantee the integrity and responsibility of both its sellers and its buyers. The practice is perfectly defensible. Who, after all, wants to deal with an annoying customer, who complains about not receiving packages or returns them broken? Who wants to contract with a seller who cannot complete an agreed-upon deal, or who ships subpar products?

Similar concerns apply across digital ecosystems. After dealing with the Cambridge Analytica scandal in 2018, Facebook announced that it had started giving users a "trust rank" based on their propensity to flag verifiably true news stories as fake. Around the same time, the housing rental company AirBnB, which already uses renters' credit scores to give them an initial rating, was granted a patent for a "trustworthiness and person compatibility" score. According to the patent, "text authored by the person or that provides information about the person" can be used to "indicate that the person has created a false or misleading online profile, provided false or misleading information to the service provider, is involved with drugs or alcohol, is involved with hate websites or organizations, is involved in sex work, has perpetrated a crime, is involved in civil litigation, is a known fraudster or scammer, is involved in pornography, has authored online content with negative language, or has interests that indicate negative personality or behavior traits."[44] Most organizations are interested in weeding out the most undesirable among their users, employees, citizens, claimants.

But even in the most totalizing systems, there is always an outside. Those who try to evade being measured and classified, as well as those who perform poorly by the system's standards, face high costs, unsuitable matches, and, increasingly, outright exclusion. Industrial capitalism has its industrial reserve army and its *lumpenproletariat*. Digital capitalism has its stubborn off-the-grid dwellers, cash economy, and, as it were, its *lumpenscoretariat*.[45] Excluding people who are deemed "too" untruthful, risky, deviant, or demanding—however these traits are defined and evaluated, usually in relation to some specific value outcome—is just a normal part of business. But algorithms allow these efforts to be carried out at scale, and to stick over time. A score that circulates, is replicated, and becomes consolidated into other indexes is far more powerful than a reputation that is confined to a file cabinet, a reference book, or an agent's memory. In Chapters 4 and 5 we turn to the material shape and economic implications of this widespread institutionalization of ordinal reason.

4

The Great Unbundling

There's only two ways I know of to make money:
bundling and unbundling.

—Jim Barksdale, quoted in Justin Fox, "How to Succeed in
Business by Bundling—and Unbundling"

DIGITAL TECHNOLOGIES FOSTER NEW STRATEGIES OF ACCUMULA-
tion. The infrastructure that makes the Maussian bargain
possible—the "gift of everything"—allows firms to collect
their data and begin to identify the market-specific positions—the "classification situations"—that can be turned
into revenue. In this chapter and Chapter 5, we develop an
analysis of these strategies and their consequences. In the
first place, the substrate of data must be converted into
streams of payments. This is a significant challenge. Given
the nature of data collection, there are strong tendencies in
these markets toward something that looks like classical
price discrimination within a framework that, if not truly
monopolistic, at least favors the consolidation of a few
large firms. Meanwhile, users and consumers tend to be
disaggregated into more fine-grained revenue streams. As
the pressure to monetize them becomes stronger, the terms
of the initial bargain change. What began as a flow of data
freely given in return for a service provided at no cost
tends, over time, to become a paid service in which data

about you (and especially your transactions) is still collected and used anyway, both for and against you. Ultimately, the potential for extracting revenue streams and rents of various kinds from people pushes companies toward commodifying the data they collect into ever more abstracted products traded on new kinds of markets.

We call this process "the great unbundling." Its key feature is that money is no longer anonymous. Because its circulation can be traced, it becomes a kind of ledger. Economic transactions become data bundles. The characteristics of the product, of the transacting parties, and of the transacting medium are known and recorded. Price is no longer unique, but adapted to the who, where, and when of purchasing, as understood by a matching algorithm. This allows economic rights to be disaggregated, rebundled, and sold off with a degree of precision that was previously unattainable.

Informative Payments

We have argued that the emergence of a social substrate for data generation and analysis enabled new modes of stratification. As we noted in Chapter 1, markets—especially financial markets—were among the earliest places where large volumes of useful, meaningful numerical data were produced just as a matter of course. To begin with, those quantities were available in lists, ledgers, and daily or quarterly reports. For the world to become properly financialized, these numbers needed to also become properly "datafied."

That is, the data had to appear in a form that could be automatically processed and had to flow at a speed as close to real time as possible. From the time of the paper stock-ticker onward, the financial sector itself led the way in meeting these demands. The rise of finance as an industry was as much a sociotechnical process driven by rapid increases in data availability and information processing power as it was a matter of economic efficiency or a political project. Forward-looking brokers and market operators embraced the promise of computer networks early on. As early as the 1960s, astute commentators grasped their likely consequences.[1] But the great migration from the pit to the screen did not get underway in earnest until the emergence of electronic quotation and later trading platforms in the 1970s and 1980s.[2] Today financial trading is a largely automated activity. In volume and importance, if not in spectacle, the steady hum of machines automatically placing and taking orders has largely supplanted the frantic activity of the pits.[3] Geographically distributed networks of computers have replaced trading rooms, a transformation accelerated by the COVID-19 pandemic.

Meanwhile, in consumer markets, the successful adoption of electronic payment systems—from credit and debit cards to retail charge cards and store loyalty cards—spearheaded "the proliferation of transactional data" and the rise of modern consumer surveillance.[4] In a similar vein to Oscar Gandy Jr.'s ideas about the "panoptic sort," which emphasized the centrality of money and credit to the advent of "surveillance capitalism," the historian Josh Lauer reminds us that "payment systems were held up as archetypal information caches" by the likes of Vannevar Bush in the 1940s. Bush was a visionary engineer who anticipated the centrality of information to science and society and became an influential adviser to and administrator within the US federal government. An appreciation for the significance and immense value of transactional data continued on down to the likes of Google's chief economist, Hal Varian, who emphasized the potential uses of devices that enable transactions while also recording and providing a basis for analyzing them.

Well before the advent of computers, company paper, payment cards, store-issued tokens or metal plates (embossed with a name, address, and customer number) functioned as means of personal identification as well as media of exchange. But these records were not conceived as "data" that could be mined for specific insights until the American Express company started digitizing its customers' sales receipts in the 1980s.[5] "Our product is information," a 1982 ad in the *Wall Street Journal* claimed; "information that charges airline tickets, hotel rooms, dining out, the newest fashions, and even figures mailing costs for a travel magazine; information that grows money funds, buys and sells equities, and manages mergers; information that pays life insurance annuities, figures pricing for collision coverage, and creates and pays mortgages; information that schedules entertainment on cable television and electronically guards houses; information that changes kroners into guilders, figures tax rates in Bermuda, and helps put financing together for the ebb and flow of world trade."[6] Through their card payments, individuals and corporations had become legible in a new way. Banks, retailers, and card processors soon followed suit and developed their own strategies for eliciting and mining granular transactional data.[7] Once liberated from the constraints of paper, and held instead as electronic databases, this data could be queried, analyzed, and matched with other records, integrated to build personal profiles, aggregated to define new kinds of populations, and, of course, bought and sold as an asset. The path to the new way of doing things was paved with failures and scandals. But it quickly became clear that, in its new form, payment data had value of its own, quite separate from the value of the systems that helped produce it and the exchanges it recorded.

A consequence was a kind of inversion in the relationship between finance and information. Knowledge of transactions and assets had been a kind of data, but now data became a kind of asset. While records had been available for some kinds of analysis, the ratio of results obtained relative to effort required was usually poor. With a properly computable substrate, however, the shape of the trade-off changed radically. The new business wisdom was encapsulated in a metaphor that quickly became a cliché. This was the idea that "data is the new oil." Perhaps surprisingly, technology companies themselves did not come to this realization right away. The basics of user tracking technology were in use from the very beginning of the internet, built into the notion of a server log file. On the World Wide Web, browser cookies were deposited on a user's computer by websites, initially as a record of their preferences or activity that could be made use of during later visits. But the possibilities were so much greater than this. As the data imperative took hold, platforms sought to augment their own troves of online data with information about people's offline behavior. Facebook's "partnerships" with data brokers (from 2008 to 2013 or so), Google's proliferation of multiple services provided through a single user identity, and Amazon's later purchase of the organic food giant Whole Foods should be understood in that way.[8] Soon the leading platforms were all setting up their own payment systems as well, and sometimes their own currencies. Transactions were not anonymous anymore. They were stamped with metadata. Money itself started to become more like information, explicitly playing the role that some economists had long argued was its most important function.[9] Considered as a natural extension of company accounting, the existence and utility of transaction records has a long history, of course. Their use in the context of criminal investigations is long established. But the consequences of richer and essentially ubiquitous transactional data for ordinary market activity is easy to underestimate. It changes the character of what money is. Its convenience as a medium of exchange takes a back seat to its usefulness as a source of information. With that in hand, the great unbundling can begin.

Market Modulations

When Friedrich Hayek articulated his critique of central planning, he argued that the main economic problem facing society is how best to use that vast quantity of knowledge that is the collective product of social activity but which is also, by its nature, inaccessibly distributed across individuals. Knowledge is dispersed throughout society, resting in bits and pieces in the heads of myriad economic actors in a way that is "not given to anyone in its totality." Hayek went on to argue that, in a competitive economy with abundant information, the price system is the most efficient way to make this distributed knowledge available. Prices communicate signals about the relative positions of all economic actors, allowing them to coordinate far more quickly than could be achieved by any sort of bureaucratic effort to collect, analyze, and act on this information.[10] Price signals propagate through the economy at great speed, connecting market actors, allowing them to influence one another, and thereby coordinating the entire system. In comparison to this magic of competitive, price-setting markets, Hayek argued, a deliberate system of central planning is clunky, inaccurate, partial, biased, and, above all, painfully slow.[11]

Crucially, Hayek saw that the theoretical superiority of price coordination applies only when information about prices circulates easily. When it does not, markets are plagued by price dispersion and waste. In those circumstances, the "law of one price" does not apply. As it turns out, such situations are extremely common in real life and well documented by economists, sociologists, and anthropologists.[12] Hayek himself was well aware that social networks and stable partnerships between experienced traders were essential to the efficient transmission of knowledge, and thus to market coordination at large. In an actually existing market infrastructure like this, the role played by pricing is a long way from Hayek's ideal. But it nevertheless seemed as though the core choice was between more bureaucracy or a more purely functioning price system. Hayek thus insisted on a stark dilemma—central plan or free market—and provoked an intense political and economic debate that echoed down through the decades in various forms, as social scientists and political theorists debated the relative merits of markets and their alternatives. The rise of organizations that thrive on the social substrate of social data has rendered much of this debate moot. Evgeny Morozov remarks that, relative to data now routinely produced, the information transmitted by prices is "condensed" and a relatively poor guide for many kinds of exchange. Because so much additional information can be brought to bear on transactions, digital technologies allow the possibility for either rapid, direct, nonmarket coordination, or for more efficient and more targeted "bespoke" forms of market coordination, where transacting parties can be matched on a set of qualities that is both wider in scope and more particular in detail.[13] So much so, indeed, that the concept of "bespoke" has become a branding mantra deployed by everyone with a product to sell, from medical treatment to wine, shampoo, or even water.[14]

In such a system, price may be just one among many variables that are both relevant and rapidly communicable.[15] Or it may not be an independent signal at all, but a finely adjustable feature to be deployed in a broader strategic game. In the technology sector, what Shoshana Zuboff calls the "division of learning" (that is, the extreme asymmetry that accompanies the distribution of all of this information) consistently favors corporations in their dealings with users, employees, or clients.[16] They just know more and have a better view of the terrain. This, in turn, tends toward concentration of market power rather than a landscape of ongoing competition between peer firms and regional ecosystems.[17] Cédric Durand and Yanis Varoufakis have used the term "techno-feudalism" to describe the new dependencies that result from this process of concentration. "Feudalism" evokes a rent-based, rather than profit-based, mechanism of value extraction and the loss of autonomy of the individuals enrolled in it.[18] Yet it is not that these markets are inevitably stagnant, intrinsically backward looking, or that the dominant players in them are fixed for all time. Unexpected technical developments, successful entrepreneurial activity, or unwise strategic decisions still have the potential to upend even the largest players. Nonetheless, the tendency of the system as a whole seems to be toward the reproduction of a few really large firms—those that have mustered enough venture capital for long enough to scale and survive the startup bloodbath and now generate enough capital to keep rivals at bay.[19]

Leaders of the tech industry stand ready to defend this trajectory. Invoking Joseph Schumpeter's definition of entrepreneurship as the search for monopoly profits, PayPal founder and billionaire venture capitalist Peter Thiel makes the case with perfect clarity. The son of German émigrés to South Africa and California, Thiel first tried to make an intellectual mark as a disgruntled critic of multiculturalism before finding fame as an investor guru.[20] In that capacity, he may be best known for his remark that "competition is for losers." Thiel writes:

> So why are economists obsessed with competition as an ideal state? It is a relic of history. Economists copied their mathematics from the work of 19th-century physicists: They see individuals and businesses as interchangeable atoms, not as unique creators. Their theories describe an equilibrium state of perfect competition because that is what's easy to model, not because it represents the best of business. But the long-run equilibrium predicted by 19th-century physics was a state in which all energy is evenly distributed and everything comes to rest—also known as the heat death of the universe. Whatever your views on thermodynamics, it is a powerful metaphor. In business, equilibrium means stasis, and stasis means death. . . .
>
> . . . Every new creation takes place far from equilibrium. In the real world outside economic theory, every business is successful exactly to the extent that it does something others cannot. Monopoly is therefore not a pathology or an exception. Monopoly is the condition of every successful business.[21]

Monopoly is presented here as a discovery engine essential to the process of innovation. And indeed, economic research in the Schumpeterian vein supports this argument, at least to begin with.[22] Many other classical texts in economics and political economy also see monopoly as the natural tendency of capitalism.[23] None of this is new. But as Thiel's broadside against the discipline implies, economists *also* argue that monopoly fundamentally alters the terms of engagement between corporations and the people they interact with. It allows firms to dictate the terms of contract—whether that contract is about trade, service, or employment—and use that power to extract rents, defy existing laws and regulations, and violate social expectations.[24] The higher the platform's market share, the more it is able to increase its "take rate" of intermediation fees charged to sellers, drivers, workers, and the like. For instance, empirical research shows that "requesters" (i.e., employers) in online labor markets have market (or monopsony) power, too, even though these settings ought to lower search and switching costs for workers. Wages are squeezed. User surplus becomes employers' and platform surplus.[25]

The software industry is rife with monopolistic tendencies, too, due to the scalability enabled by low distribution costs and the network effects that produce growing utility. This, arguably, is even more true of software that continuously learns by itself, since positive feedback loops tend to naturally reinforce market advantage. Viktor Mayer-Schönberger and Thomas Ramge call this "the feedback effect."[26] Plainly stated, "the more people are using Google, the better it becomes, because every search is in some sense a tinkering and improvement in the service."[27] This natural advantage, built into the technology, also characterizes generative artificial intelligence models like ChatGPT and DALL.E. There, as elsewhere, the pursuit of network effects initially motivated a Maussian bargain approach. Given these models' voracious appetite for processing power and their parent company's reconstitution as a for-profit organization, it was short-lived.

The value of feedback effects to an organization reinforces its data hunger. Data abundance, in turn, shapes its market strategy. Once a platform succeeds in inserting itself into everyday digital interactions, the way Amazon did with online shopping or Google did with search, it has strong incentives to not only demand more data but also use it in ways that bolster its position—which can be at odds with personal and public welfare.[28] Facebook used its market intelligence to identify and buy up promising startups, its user data to attract developers and content providers, and the developers and content providers to attract users, until everyone was corralled inside its ecosystem and it pivoted to aggressively push ad content. Amazon collected and used its customer and transaction data to undercut its own sellers, which it had attracted to the platform by promising generous terms and access to a broader market. Not only did these terms (and the sellers' investments to optimize themselves for Amazon) rapidly vanish, but the company started competing with suppliers by cloning their most successful products, using its internal advertising engine as an advantage in the sale process.[29] In parallel, Amazon's search outcomes and user recommendations became increasingly ad driven, and more and more self-serving toward in-house brands.[30] Google used its dominant position in search to prop up its advertising business by tying Google Ads, which routes demand from advertisers, exclusively to DFP, its publisher ad server. According to a 2023 US Department of Justice complaint, the move resulted in Google's publisher ad server controlling 90 percent of the market by 2015 (up from 60 percent in 2008), allowing the company to artificially inflate prices. This monopolistic shift in the political economy of publishing dramatically undermined the viability of ad-reliant news organizations while serving as a conduit for the rise of well-funded imposter look-alikes, with dramatic consequences for the so-called public sphere.[31] One way or another, all of these organizations used their own network-based position to increase their own social indispensability and intermediary power over the distribution of knowledge or goods. The double dependency of *both* consumers / users and producers / advertisers on this intermediation (or what Tim Wu calls the platforms' control over some "master switch") allows them to extract as much surplus as possible while often destroying the quality of the service they provide in the long term.[32] Note that this behavior is not unique to US firms. In the middle of the pandemic, the Chinese government unleashed a "regulatory storm" against anticompetitive practices within its homegrown tech sector, such as the social media company Tencent "[blocking] WeChat users from sending links to its rival Alibaba's e-commerce websites."[33]

This ability of data-rich organizations to gather market intelligence has also fueled a shift in strategies for profitability. A firm will act differently toward its customers, and it will think differently about the prices it quotes them, if it can know things about their character, their desires, or their material situation. To use Gilles Deleuze's concept, it can *modulate* everything about that market interaction through technologies of control.[34] If it is possible to know a potential buyer's disposable income or their travel plans, a prospective employee's reservation wage or their likelihood of staying in their job if hired, or any other preference or behavioral tendency that might be relevant, then price setting becomes a very different process. Accurate data promises better "personalization," which in turn opens a path toward a more fine-grained form of price discrimination. Prices can be automatically adjusted not only to prevailing market conditions, but to the algorithm's best guesses about what synthetic microcategories of people might be willing to pay. In the strikingly direct words of a *Harvard Business Review* article, "We're in a new era of supercharged price discrimination, made possible by two major scientific and technological trends. First, AI algorithms—often trained on highly detailed behavioral data—enable organizations to infer what people are willing to pay with unprecedented precision. Second, recent developments in behavioral science—often invoked with the tagline "nudge"—provide organizations greater ability to influence their customers' behaviors."[35] There is a certain amount of exaggeration here because, of course, these methods do not really know the precise preferences of every specific individual. Still, the level of resolution that price setting might work at has indeed been changed. When they consider ways this power might be abused, the authors of the *Harvard Business Review* piece recommend that corporations apply ethical principles to their pricing strategies. But this mistakes the rule for the exception. Price discrimination and dynamic adjustment on the basis of available information are not some aberrant deviations from some general norm of fair pricing. Rather, they are the natural situation of markets in the age of personalized digital affordances. If companies have information at their disposal that lets them discriminate on the basis of price or wage, then that is what they must do. Rather than offering a single "market price," it makes sense for firms to try to make better guesses about what different sorts of people are willing to pay or receive. This insight applies across markets. For instance, insurers may see the traditional challenges of their industry fade away, while problems faced by customers become ever more sharply defined. Insurance contracts may be adjusted to reflect a dizzying array of situations. What were once threats of adverse selection and moral hazard for insurance companies can be transformed by the flow of data into problems of costly premiums and insurability for customers.

From an economic perspective, we may still have an efficient allocation of resources. The difference is that the combination of market power and automated, fine-grained segmentation tools means that corporations are in a position to squeeze out far more of the surplus on both the buy *and* the sell sides. Popular new software helps sellers, landlords, or employers automatically set prices, rents, or wages. With these sensitive calculations removed from messy interpersonal negotiations, there is evidence that some of these products push the envelope as far as possible.[36] Still, whether their effects are, on the whole, regressive or redistributive is an empirical question. It depends on what kind of data is being used, and how.[37] In product markets for instance, a more perfectly price-discriminatory world could very well benefit those of lesser means by giving them access to the same products at lower prices. But discrimination along some other dimension might have sharply regressive effects. For instance, perhaps our data can help us to identify a class of people who will be tempted by a particularly rotten deal, whether for reasons of poor literacy, straitened circumstance, social stigma, or citizenship status. Economists and legal scholars have accumulated substantial evidence that such practices are routine and quite profitable.[38] But given the unequal distribution of such risks throughout society, their negative consequences are also likely to weigh more heavily on specific segments of the population—which is to say, the poor, and specifically ethnoracial minorities, who also have a long history of being institutionally segregated into subpar services and are still targeted for subpar deals.[39] This is how price discrimination ends up overlapping with familiar forms of social discrimination.

The same information-rich practices have also become normalized in the domain of workforce management, with very few legal restrictions to date.[40] Human resource departments at tech firms famously collect extraordinary amounts of data on their own workforces that help them develop new analytics tools, run experiments on employees, and test all sorts of management theories. The buildings themselves have been designed with this kind of purpose in mind, echoing a long tradition of firm-sponsored scientific studies of labor control and productivity. There is nothing remarkable here—just more data, which leads to more possibilities.[41] To be sure, the new data-driven hiring and management strategies, and even the "platformization" of workers, might produce opportunities for people who might have been otherwise shut out of the labor market. But they can also cut down dramatically on workers' autonomy, distribute work schedules to maximize profit, anticipate who has a higher likelihood of quitting their jobs, calculate pay on the basis of smaller and smaller fractions of time worked, or even remunerate workers based on an automatically generated estimate of what they might be willing to accept given their rating and the specific conditions the data suggests they might face.[42] Ever finer wage discrimination and dynamic wage setting relies on the same economic framework as price discrimination and dynamic pricing.

Almost all firms, in fact, have become "ruled by data" in some manner, even if this only extends in practice to rule by the *idea* of acquiring data.[43] Now, the possibilities opened up by the world of granular data and powerful analytics cannot simply be willed into existence on the strength of their potential benefits to firms. Imagining the potential for more fine-grained price discrimination enabled by the algorithmic analysis of behavioral data is not the same thing as a stable, operational system that actually does the job. The gap between a slide-deck pitch and a well-functioning production server is where some of the most difficult engineering challenges must actually be solved. It is also where fast-talkers, be they market entrepreneurs or social theorists, end up taking advantage of the slippery character of terms like *artificial intelligence* or *machine learning*. To say you have an "algorithm" for accomplishing something is not the same thing as building a system that in fact accomplishes your goal. For example, the management of the real estate firm Zillow discovered to their cost that algorithmically exploiting an apparent information advantage in the housing market is substantially more difficult than it might appear.[44] It is here, also, that the more "neoinstitutional" aspects of datafication live. If an engineering problem is not, in fact, soluble, then what may take its place is some sort of Potemkin procedure, a ritual simulacrum that will have its own consequences.

Streams of Income

In the world of physical goods, the blending—or bundling—of software and hardware has been paralleled by an *unbundling* of the rights associated with each. When a company sells a physical but datafied good, the buyer owns the physical item (e.g., a car, a refrigerator, or a smoke alarm), but the seller may retain ownership of both the software and of data streams associated with its use. In some cases, the item may come with additional physical or hardware capabilities that must be unlocked in software for a fee. Data from the device might be sold on to a third party, or used to develop and pitch ancillary services, or both. Consumers are by now fairly well habituated to this sort of thing in the context of smartphones and computers. You buy a gaming console (that is, a piece of physical hardware) and then pay to download a game (a piece of software), perhaps one that also has a subscription component (an ongoing service) that includes a requirement that the console be connected to the internet while it is being played (a remote server is providing functionality necessary to play the game, but also an opportunity for monitoring). As ever more kinds of goods become datafied, however, responses to this sort of model may range from puzzlement to outright anger. It is one thing for a phone to demand a software update, or for a PlayStation to require an internet connection. But when your refrigerator, dishwasher, or doorbell do too, things may seem a little strange.

We can think about this process from either of two points of view. On the one hand, there is the intuition that the company selling the device has found a way to control or cripple it in a way that allows it to extract additional profit from the user over and above the purchase price of the device and the actual costs of making and selling it. From this angle, the business model is a form of "rentierism."[45] Economic rents are payments for some factor of production above and beyond the marginal cost of providing that input. In other words, rather than just sell you the thing, the company wants to find a way to have you keep paying for it. If the company can make an otherwise functioning phone or TV or thermostat stop working whenever it likes—because you refused to install their software update, for example—then the consumer has a good case for feeling taken advantage of. The intuition is even easier to see when the physical functionality is in some sense fully present in the device when it is purchased, but is not enabled simply because the user has not paid for it. A Tesla Model S, for example, may ship with performance capabilities that require additional payment in order to be unlocked via software. The sense that the company is unfairly extracting a rent here is easy to understand.

Although expressed in terms of the relative costs of bringing factors into production, the concept of an economic rent is rooted in a visceral sense that a principle of fairness is being violated. The producer is extracting this money just because it can, not because the rent is really required. Normally, the economic argument is that firms can only be expected to take advantage of such opportunities, and that they will do so for as long as they can, but market competition will eventually bring things back into line and erode opportunities for rent taking. Hence the concept is typically deployed to attack possible barriers to that competition, such as occupational licensing, patents, or other forms of benefit deriving from the brute fact of legal ownership.

From another point of view, however, what is happening here is that, far from being stymied, market competition is simply being given its full expression. If we think of what is being sold not as a single entity but rather as a collection of capabilities, functions, and features, then buying it just means buying the array of things one might do with it. All that the new technology does is make it possible to further refine and more clearly delineate—and price!—each particular element in the bundle of usage rights that the purchase conveys. From this perspective, products are being datafied not to illegitimately capture rents but to independently price features in a way that perfects the market for them. And, after all, these goods are not simply physical machines. They contain software that needs to be maintained and updated. This is an ongoing cost that needs to be covered somehow. The users of datafied products pay both with their money and with their data. They subscribe to a service, and they allow that service to collect data on their activities. If they suspend that connection (if they fail to pay up or log in, for instance), the physical object becomes inoperative for them.

In the case of products that, from the individual's point of view, are purely software applications—a music streaming service, say—the first step in this process is the conversion of the terms of the Maussian bargain. Across many different kinds of services, the gift of personal data in return for a free service is eventually reorganized into the establishment of a paid subscription tier. In the context of free services, it has long been observed that "if you are not paying for the product then you *are* the product." But, as we discussed in Chapter 1, the scale and growth rate of many free services can make it hard for direct advertising to pay the bills. And once companies have achieved a near monopolistic position, the temptation to capitalize on it is too strong. They succumb to the itch to work both sides of the market by wanting to charge users for what was originally given away for free while still selling or monetizing the data they collect about them. From Flickr to Twitter, the history of web services is littered with examples of resources whose popularity is built on sociable free entry but whose later phases descend into increasingly desperate ways to generate revenue.

In a nondatafied world, a successful sale traditionally comes with a transfer of ownership that severs the necessary but temporary connection between buyer and seller. With connected and software-bearing technologies, however, the transaction is only the beginning of an open-ended relationship. The user remains tethered to the manufacturer or the service provider when they use the machine or even, simply, by keeping it powered on.[46] What consumers *cannot* generally purchase is the right to access the software that powers the device or to repair or update it themselves if it stops working. These are the exclusive prerogative of the manufacturer and its network of authorized dealers. If the company goes under, fails to properly upgrade its software, or requires that its customers agree to its new terms of service, people may find themselves with a device that is unusable, incompatible with other systems, or suddenly collecting a disturbing amount of data about them.

These tendencies are not confined to phone apps or household gadgets. A now canonical example is the American heavy equipment manufacturer John Deere, which has sought to become a leader in "smart agriculture."[47] Datafication, the company claims, will be to twenty-first-century farming what mechanization was to nineteenth-century agriculture. It is a technological revolution that will massively increase productivity and permit a more efficient use of resources (such as water) in an era of climate urgency. John Deere has outfitted new generations of tractors, harvesters, and other agricultural machines with sensors, cellular transmitters, and software that is on by default and cannot be easily turned off or tampered with. In January 2022 it unveiled a tractor that it claimed "can plow fields, avoid obstacles, and plant crops with minimal human intervention."[48]

Again, the core impulse is familiar. Agricultural corporations have long sought to secure the dependence of farmers through the genetic manipulation of seeds, planned obsolescence of machinery, or simply through access to parts for maintenance. Many farmers have pushed back against the computerization of their means of production not by rejecting software as such but by turning the "right to repair" farm equipment into a potent political issue.[49] Others, meanwhile, try their luck in the overheated market for older, computer-free machinery; or they turn to do-it-yourself videos and websites to learn how to hack their own equipment using third-party code that technically violates the terms of their software license with John Deere.[50] Most people do not resist the datafication of their machines and devices in this way. Regulatory protections against companies' control of repairability are (so far) rare and hard to enforce. Instead people tend to be more fatalistic in the face of technological upgrades, sometimes welcoming them with trepidation. Rather than wanting to tinker with their devices, they prefer it when their cars are more like appliances and their appliances are more like iPhones.

For both physical and virtual businesses, data is a valuable asset on a corporation's balance sheet in more than one way. Good data can help increase profits through product segmentation, supply chain optimization, customer targeting, and so on. But it can also be the foundation for the development of derivative financial services, such as credit, insurance, or market intelligence. The linking of a credit offering to a manufacturing, service, or retail sale became a sizable—indeed fundamental—driver of corporate profits in the nonfinancial sector in the first decades of the twenty-first century.[51] In 2004, for instance, the *Wall Street Journal* remarked that General Motors was already more a bank than a carmaker.[52] Its lending arm (then known as General Motors Acceptance Corporation or, more commonly, GMAC) was making more money than its manufacturing arm. In 2017 the newspaper suggested that the same was now true of John Deere. In the midst of declining or stagnating incomes in farm country, the company expanded its lending activities. Short-term loans for crop supplies and leasing contracts for equipment potentially led to long-term vulnerabilities for farmers, but they shored up the firm's short-term revenues. Wall Street seemed pleased with the redirection: "The financing arm has shielded [John Deere] from the worst of the farm slump, keeping factories and dealers intact and investors satisfied with profits. Despite a 37% drop in sales of its farm equipment since a record high in 2013, Deere's stock price is up 72% from its recent low in early 2016."[53]

Credit-based financialization, as we have seen, is by now old news. But the scale at which it may now be deployed is not. Mobile technology has transformed the consumer credit market, from the most fringe and predatory outlets (cash advances) to the most established (banks). Payday lending apps will automatically process small, expensive loans in exchange for a monthly fee and intrusive access to a person's payroll and bank account information. Many digitally based companies have partnered with these new lenders to propose short-term credit to their own employees. Gig workers, who are typically paid "in 'batches' after completing multiple gigs, or immediately upon completing a gig,"[54] are a prime target for systems that accelerate payment or deliver quick credit for a fee and/or in exchange for data. Online customers are also easily reached, with offers to *delay* payment on similar terms. Mundane purchases—such as a pair of jeans—can be routed through buy now, pay later schemes at the point of sale.[55] Speed and convenience are key. On the demand side, the ease and privacy of smartphones makes predatory finance look not so predatory. So does its integration into the warp and woof of everyday digital entanglements. The exposure of waiting in line at the payday lender is gone. And on the supply side the good deal is also easy to set up. With enough data on its users or employees, any company can think of itself as a lender.

Credit's integration with tethered commodities gives it much greater potency than before. With an ongoing connection to the car or tractor enabled by default, the manufacturer effectively has a persistent link to the owner and operator as well. This can be used to monitor credit compliance and even compel loan repayments. With self-executing contracts and location information, the manufacturer-as-creditor can impose automatic penalties or repossess physical assets without having to travel the costly route of debt collection. The costs of this reconfiguration are distributed unequally across different populations. Buyers with poor credit already face higher-interest loans and demands to put more money down. But they might now also have to deal with "payment assurance devices" embedded in the goods they buy. These devices typically combine a GPS tracker with a "kill switch" that can disable their vehicle should they miss a payment.[56] On the seller's side, the costs of collateralizing loans and recovering assets could very well plummet, further easing and encouraging the process of managing a market in credit.

For both financial and nonfinancial firms, the payoffs of datafication do not stop at the extension of credit. A fleet of tractors will have some value as a collection of physical goods, or as collateral, certainly. But the data they emit may be more valuable still. Data flows become income streams. For instance, a manufacturer might position itself as a financial intermediary through which farmers can sell their crops. Or a trading platform might sell its information to its preferred market maker, an example we will develop in Chapter 5.

Insurance also looms large as a means of monetizing data from fleets of vehicles. Tesla makes and sells cars, but until 2021 it could not turn a profit on them without the sale of regulatory offsets (a financial product) to other car manufacturers. Even today, its business model relies heavily on auxiliary financial activities. In the fall of 2021, Tesla unveiled its own insurance division, which it anticipated would contribute a large share of revenues to its future operations. The reasoning is straightforward. The data collection embedded in most new cars allows for more efficient claims processing. It also opens the possibility for insurance underwriting to become much more personalized and dynamically priced.[57] That is, car insurance premiums will be adjusted to reflect a specific person's driving behavior (known by measuring their propensity to step hard on the brakes, run a red light or a stop sign, use a phone while driving, etc.), the condition of their vehicle, and the journeys they usually take. In a way this has always been a goal of insurance pricing, but things may change qualitatively when the information insurers need is supplied directly by the car rather than via a polite inquiry to the owner. (And for those whose car isn't smart, most insurance companies offer a discount in exchange for using a telematic sensor or a phone app.) When these technologies are embedded everywhere and everyone is surveilled in this way, insurance premiums will depend on the specific risk profile as measured and scored by the sensing algorithm. But what remains of the purpose of insurance—to socialize risk—when everyone pays the price they "deserve"?

Collecting and processing more data reduces the informational asymmetries (those of moral hazard and adverse selection) that make insurance a risky business. But shifting from socialized to individualized risk also transforms the very purpose of insurance. This may not be so bad where car insurance is concerned,[58] but in other domains, such as health or place of residence, the most significant sources of risk—and thus the proper allocation of responsibility—may lie outside the individual in the natural or social environment. The fact that these structural forces cannot easily be measured does not mean that they can be conveniently ignored. Doing so not only excludes people unfairly but also threatens the way that insurance systems can act as a prosaic but intensely practical manifestation of solidarity. We shall return to this point in our discussion of changing concepts of citizenship in Chapter 7.

Meanwhile, the "pretense" (to use Hayek's word) that "only what is measurable is relevant" is problematic in another way.[59] It moralizes the data imperative and legitimizes the hunger for data for its own sake. Again, it still matters whether all this data collection is, in fact, worth it. Putting the necessary sensors in a vehicle is not free. The reliable collection and proper analysis of the data is not devoid of error either. But these systems are only getting cheaper.

This general process of layering and abstraction, explored more fully in Chapter 5, tends to make soft-service providers and tangible manufacturing industries look more and more similar. Like car insurance, the business of health insurance is increasingly grounded in detailed telemetry from physical devices such as fitness trackers and smart watches. Individual consumers who choose wearable technology are rewarded with lower insurance rates. Firms that force them on their employees might be too. The data generated by the devices can then be mobilized proactively to modulate people's behavior by issuing warnings, daily targets, emergency interventions, and so on. Measured against these benchmarks, individual records—and thus premiums—may be updated continuously as new information comes in.

From the consumer's point of view, these kinds of services may be welcomed as helpful, empowering, or even lifesaving. They also open the door to scaled-up academic and scientific research about people's behavior and health. The less scrupulous sorts of firms (and researchers) will want to grab as much data as they can, even if that is more than the user realizes they are giving up. But even those organizations that have a care for their customers' privacy—the ones that carefully ask for permission whenever a change is made, or do all of the most sensitive processing on the local device rather than a central server—will still tend to move down a similar path. The temptation to disaggregate in order to monetize is very strong indeed.

The careful unbundling of data streams and associated cash flows is a striking instance of how modern financial economics conceives of all economic relations. Echoing Michael Jensen and William Meckling's quintessentially neoliberal description of the corporation, we could say that unregulated digitization has made it possible for everything to be reinvented as "a legal fiction which serves as a nexus for contracting relationships."[60] Concretely, this process is facilitated by the fact that economic contracts are now embedded directly in software at the time of purchase. From this perspective, a refrigerator, a tractor, or a TV is little more than a bundle of rights that specify the distribution of cash flows between different parties (buyers, users, the manufacturer, and anyone with a derivative claim, like advertisers, credit providers, or insurers). Consent may need to be obtained in a more or less informed way, because the terms of the contract have to be agreed to in some sense. What matters is that the technology allows for more fine-grained disaggregation of services, producing flows of data that can in turn be abstracted, rebundled, and sold.[61] In this way, every producer of goods becomes a technology company, every technology company becomes a service provider, and every useful service becomes a stream of data that can be turned into an asset. That last step involves an act of abstraction, where the unbundled threads of particular exchanges—each individual contracting relationship—are abstracted out and gathered together by kind in order to be sold as a specific kind of revenue source. This kind of abstraction, a prerequisite of financialization, turns out to be a natural complement to the kind of abstraction that software makes possible.

5

Layered Financialization

FINANCIALIZATION IS "A PATTERN OF ACCUMULATION IN WHICH profits accrue primarily through financial channels rather than through trade and commodity production."[1] As a tendency, it takes two main forms. The first is a rise in the share of corporate profits that comes from the financial sector, broadly construed.[2] The second, analyzed at the end of Chapter 4, is a rise in the share of revenues generated by portfolio income relative to productive activities within the nonfinancial sector. Beyond this, the term *financialization* connotes the diffusion of broadly "financial" ways of thinking about the economy—and, indeed, the world at large. In this more expansive sense, it means a focus on capital appreciation, on the increasing value of the prices of shares and other financial assets. A financial lens sees the world as an investment portfolio. Anything and everything might in principle be converted into an asset of some sort and made tradable on a market.[3]

How is the tendency toward financialization affected by the ability to augment devices, organizations, and indeed people so that they continuously emit data about themselves? Right away, these technologies enable things that we could not do before. Everything from fitness regimes to farm management can be monitored and evaluated. The initial purpose of this monitoring is to feed information back to the people making use of the devices. Perhaps those people (or their devices) can also be nudged in the direction of some goal, whether that is set by the local user or by whoever is doing the monitoring. But these flows have additional potential in the aggregate. When suitably abstracted, all of this new information becomes interesting in its own right as a kind of overview of what is happening with this category of device, class of person, or kind of setting. It also makes this information more tractable and more useful. It might be deployed to gain an edge on one's competitors. Most interesting of all, it might be used to open up entirely new lines of business. As we saw in Chapter 4, unbundling some product or service into its individual threads or streams of data in principle makes each of them monetizable. This can be a profitable move, but it comes at the risk of making the customer feel they are being nickel-and-dimed for every action they take. After the unbundling comes the rebundling, the moment when individual streams can be regathered but also abstracted into a new category and sold as an asset on a different sort of market.

To return to an example from Chapter 4, a company that makes tractors or combine harvesters may end up with streams of data on the activity of many thousands of individual pieces of equipment. That information is not just useful for reporting the state of the machine to its owner, for issuing reminders about maintenance schedules from the servicer, or even for policing loan repayments by the credit arm of the manufacturer. It is also a source of information about what is happening—and what is likely to happen—in various crop markets in the aggregate. Thus, in virtue of collecting data on how its machinery is being used, a manufacturer might end up, directly or indirectly, in the business of agricultural futures, either using this new information itself or selling it on to firms that can make better use of it. This might leave the firm in a situation where it hopes to profit from investment decisions or general price movements in markets that adversely affect the very customers it sells its equipment to, and from whom it collects data.

The tendency toward financialization has been recognized as a central feature of capitalism at least since the time of Karl Marx. Volume 2 of Marx's *Capital* focuses on it in depth. Sociologists and political economists have analyzed past waves, and most prominently the long surge in speculative trading and asset innovation running roughly from the development of modern options trading to the financial crisis of 2008. Here we shall argue that contemporary technologies of data collection and classification have a strong elective affinity with the tendency to financialize. Digital technologies provide a huge propulsive boost to the process of abstraction that undergirds the creation of new vehicles for investment. Furthermore, new technologies, through their Schumpeterian promises to destroy settled industries and create new ones, also open up uniquely speculative spaces. The tech industry and its financial backers depend less on secure expectations of future cash flows and more on a constant stream of hopeful believers, both large and small, who will commit their money to buying up shares when companies go public. It is financial speculation that sustains the effort to deploy new technologies at scale.[4]

Layering Abstractions

In Chapter 4 we saw how embedding information technology in everything from refrigerators to combine harvesters has created new opportunities for firms. At the simplest level, the data facilitates maintenance or allows some service to be provided directly. But much broader possibilities immediately suggested themselves to companies. The first and most obvious is surveillance, and the possibilities for both customer service and customer control that come with remote monitoring. The prospect of aggregating streams of data and treating them as the basis for new sorts of assets, and thus new sorts of markets, is far more interesting. The data itself becomes a product to be sold to interested parties.

This layering of abstractions underpins the process of financialization. It begins at the ground floor, as it were, with the creation of commodities themselves. To turn tangible objects into tradable goods, one must find ways to control, minimize, or erase their individual particularities so that they can be made functionally identical, interchangeable, and comparable. This process is a social achievement that requires extensive underpinning and framing by institutions.[5] A commodity's qualities must be clearly specified, and its quantities precisely measured. Bushels of red winter wheat, barrels of light sweet crude oil, shares of common stock, grades of mortgage-backed securities, and pairs of Levi's 501 jeans are all commodities with varying degrees of standardization and tangibility. Again, harking back to Marx, the commodity comes to market in what Luc Boltanski and Arnaud Esquerre call "the standard form."[6]

Standardization partly explains why people are often unconcerned about the social conditions under which specific items are produced. Commodities present themselves as interchangeable things whose value is fully expressed by the price one pays for them. As a rule, the specific history of any particular thing is of no interest. All that matters is that it is a proper instance or token of its type. Standardization also allows for particular commodities to be abstracted up into new classes of tradable instruments, layer by layer. The more homogeneous an item of merchandise, the more liquid its market can be. Highly liquid commodities can circulate further and be transacted in a general marketplace, an auction house, or an exchange.[7] Traditionally, exchanges were physical spaces, places where traders met and haggled. But these have mostly been reorganized or replaced by various kinds of transaction management systems. These systems circulate information and make it easier for prices to converge. They also allow markets for secondary, or derivative, exchanges and financial claims to be viable. In this "investment form," commodity exchange becomes a nexus of contracts for future delivery or options on such contracts that can themselves be traded on a market.[8] Indeed, the "higher" or more abstract the derived form, the more platonically homogeneous it will tend to be, and thus the more liquid and fluidly tradable it can become. The history of derivative financial markets can be quite literally pictured as a process of steadily layered abstraction, beginning from the tangible stench of particular pigs and cows massed and breathing in stockyards, moving out, away, and up to the pure abstractions of derivatives and futures markets in standardized pork bellies or feeder cattle and far beyond. The abstractions associated with information technology help make new layers possible. Any physical property, any aspect of work or everyday activity, can be unbundled and transformed into a flow of information that can be measured, divided, and classified. In both physical form and metaphorical scope, we see a seemingly never ending logic of "miniaturization," of increasing focus and specificity.[9] For example, service labor is disaggregated into targeted and efficiently allocated microtasks tracked by devices worn on the body or embedded in physical objects necessary for work. A car ride via Uber, a sorting task on Amazon's Mechanical Turk, a microcontract with a vendor, or any one of many other kinds of labor become what Veena Dubal calls "digital piecework."[10] The same process of fine-grained standardization applies to personal data harvested from multiple sources. This is the "workless labor" of users, in Ori Schwarz's felicitous phrase.[11] It is harmonized and structured for auction on advertising markets. Data management platforms translate incoming bits of information—a keyword search, an imputed emotional state, some data on geographical location—into targeted actions and opportunities, all in real time. In the moment it takes a web page to load, tiny advertising auctions are opened, bid upon, sold, and immediately executed. The result of all this is a specific ad selected by the auction protocol and shown to the end user. Each event happens at the direction of a networked, global, and instantaneous computing infrastructure that bears much resemblance—in its physical materiality, its liquid operation, and even its hyped-up, speculative logic—to modern financial markets.[12]

Bits and pieces of information are thus more than inputs in the process of producing services such as management or advertising. They also support the making of what Marx called "fictitious capital." These are the classes of financial assets that secure claims to future revenues. People trade for many and varied reasons. Some may actually want to take delivery of the underlying physical goods, from cattle feed, to palm oil, to real estate properties. Others—speculators—are far more interested in the activity of the market itself, abstracted as it may be. Digitization facilitates the bundling of any real capital into securities that can be traded on their own terms. Cattle feed futures, real estate securities, or cargo freight finance certainly benefit from this process.[13] But so do new streams of data about one's person. As we move up the ladder from the ownership of shares to options to derivatives and beyond, the scope and efficiency of financialized trading depends on the steady flow of data. As new layers are added, new opportunities open up to price the flow of information between and across them. A side effect is that highly abstract market spaces can be made available to individuals in an immediately accessible way, even if newcomers have little real idea of what is happening beneath the surface layer. In this sense, abstraction is also disintermediation. For example, a brokerage facilitates access to specialized financial markets. Occasionally, it might allow some individual investors to trade in financial markets for a commission. Perhaps it also acts as a market maker itself. The digitization of trading and the appearance of a powerful networked computer in everyone's pocket changed this dynamic quite radically. Brokerages like Robinhood realized they could recruit so-called retail investors and encourage them to speculate on the stock market using a friendly phone app. They did not charge them any commission. In their own words, as a zero-commission broker the company would make its money mostly through "a routing system to incentivize the market makers Robinhood has relationships with to compete for order flow based on the amount of price improvement obtained. This algorithm, known as the smart order router, prioritizes sending your order to a market maker that's likely to give you the best execution, based on historical performance."[14] It also generated revenue "from lending margin securities to counterparties"—that is, by loaning out shares to short sellers.

A system like this, known as payment for order flow, allows a brokerage to take a very small per-transaction cut of a contract by directing it to some particular market maker or exchange in order to execute the trade. At a sufficiently large volume, and with the ability to take sufficiently fine cuts of trades, payment for order flow is an attractive proposition for brokers. For investors, the absence of a commission means the trade is cheaper, but it also means the broker's interest shifts from assisting the investor to directing the contract to whichever market maker can profit the most from the trade. This is another way of saying that the broker's source of profit depends on the retail investor being relatively ill informed.

During the first year of the COVID-19 pandemic, Robinhood was the focal point of a huge surge in speculative investment in so-called meme stocks. These stocks were generally uninteresting as investment opportunities but were targeted purely in order to run up their price. They included, most notably, the mall retailer GameStop and the cinema chain AMC. Speculation was fanned by enthusiastic discussion online, specifically on Reddit, and further enabled by commission-free trading on Robinhood. This wave of small retail traders allowed Robinhood and its preferred market maker, Citadel Securities, to do a roaring business. Profitability depended more or less entirely on there being a substantial number of retail investors without a solid grasp of the risks they were exposing themselves to, particularly when it came to options markets.[15] The frenzy ended, as is often the case, with the temporary suspension of trading in the stock and the near collapse of the broker, Robinhood, which needed a large injection of cash from Citadel to save it. A string of public and political recriminations followed.[16] As in earlier cases, Robinhood had enacted each step of the Maussian bargain with aplomb. It provided something delightful to people as a gift; it profited hugely from the substrate of data that flowed back in return; and it rode the resulting flood of gleeful, effervescent sociality to its significant financial benefit. At least, that is, until the wave broke.

Events like this bring out the way that, in an ordinal society, the process of data-driven abstraction and sorting tends to loop back out to the world of individual identities existing in a similarly digitized social medium. On one side, the processes of data-dependent abstractions that we have been describing produce ever more exotic financial instruments whose structure and inner workings are difficult for nonspecialists to grasp. In a previous era, trade in these products might have been confined to elaborate, technically complex, but also highly restricted market settings. Now, however, these financialized abstractions easily reintegrate with the world of socially driven investor excitement. This also greatly expands the scope for fraud. Meme stocks, crypto coins, nonfungible tokens (NFTs), and other products are fed back into the pool of digital users, who can themselves be seen as occupying classification situations based on how their participation in the market can make someone a profit. To put it only a little too sharply, it is the phone in everyone's pocket that allows both sides of this process to happen. Highly financialized abstractions do not simply disappear into a tiny sphere of speculative but expert traders in a corner of the market; they fuel a general economic effervescence, one that is often pitched in terms that pander to people's love of autonomy, choice, and freedom.

Popularizing Protocols

The appeal of Robinhood was as much political as economic. The absence of a commission and the app's friendly interface enabled small-time, often young, inexperienced investors to participate in what seemed like a relatively exclusive kind of economic activity. It encouraged them to think of themselves as a risk-taking, savvy, even cunning sorts of persons who were moving in a world dominated by enormously more powerful players.[17] The connection to social media—by way of Reddit and other user forums— allowed these amateur traders to band together as they tried to move the market in their direction.

They lost in the end, of course. They were taken advantage of by the very platform that was supposed to be liberating them. But their determination to live up to their image of themselves did not die. It just drifted further toward the even more disintermediated, volatile, and risky world of decentralized finance. Here, at what is presently the frontier of organizational abstraction, there are supposedly no states, no banks, and not even the comforting face of a Robinhood to hold the door open for entry. Money itself is to be disintermediated into what Koray Çalışkan calls "data money." These are payment systems backed by transaction records that are public but encrypted, running on a global network of computers. They are "distributed ledgers."[18] The cryptographically verifiable, decentralized, and nominally low-friction nature of these systems is supposed to make them trustworthy. In practice their pseudonymous (or in some cases fully anonymous) character tends to facilitate all sorts of illicit trades. We might say that if the wealth of those societies in which finance prevails appears as a giant network of computers, the single digital ledger entry appears as its elemental form.[19] Modern finance is electronic. It not only depends upon but fundamentally just *is* the protocols or conventions governing the treatment, formatting, recording, and circulation of data within a network.

The protocols for distributed ledgers might be thought of—and indeed are often promoted as if they were—a kind of political constitution. They set the rules by which a community regulates exchanges and maintains itself in an orderly manner. What they lack in institutional facticity they make up for in collective fervor. Unlike fiat money, which has become globally taken for granted and is very deeply entrenched in economic life, a distributed financial system still needs to actively produce self-conscious belief in itself. This belief is a matter not only of confidence in the protocol's technical soundness but also faith in the future prospects of the community of people and organizations that maintain and use it. Like all forms of finance, but in a far more explicit and active fashion, decentralized finance is a "rhetorical fabrication" held together by myth, romance, and narrative.[20] New products, services, and investments must be relentlessly championed, publicly shored up in moments of doubt (BTFD, or "buy the fucking dip"; HODL, or "hold on for dear life"), and zealously defended against competitors, skeptics, and, above all, regulators.

Crypto advocates express broad contempt for the institutions of central banking and the monetary elites who staff them. It is not irrelevant that the bitcoin white paper—the first to articulate the cryptographic method by which the movements of every bitcoin are logged into a public ledger—was published on October 31, 2008, barely a month after the spectacular bankruptcy of Lehman Brothers. Bitcoin's software, released by the pseudonymous "Satoshi Nakamoto" in January 2009, theoretically enables people to safely engage in direct and unmediated transactions without the need for individual trust or institutional scaffolding.[21] They can bypass private banks and thus also the public system (of central banks) that backs them up in the last resort. At least, that is the idea. Even though bitcoin mining can be done on any computer, in practice mining pools rapidly became remarkably concentrated.[22]

The rise of cryptocurrencies fed on market populism. It was born of the desire to upset the existing monetary order by denouncing fiat money as nothing but a political fiction— which it is, albeit an exceptionally long-standing and time-tested fiction.[23] But it also mobilized the power of the social substrate to replace that settlement with its own, no less political, vision. As Stefan Eich puts it, "cryptocurrencies are part of a struggle over the political status of money in an age of financialization."[24] Casting doubt on the stability of the US dollar was a constitutional move for Bitcoin, expressed in the original white paper. Since then the pummeling of official currencies and central banks has been relentless, with prominent crypto coin holders stoking panic on social media at every economic jolt. This is not simply a matter of principled commitment, of course. Their fortunes depend on it.

The cultural work being done to popularize the token economy manifests as yet another metamorphosis of the volatile fusion of anarchism, libertarianism, and formal organization that has sustained the tech industry since its inception. In 2013, then nineteen-year-old Vitalik Buterin, a Russian Canadian programmer, argued that practical applications of Bitcoin's blockchain technology could extend far beyond the design of a new currency (though he himself quickly unveiled a digital currency for Ethereum apps, Ether, or ETH). He thought it could power decentralized, user-governed organizations of all kinds.[25] The idea took a life of its own. Chains, tokens, and communities multiplied, spreading ideas about the tyranny of all centralized powers and the inalienable sovereignty of individuals acting in and through the market to govern their own lives and accumulate assets.[26] In this celebration of self-sufficiency and spontaneous order, token promoters appealed to political sensibilities on both the left and right. On the one hand, decentralized forms of social coordination and governance revived the fantasy of the self-sufficient commune. We see it, for instance, in talk of "decentralized autonomous organizations" that are supposedly run by the mass of token holders according to some fixed protocol enforced by its own code.[27] On the other hand, decentralization also has a clear elective affinity with the bunker mentality of the Far Right, seemingly offering protection against the risks of demotion, deplatforming, and repression by the state and its corporate intermediaries.[28]

Underneath the ritualistic defense of the little guy—now flattered as a protean creator—against the power of the state and the corporation, the built-in power of the largest miners and most important developers always threatens to turn these grassroots utopias into communities that are dominated by a small group of stakeholders. Since the point is to create an unfalsifiable and anonymous ledger of transactions, its champions resist any action that might tamper with it—especially one that threatens the distribution and initial allocation of property rights.[29] They also seem determined to ignore the old Durkheimian insight that, no matter how carefully specified, contracts cannot enforce themselves. It is easier to avoid the implications of this fact when a relatively small number of people are, in fact, running the show.

Banking on Speculation

By mid-2023, the market-tracking service CoinMarketCap listed about twenty-five thousand cryptocurrencies traded across more than six hundred exchanges. Of these, the largest by a long shot were Bitcoin and Ethereum, which between them made up about 60 percent of the market. Both the estimated total market capitalization and product share fluctuate a great deal. Over the years, the market has repeatedly suffered scandals and huge crashes, with the big coins at times losing up to three-fourths of their value and smaller but still significant offerings being wiped out. When these markets rise, the excitement and buzz is palpable and relentlessly amplified. When they fall—or when entire exchanges disappear overnight, as with the FTX debacle—reaction swings from despair at the scale of losses, to relentless efforts by evangelists to rally support, to grim satisfaction from those who have maintained all along that the whole thing is a nonsensical scam.

For some commentators, the present wave of speculation is more than just a familiar convulsion of a market gone wild. Mark Andrejevic argues, for example, that the universalization of predictive capacity has primed the "full range of social and political life" for speculative activity.[30] Similarly—though the specifics of their arguments vary—Laura Bear, Michel Feher, and Aris Komporous-Athanasiou all see speculation writ large as the episteme of our time.[31] It seems to be the natural condition of an economy dominated by increasingly global, increasingly rapid, and increasingly open circuits of capital.

Despite being built on the idea of immediately auditable, transparent, and verifiable transactions, cryptofinance seems like a bubble constantly at risk of bursting, or a vehicle for sometimes organizationally complex but always conceptually familiar swindles.[32] The history of finance is littered with episodes of money mania, blind panics, and spectacular scams.[33] The most interesting cases are ones in which financial instruments that initially seemed exotic, dangerous, or absurd became properly integrated into the financial system. Could crypto be like this? The development of option pricing and its associated market offers a comparatively recent example of the typical sequence at work: First, generate excitement—and skepticism—about something new. Then, float upward on the bubble as it expands. In the process, lobby the authorities to recognize and perhaps regulate the resulting activity so that it can become a legitimate form of trading rather than a species of gambling.[34] The most distinctive claim of cryptofinance is that it will be able to stabilize and institutionalize itself, to reach the point of ubiquity, legitimacy, and availability, without that last and usually necessary step of becoming integrated into a financial system ultimately overseen by the state and central banks.[35]

In its present form, cryptofinance rests on three main processes. First, artificial scarcity is maintained through the mathematics of cryptography. Second, a vision of automated self-governance and value is propelled by networked media. And third, the growth that comes from popularity is fueled by the power of leverage through debt. Financial engineering enables the built-in restriction of supply. This is visible right across the spectrum of crypto, from Bitcoin's intrinsic coin limit, to exclusive tokens tied to membership in decentralized autonomous organizations, to the ex nihilo creation of crypto-native assets such as blockchain entries for digital objects (or NFTs). The hopeful logic here is that "the math [will secure] the economy, which in turn [will motivate] people to use the math."[36] As speculative investments in socially constructed objects of value go, there seems to be something reassuring about the idea that the coins or tokens are built on a complex chain of publicly visible computation. Cryptography, say its advocates, does not lie. It is, after all, a kind of mathematics, the language of reality itself, and thus has an existence far more deeply rooted than mere social assertion. In the words of Wikipedia founder (and occasional crypto critic) Jimmy Wales, "you can't ban blockchain. It's math."[37]

Mathematics is essential to finance, but is also just the beginning of it. Though founded on calculation, financial markets are *moved* by something much less pure. Speculation depends on sociality—on rumor, conjecture, and, above all, on the erratic movement of crowds. It runs on stories shared by people willing to part with their money or move it to one place rather than another. All monies and all assets require a "community of shared belief to 'work,' to exist as something recognizable as money."[38] In the case of crypto, there are no tangible items being exchanged beyond a very special sort of ledger entry and the shared belief that it is valuable. In the absence of any underlying "fundamentals" to constrain market movements, cryptocurrencies and crypto assets are especially dependent on the availability of cheap money, and on the self-validating energy and collective dynamics of "social avalanches."[39] The processes at work are as old as finance itself.

In practice, the abstractions of distributed ledgers and cryptographic methods must reenter the world socially. Channels of communication range from highly specialized, organized advertising campaigns all the way to more diffuse streams of talk, buzz, and excitement. Crypto subcultures have proliferated, whipped up into a state of febrile excitement by low borrowing costs and through means and methods familiar from any wave of speculative activity.[40] The point of each crypto project is to attract a steady flow of curious people who might be willing to open their wallets. Thus, a community of faith must be assembled. Prophetic names, unique purposes, remarkable designs, and esoteric rituals—all backed by advertising cash—give coins special meaning. Participants are glued together by economic fate, by the moral imperative to hold on to their assets, and by "practical affirmations of worth" that they hope will "bootstrap" the coin's economic value.[41] Gifts, once again the most basic and powerful means of establishing a relationship, help maintain confidence and periodically rekindle the special nature of the bond between issuer and holder. For instance, believers who have been present since the beginning may receive additional coins, rights, or derivative products. NFT vendors tried to generate demand by giving tokens away for free, a practice known as "airdropping."[42] Advocates with outsize influence exhort the faithless to join and call upon their followers to muster round-the-clock reactivity. In the case of people like Elon Musk, for instance, these are millions of literal followers on social media. Endorsement by the occasional "whale" (a person or entity with a high stake) appears like a powerful vindication. Members are rewarded with feelings of both belonging and exclusivity, with fantasies of ownership or decentralized governance, and perhaps with the ability to further leverage themselves into ever more stratospheric regions of crypto-native "value." New territories proliferate in virtual universes that new fiat assets claim to rule.[43]

Despite their name, cryptographic coins and exchange in NFTs are not the end of financialization's layering process. Markets can continue to expand both horizontally and vertically. Multiple coins of various types and with various properties (such as their alleged stability or ease of convertibility to dollars) proliferate in one dimension, leading to familiar-looking diversification and arbitrage markets. Meanwhile, and notwithstanding their nominally nonfungible status, tokens can themselves become objects of fractionalized ownership and futures speculation.

This entire world arose—and, for now, continues to exist—in a self-referential network where transactions in crypto are almost all transactions for other crypto assets. The question is whether the connection with state regulation will be made by any path other than criminal prosecutions on a case-by-case basis for securities fraud and outright larceny.[44] The crypto protocol, like other "codes of capital" before it, seeks to create value by classifying digital tokens as wealth-generating assets.[45] But willing tokens into existence is not enough to guarantee their institutionalization and the protections that come with it. The conspicuous enrollment of celebrities can generate excitement about a speculative investment in an otherwise opaque financial product. Making a cryptocurrency redeemable for anything besides ransom notes and other versions of itself is a different matter.

While the birth and early growth of crypto finance was motivated by a loud rejection of state-based finance, further development without the support of the state seems like an impossible task. We have seen this on both ends of crypto finance. Demands for regulatory oversight (and thus legitimation) have become more pressing. As people's money becomes increasingly tied up with crypto assets—and as naive investors are repeatedly ripped off on a small scale, or entire parts of the market collapse on a large scale—pressure for institutional protections have grown. A 2022 investor lawsuit against the crypto platform Coinbase argued that tokens are similar to securities, and the platform should therefore be regulated in a manner analogous to traditional securities. It was tossed out, but in 2023 the US Securities and Exchange Commission sued both Coinbase and another crypto platform, Binance, for operating an unlicensed securities exchange (a claim Binance's leadership had gleefully cheered in internal email communications).[46] Investors and intermediaries have come to realize that the fate of digital tokens depends, ultimately, on their backing by some legitimate political entity that can offer legal protection. In Katharina Pistor's terms, the legal code must act as a backstop for the digital one.

So far, most governments have been cagey when not simply hostile. Some have deployed cryptocurrencies in a hazardous gamble to attract foreign speculators or mitigate the effects of national inflation, with very poor results. In 2021, the government of El Salvador made Bitcoin legal tender alongside the US dollar. This was a risky move and it immediately backfired. Meanwhile, facing hard sanctions from the United States, along with hyperinflation, Venezuela has pushed hard to institutionalize the "petro" as a national token backed by natural resources, primarily oil. In war-torn Ukraine, blockchain-based alternatives to a nonfunctional banking system were used in fundraising efforts to support both the country's defense against the Russian invasion and the emigration of displaced citizens. But all of these moves spring from various kinds of desperation, and in places where the state itself is under pressure as a viable entity. Where this kind of urgency is not necessary, the struggle over the future of money and finance takes the shape of a well-funded political movement, advancing its interests through advertising, advocacy, and lobbying in national and state legislatures. In the United States, crypto platforms and their venture capital backers have targeted politicians for favorable rules and tax incentives in the hope of charting a viable path for crypto activities.[47] For all the talk of autonomy, self-auditing, and freedom from the dead hand of regulation, leading advocates know that their survival depends on integration within some preferably weak but definitely legal regime that would leave their capital gains more or less intact.

A populist rhetoric of revolution is still deployed when required. In a keynote speech at the 2022 Bitcoin Conference, venture capitalist and PayPal founder Peter Thiel brought the showdown over the soul of finance to a dramatic high. As a performance, the speech has the air of a religious revival led by a not particularly expert pastor.

Painting himself, a billionaire in his mid-fifties, as the leader of a "revolutionary youth movement," Thiel throws a couple of one-hundred-dollar bills to an adoring crowd ("crappy fiat money. . . . I thought you guys were supposed to be bitcoin maximalists. . . . It's kind of crazy that this stuff still works") before launching into a takedown of the crypto-skeptic "finance gerontocracy" that has dominated for the previous forty years. He dubs finance's late and opportunistic embrace of environmental, social, and governance goals a "hate factory" designed, much like "the Chinese Communist Party," to "name enemies" and undermine the (energy hungry) development of the crypto industry.[48]

This sort of thing is only necessary because cryptocurrencies have failed to prove themselves, even as a technology. Bitcoin is terribly slow at verifying transactions and consumes huge amounts of energy.[49] Boring old payment systems have been successfully digitized and are integrated with ordinary economic life in many countries, carrying a comparatively enormous volume of transactions far faster and at a fraction of the cost of crypto alternatives. The main technological advantage of the blockchain, its encryption, does not require any kind of privatization. States and the European Union are considering their own digital currencies. Meanwhile the crypto market itself is riddled with scams. Its most high-profile champions have a habit of getting indicted, or of hitting the Eject button just before things go bad for the masses. It turned out that, a month before his barn-burning speech at the 2022 Bitcoin Conference, Thiel's Founders Fund had disposed of almost all of its Bitcoin holdings, just in time to avoid the crash that arrived in May of that year.[50]

The wave of crypto speculation expresses and reveals the dream of hyperliquid capital. This is the fantasy of a "hyperfinancialized" economy where everything is "poised to become an asset class for speculative investment" that may be circulated everywhere, instantaneously.[51] Its promise, unfulfilled but perennially enticing, is that the whole infrastructure of the internet could be turned into a ledger that is also a casino. In that space, all physical and digital things, including the most mundane and ephemeral items, may be linked to a tokenized receipt or property title, now understood as a tradable asset of its own. Every organization would be able to create securities by putting the data it produces on the blockchain. Everyone could collateralize their own sliced-up, digitized, or digital life, literally turning their own person into an object of financial investment and thus speculation. Just as early web evangelists dressed up in clunky versions of their imagined cyberpunk future, crypto enthusiasts have tried to enact their dream as a kind of stunt. In the midst of the COVID-19 pandemic, a twenty-three-year-old Frenchman named Alex Mesmaj tokenized himself, selling digital certificates to a share of his future earnings, and used the proceeds to— what else?—fund a move to the San Francisco Bay Area. To be fully consistent, he perhaps should have moved to Miami instead, or San Salvador.[52]

Absurdities like this should not obscure the fact that the energy and resources deployed to realize this future have been enormous. The forces unleashed by the blockchain and its attendant contractual instruments—the combination of technological innovation, economic greed, and political animus—are unlikely to prevail in the form envisioned by their most vocal promoters.[53] But the philosophy that animates them is deep rooted and resilient. Most recently, its advocates have turned away from decentralizing finance and toward a new target: decentralizing society. Securitizing the soul by way of stable digital identities is the next step in the substrate-making process. Who are you, deep down? And can you prove it?

6

The Road to Selfdom

THE IDEA OF MODERNITY HAS LONG BEEN SEEN AS HAVING two contending aspects. On one side, the side of social organization, is the domain of rationalization and control. This is the modernity of bureaucracy, science, technology, and planning. It is the technocratic, Saint-Simonian vision of a society run on rational principles and devoted to the elevation of humanity in the abstract. Here the administrative task of modern organizations is to know and manage their subjects. On the other side, the side of the individual, is the domain of experience and expression. This is the modernity of the Romantics, of the full and authentic realization of the self and all its powers. Here the existential task of modern individuals is to know and create themselves.

Utopian or emancipatory tendencies in social theory seek to have both of these dimensions at once. In his analysis of this tension, the political theorist Marshall Berman names "the politics of authenticity" as "a dream of an ideal community in which individuality will not be

subsumed and sacrificed, but fully developed and expressed." In Berman's telling, this broadly romantic politics became submerged from the middle of the nineteenth
to the middle of the twentieth century. It was covered over
by arguments where "radicals and their opponents [both]
identified the capitalist economy and the liberal state with
'individualism' and equated radical aims with a 'collec-
tivism' that negated individuality." It was the "cultural explosion" of the 1960s, Berman asserts, that forced the idea
of individual authenticity back to the center of politics. The
New Left brought radicalism "back to its romantic roots."[1]
Its visionaries wanted the benefits of a decentralized and
differentiated division of labor, but without the administrative caging, stultifying overspecialization, or market in-
strumentality that came with life under capitalism. New
technologies would transform society into a kind of anar-
chically cooperative and productive network. But, as it
turned out, it was the Right, and especially the Libertarian
Right, that ended up most effectively capitalizing on these
ideas. It sought something like the same thing, but from the
other side. It insisted that it wanted individual freedom
and authenticity, too, but by way of a coordinating framework through which people could be identified and
rewarded without limit if they deserved. New technologies would instead enable an exuberant, individually oriented market populism. In Chapter 5 we saw how networked technology and expressive individualism were
harnessed by the likes of the brokerage firm Robinhood
to support and supercharge new forms of digitally medi-

ated financial effervescence. We now turn to how these same forces are reorganizing political life.

At its core, an ordinal society is about individuals. Organizations are compelled to engage in data-driven learning about individual people, abstracting that knowledge to sort them into classification situations, creating the eigencapital that individuals benefit from across institutions. How do these institutional tendencies intersect with long-standing debates about individual flourishing, the role of knowledge in society, and the shape of political life? In Chapter 1 we saw something of how these disputes played out as the World Wide Web emerged. In this chapter we show how the ordinal society is predicated on the maturation of a distinctive conception of the individual. We shall argue that a resurgent politics of authenticity, understood as the public assertion of a distinctive form of personal sovereignty, can be seen in three key arenas. The first is in the changing character of privacy; here a combination of mandatory authentication and presumed public visibility empowers a self that is sovereign but not private. The second is in the sphere of institutionalized expertise; here presumptions of official bad faith and the availability of information to individuals empowers a self that is its own source of research and expertise. And the third is in the world of the public sphere; here the valorization of differentiated, authentic identities, on the one hand, and algorithmically mobilized masses, on the other, empowers a self that is emotionally alert but resists conventional mechanisms for generating social solidarity.

Authenticated Exposure

We can begin with disputes over the meaning of privacy. The expressive impulse of romantic modernity is that persons should be truly themselves. The administrative demand of high modernity is that they should be properly identifiable. These first-person and third-person perspectives on the lives of individuals are, in fact, deeply connected. The politics of authenticity is entwined with the politics of authentication.

The most familiar manifestation of the idea of privacy is defensive. People should be protected against invasive efforts to collect data about them. Critics beginning from this premise see digital capitalism as fundamentally anti-liberal in nature. They point to the technology sector's general disregard for privacy and its manipulative interference with the formation and pursuit of people's goals and desires. We have already seen this line of analysis in Shoshana Zuboff's critique of the "instrumentarian power" of "surveillance capitalism," for instance, and more broadly it appears in debates about privacy law.[2] Generally speaking, in these accounts privacy is seen as both an inherent individual right and a substantive good to be preserved and defended. In addition to the argument's own merits, there is substantial public support for this approach. When given the chance to voice their opinion in surveys, people say they care about privacy. If the default is to not be tracked, and being tracked is a matter of opting in through some deliberate choice, people will typically not choose to do so. (Although the tendency to simply accept the default option is something that is true of choice making generally.) The difficulty arises less with the general notion of a valued right to privacy and more in the details of what people think this entails. The substantive content of privacy has changed over time, and attitudes have coevolved with technological innovations. Privacy is very much a moving target.[3]

The principal reason it moves is that while, at its upper limit, existing and being recognized in the eyes of others is a kind of narcissism, at its lower bound it is an essential feature of being a person. To be in society is to be visible to others, to be recognized as such, and to see others visible to you.[4] As technologies of visibility change, so too do the baseline conditions of social existence and participation. Erving Goffman's dramaturgical analogy naturally suggests itself. Society is a kind of theater. Online society is no different, and indeed may be all the more theatrical because the representation of oneself—in whatever virtual form—is selected and directed from behind the camera. Like any other social setting, it is a place of interaction and self-crafting, with its own commonsense, social rules, blind spots, set dressing, and stagecraft. These familiar processes are mediated by or inextricably intertwined with whatever technologies enhance them. Because surveillance is now everywhere, people are generally aware—and are educated to be aware—that they will always be visible to some degree. Most people do not choose to disappear off the grid. Instead they end up living with the reality of their more or less transparent lives. The careful management of one's own visibility to others—for instance by selectively sharing one's location or allowing private posts to be seen—is an opportunity to unflatten the free-for-all of digital ties and organize one's social life into varying levels of closeness and trust. Sometimes visibility can be a direct benefit to oneself, as surveillance is turned into a source of private information about, say, one's own health and fitness.[5] This typically has some sort of social component, too, as people are encouraged to share their activities or progress with friends. A very few people turn the performance of themselves into a small business as they seek attention from and influence over others. For most, though, the ability to opt out of surveillance is constrained by the desire to participate, to be where social life is happening, even if their desire to be monitored is not that strong. The absence of privacy is expected, disliked, and tolerated—all the more since corporations, too, carefully design interfaces to cultivate a sense of ignorance or helplessness.[6]

From the earliest studies of online identity, the possibilities opened up by new modes of interaction, coupled with the persistence of the ordinary business of self-presentation, invited sharply negative judgments. These assessments tended to become more ambivalent over the long term. Critics asked whether new modes of online interaction made social life more active, self-conscious, and freeing, or whether they instead produced a world that was more coerced, artificial, and disciplined. Scholarly accounts hedged their bets.[7] Empirical studies tended to fall back to detailed accounts of technology in use, describing complex assemblages of people and devices.

If there has been a real and significant shift, it has been in the degree to which components of individual identity and self-sameness are now portable across institutional settings.[8] These portable units are what Gilles Deleuze called "dividuals," the data-based avatars of individual identity that can be distributed across systems of control. The spread of "dividual units" of identity is significant because anonymity and personal freedom are related both psychologically and organizationally. At its absolute limit, anonymity is a sort of hermetic oblivion: you exist, but you are not in any way visible to others. In a less stringent manner, forms of "public anonymity" provide a kind of participatory freedom. These are more properly thought of as some form of pseudonymity. Named identities exist and persist over time and in public, maybe to a spectacular degree, but it is difficult to connect this public identity to any specific person or people behind it.

A further step away from perfect anonymity and robust pseudonymity brings us to what might be called "interstitial liberty." Here it is not that people are truly anonymous but that the information available about them is sparse, fragmentary, or hard to gather. Interstitial liberty arises from failures of design or from technical limits on the logistical capacity of organizations to keep track of people. This sort of freedom bubbles up out of the cracks between organizations that will not or cannot efficiently talk to one another. Much more common in the past, it is the freedom to move far away and completely start over without being followed by one's background. Negatively, it is the freedom created by records stored on old computers in outdated file formats that are impossible to search or cross-reference; or the freedom that flows from there being no "permanent record" of your existence that is accurate, comprehensive, and accessible. As surveillance systems consolidate and become more pervasive, the mesh of the digital network becomes finer and this kind of liberty tends to disappear. The possibility of anonymity comes to depend instead on the deliberate development of systems and procedures explicitly designed to ensure it. Interstitial liberty dries up as the gaps between systems are closed. Aspirations to recover something like it can be seen in the effort to create some sort of "right to be forgotten."

What are the consequences for the self? The shift from a world of interstitial liberty to one of relatively easy identifiability, and then subsequently to one of obligatory authentication, tends to displace the playful freedoms and pleasures of "decentered identity" that early computer users found so enjoyable about "life on the screen."[9]

More than any other company, Facebook successfully reframed the web as a space where real people ought to present themselves as themselves. Against competitors such as MySpace, it seemed to be the more genuine platform. It vowed to fight against the less trustworthy and more dangerous world of anonymous or pseudonymous identities. Facebook tried hard to make people use their real names and encouraged them to document and report on their lives for the benefit of their friends, and then their friends' friends. In doing so it deliberately connected a person's online presence with their offline world, especially for the overwhelming majority of people who did not already have any sort of "web presence" to begin with. It grew outward from the top, beginning with the most exclusive institutions of American higher education.[10] It was, after all, born at Harvard University as a student-only database of personal profile pages. (This was after its very earliest incarnation as a means to rate the physical attractiveness of women students.) This seemed quite mundane to people who had spent their high school years building public résumés and who were getting comfortable with their social status as Harvard products.[11] TheFacebook, as it was called, looked like nothing more significant than the school's freshman register, except for the fact that it sat on the network. This connective power, combined with the real people in the database, turned it into a force of its own and a focus of collective attention.

Safely enclosed within the university's network, Facebook's narrative of personal authenticity was both enjoyable and not restricted to hopeless computer nerds. As Charlie Cheever, a Harvard alumnus, recalled in an interview with Alexis Madrigal, "'That was really the first time that people ever made an account with their real name on it.' . . . Before TheFacebook, 'pretty much everything was like "Username: mds416." It was considered unsafe to use your real name. Cybervillains would come to your house and kidnap you."[12] Madrigal concludes: "TheFacebook borrowed some of the intimacy of the college environment to make this fairly radical step away from privacy feel safe."[13] As the network grew and other digital intermediaries established themselves, people were socialized into the blurring of public/private boundaries and the "context collapse" characteristic of online environments.[14] Newly arriving students were born into it. A certain kind of transparency became the norm, even if it was not always wholly "authentic." Rather, like any social setting, joking, ironic distance, role-play, playfulness, and cynicism coexisted with more heartfelt uses of the emerging platform.

From the point of view of institutions, questions of identification and authenticity present themselves as problems of control. Access must be managed, populations governed, and conduct regulated. Our methods for verification have evolved over time, just like our concepts of privacy. Elaborate but conceptually simple practices of spying, eavesdropping, or testimonials gave way first to special documents, hard-to-counterfeit objects or obligatory registration systems, and then, in turn, to electronic tags, indelible or unforgeable biometric markers, which in some futuristic versions can be exchanged for some privately issued crypto tokens.[15] This trajectory, certainly in its most recent developments, may make it seem as though the sphere of control is expanding inexorably. In 2023 many solicitations for authentication—a camera to stare at, a finger to press on a surface, an ID card to pull out of a wallet, a login name and password—are still visible and intentional. But others are much more insidious. The "electronic eye," in particular, appears increasingly inescapable, totalizing, and intimate. The voice or face "catchers" work unobtrusively in the background, embedded in the physical environment.[16] They are barely noticed, if at all.

Their impulse toward sociability notwithstanding, people do push back against being constantly seen and recognized.[17] Technological advances toward forced transparency and mandatory authentication tend to provoke their own countermovements. Strategies for evasion vary. Collective strategies go from mobilizing to secure databases, to banning sensors from public spaces, to destroying materials and records. Individual strategies rely on encryption, multiple identities, avoidance, sabotage by way of false or misleading information, or calculated efforts at disappearance.[18] Though these methods may be successful, a world with a high baseline of visibility makes them ipso facto suspicious. Why would someone work so hard to evade scrutiny if they did not have something illicit to hide?

For individuals, privacy threatens to become not the preservation of interstitial liberty but rather the accumulation of secrets, and secrets are associated with stigma.[19] Meanwhile, for organizations, and especially the state, almost the opposite process takes place. Led by the development first of "official secrets" in government, and subsequently "trade secrets" in business, legitimate forms of organizational secrecy continuously expand, whether in the name of national security, market competition, or simply the need for "confidentiality."[20]

Secrets eventually get spilled. People get doxed. Sensitive records get hacked. At its worst, what Bernard Harcourt calls the "expository society" revolves around a distinctive kind of power.[21] This is the capacity to not only surveil and manipulate but also to be a voyeur, to incriminate, expose, even blackmail. As David Lyon puts it, "not only being watched but watching itself has become a way of life."[22] As has, arguably, watching oneself being watched.

In one of the most famous passages of *Being and Nothingness,* "The Look," Jean-Paul Sartre describes the peculiar vulnerability that develops when someone goes from seeing (being a self with a perspective on the world) to being seen (having to confront the perspective of another on one's self). He illustrates it with the example of a voyeur peeping through a keyhole who suddenly finds himself caught by someone watching him. The look of the other is always unnerving, Sartre argues, not only because we fleetingly recognize ourselves in it through our imagination of their judgment of us but also because we don't. We can always step back, challenge our perception of others' perceptions of ourselves, or explain them away—but we don't know what these perceptions really are. Others have the distinctive power of making us feel judged in ways we cannot fully control. Social life is all about the dread that accompanies our awareness that we can never access what the other sees. We can only guess.[23]

Increasingly, machines direct the process. "The look" hardens and gains facticity through the incremental buildup of the personal data archive, on the one hand, and the expansive reach of digital networks, on the other. In the world of "networked privacy," exposure must be assumed: a criminal or eviction record available online, a deleted tweet resurrected by screenshot, an old photo scanned and recirculated, a confidential memorandum copied, a face automatically recognized, a bit of video sent to a group chat, a categorization that opens or closes some opportunities, an online threat flagged.[24] Many of the things people ordinarily do are incriminating in principle under some law or other, or are simply embarrassing under some allegedly normative standard, especially since standards may evolve over time or sometimes change very rapidly.[25] The potentially compromising bits of information are of interest to many parties. On the one hand are representatives of officialdom in various forms: the police; insurance companies; employers; property owners and managers, and so on. Their interest is in things that are criminal or at least against the rules in some strong sense. But on the other we also have prospective, current, or former romantic partners; college admission officers; social connections; a rubbernecking general public, all looking for clues, gossip, or shame. Here we shade over into the world of community chatter about what is new and scandalous, a perennial topic of interest and also grist for the mill of informal social control. In the end, nearly everyone has a case to prove, an axe to grind, or a nose to poke. The outrageous or outlandish acts people perform to drive up online statuses, comments, likes, and views may come back to bite them, sometimes in tragic ways. The drill artists studied by Forrest Stuart face the contradictory risks that their online performances of violence will be both doubted as fake posturing by rivals *and* treated as solid evidence of authentic behavior by prosecutors. Or, similarly, the young people interviewed by Alice Marwick enjoy their social media platforms while also being aware that "our networks are only as safe as our chattiest contact."[26]

The combination of technology and idle curiosity has naturally fueled opportunistic stunts that exploit people's vulnerabilities and possibly create new ones.[27] Even without a person being the target of extortion scams or the object of deliberately organized harassment, the experience of unwanted exposure can be vicious. Under these circumstances we can better understand why one of the early legal frameworks to curb the power of Web 2.0, first recognized in France and then institutionalized in the European Union in the mid-2010s, was about the right of persons to be forgotten online—that is, to have incriminating information removed from web searches.[28] But cultural and economic pressures in favor of authenticity and authentication are just as strong, and they are backed by more powerful interests. Google resisted the European rules, arguing that the public has a right to know and that a public record is, after all, public. The rules do not apply to data collected outside the European Union. And, in any event, information is never deleted—just obscured. The personal archive keeps growing, ready to be called upon if there is sufficient reason. States have an interest in this data just as much as firms.

In principle, a world without secrets might mean the social effect of any one piece of information reaching the public consciousness would dwindle toward insignificance. Since revelations are both eagerly awaited and increasingly unremarkable, everyone may feel compelled or authorized to reveal more anyway. Personal exposure might thus become a banal event, whether it happens by force or by choice. After all, exposures now disappear from view quickly, drowned in the incessant rush of the parallel exposure of others and the continual movement of information flows. Perhaps they are reclaimed as a shareable experience, creating new solidarities. Everything becomes an opportunity to "come out."[29] In a positive reading of the tendency to fuse authenticity and authentication, a world without secrets—and overflowing with so much information—may foster indifference, a blasé attitude toward social practices, situations, and identities. It might thus be more flexible, open, and in some sense more free.

This seems naive. More to the point, it confuses the perspective of the viewer with that of the victim. While viewers move on to the next bit of exposure, victims are left with whatever wreckage remains. The sheer scale of potential exposures makes them so destructive that their ephemerality is irrelevant. It is of little comfort to the exposed that the world will quickly move on to find another victim tomorrow. Even worse, the design of search and social media make it almost impossible to stop cascades of gleeful sharing and judgment. Rather, it is designed to facilitate and amplify them. A large, loosely connected network of users combined with an absence of choke points and pernicious economic incentives makes it easy to propagate storms of abuse, laughter, or derision. Anger, indignation, and rage are the fuel of social media, or even of the media tout court. And that, in turn, helps support shadier economies where money and influence can be acquired either by the threat of *kompromat* or the actual destruction and repair of reputations—an old business, revamped for the digital age.[30]

In addition to the problems that come from having authentic secrets revealed, there are the problems associated with exposures based on some text, image, or clip that seems authentic but is not. The success of large language models in producing fluent text on demand, together with similarly rapid advances in generating images, sound, and (most recently) video from prompts, has opened up new horizons in the world of plagiarism, fakery, personation, and fraudulent representation of people. What previously required a substantial amount of time and skill can now be done rapidly, at scale, and to an increasingly high standard. The diffusion of these tools produces a corresponding demand for authenticity and veridiction from both sides. Evaluators demand to know if a submitted essay was really written by the student. An image or document circulates publicly but may or may not be authentic. People victimized by deepfakes look for legal means to prosecute their harassers, or technical methods to prove footage was manufactured.

The first step on the road to selfdom, then, is a test of personal authenticity. In the ordinal society, you must be identifiable and auditable. This demand can be imposed from above, but it is also something that people may demand be done on their behalf. Verification is both formal and informal. It is carried out first and most obviously by the state and other large organizations, but in the end the network makes everyone a potential witness. While privacy remains valued, its practical availability is increasingly ambiguous. The default orientation of most market-oriented systems is toward a kind of latent or ambient public presence that encourages sharing and always carries with it the potential for exposure. People can search for and find you; the main question is whether doing so is worth it.

Exposure is correspondingly easy; the main question is whether you can plausibly show whether what has been revealed is authentic or not.

The Searching Disposition

As we saw at right at the beginning of the argument, the dream of the World Wide Web was about the accessibility, diffusion, and democratization of knowledge. Something like this vision of universal, interconnected learning has long been central to radical, romantic, or at least "antisystemic" critiques of education and science. In the 1960s and 1970s, to pick one example from many, the Catholic sociologist Ivan Illich argued that society needed to be "deschooled." By this he meant that the functions of education and training needed to be deinstitutionalized and the cultivation of knowledge returned to a loosely connected network of people cooperatively solving problems. He thought people should discover and learn things together in the context of immediate tasks at hand. To this end he imagined "learning webs," something like a bulletin board or knowledge-matching system for a whole society:

> The user would identify himself by name and address and describe the activity for which he sought a peer. A computer would send him back the names and addresses of all those who had inserted the same description. . . . In its most rudimentary form, communication between client and computer

could be established by return mail. In big cities typewriter terminals could provide instantaneous responses. The only way to retrieve a name and address from the computer would be to list an activity for which a peer was sought. People using the system would become known only to their potential peers. . . . A publicly supported peer-match network might be the only way to guarantee the right of free assembly and to train people in the exercise of this most fundamental civic activity.[31]

Illich's critique of educational institutions has many features familiar to sociologists—particularly his insistence that much of the organizational scaffolding and formalized procedure surrounding education is an edifice of ritual extraneous to, and more or less decoupled from, the actual business of learning and doing things. For Illich, "deschooling" was about flattening and decentralizing the domain of knowledge. This was not just practical good sense—that is, a matter of more effectively bringing relevant knowledge to where it needed to be applied—but also a kind of social freedom enjoyed by people working and living their lives together, which he called "conviviality."

Utopian as such a vision might be, patches of it really do exist. Consider the case of higher-level education and scientific expertise. In this world, bureaucratic gatekeeping and market-driven licensing are, of course, everywhere, from admissions offices to journal paywalls. Nevertheless, the decentralized, network-driven, and freely "rhizomatic" character of scholarly communication is far more prevalent than one might expect. The logic of the gift also persists far more tenaciously than it has any right to, in everything from the illicit availability of journal articles to the thriving, open infrastructure of software that underpins huge tracts of research. Access to this network of knowledge and knowledge makers is restricted in many ways. But once an entrée is obtained, the mass of relatively open, connectable material (and people) is breathtakingly large. A radical observer like Illich demands to know why these benefits should not be available to everyone.

Some of the pressure in this direction has caught expert authorities off guard. For example, in the context of the university, much attention is focused on matters of unequal access to higher education, the sharp inequalities of the academic labor market, and the proliferation of administrative proceduralism. With these problems as their target, critics reasonably consider themselves on the side of truly open, substantive inquiry, perhaps advocating for it under the labels *critical thinking* or *academic freedom* more broadly. Their enemies are those who would eliminate faculty autonomy and transform universities into skill-based training centers directly responsive to the alleged needs of the economy. As real as these trends are, this stance tends to miss the degree to which the *substantive* authority of experts has also been displaced in a way that depends less on broadly "neoliberal" trends eroding university life and more on the increasingly distributed and relatively open world of knowledge.

Established scholars see their expertise as grounded by their training and the substantive knowledge they possess.

The validity of that knowledge is cemented by and signaled through their affiliation with institutions of learning that, in effect, rent their expert reputations. This can lead to a kind of complacency. Romantic and antisystemic critics have always emphasized the emancipatory character of the *structural* changes that would accompany the transition to some new mode of social organization, be it postcapitalist or postbureaucratic. In the specific case of a radically democratized future for knowledge distribution, the *content* of that knowledge, and the associated consequences for critics such as themselves, was easy to take for granted. A lack of attention to that content can be thought of as an understandable necessity given the difficulty or impossibility of writing "recipes for the cook-shops of the future," as Marxists have long been fond of noting. Alternatively, those preferring an analysis and critique of institutionalized complexes of power/knowledge might tend, in a broadly Foucauldian vein, toward radical skepticism about the very possibility of expert knowledge in the first place, or the chances of escaping that nexus at all. But for the more earnest sort of social critic, the prospect of emancipation from the constraints of the present knowledge system can easily carry with it the idea that people will eventually come around to having correct views on things—which is to say, the critic's views on things. There might also be some expectation that an appropriate degree of credit ought to accrue to those who have held these correct views the longest. While this characterization is a caricature, recent strong shifts in popular opinion in several issue areas have been based in part on a sharp rejection of expert consensus. This has exposed the uneasy tension between advocating for the democratization of knowledge, on the one hand, while retaining the expectation that people ought to listen to expert authorities, on the other. When it comes, for example, to questions of climate change, public health, or constitutional government, it is striking just how many critics of the architecture of contemporary knowledge systems have realized they are also rather more committed to the importance of credentialed, institutionalized expertise than they might previously have imagined.

Like Illich, Marshall McLuhan was a popular theorist in the 1960s and 1970s, who is now rather out of fashion. He, too, drew a direct connection between the "electronic environment" and "the end of monopolies of knowledge" in a lecture delivered in 1970: "With the end of secrecy . . . there can no longer be a monopoly of knowledge in learning, in education, or in power."[32] Although McLuhan was writing for the age of television, in retrospect his picture of things accords better with our present than his own. McLuhan's media landscape was dominated by a relatively tiny number of gatekeepers. Authoritative broadcasters periodically spoke live to a national audience all watching at the same moment. From time to time they drew on a fairly fixed stable of experts. That world is long gone. Now, knowledge never settles. It is provisory and conflicted, a dynamic, gushing, never-ending flow of data and updates.[33] Its distribution is fragmented and disaggregated. Not only are there fewer institutions doing the work of cultural integration—the way national broadcasters may once have been chartered to—but the production and distribution of knowledge is actively dismembered into small islands connected by more lateral flows.

To the extent that a shared or collective focus is a real phenomenon, it is by way of diffusion across media platforms. E-commerce platforms claim to intermediate the plentiful offerings and demands of the consumer, so that people can better find what they need or want. Likewise, the providers of commercial search engines and social media platforms may argue that they curate the distribution of information so that people can better find what interests them. But their purpose is not to distribute knowledge or even to convey news. It is to sell advertising.[34] Platforms mediate information in order to find customers. "The algorithm knows best" really just indicates "the market knows best."[35] Again, the point is not that the knowledge environment that characterized the age of mass media was uniformly superior in its effects or more principled in its foundations. Contemporary critics of those systems exposed their shortcomings at the time, as did pioneering empirical studies of the actual consumption and diffusion of news and knowledge more generally. Intellectuals decried the superficiality of mainstream broadcast and print media, denounced its dependence on the advertising industry, and protested their own exclusion.[36] But what came later has tended to undermine their position even more.

The pessimistic version of this phenomenon is familiar. To begin with, the supposed "marketplace of ideas" that followed the deregulation of print and broadcast media simply handed the megaphone to the wealthiest players.[37] But material resources are only part of the story. The "division of learning" (that is, the extreme power asymmetries that structure the production and use of information) had as its corollary the increasing personalization of knowledge.[38] This worked a deeper transformation. Digital technologies accelerated a process of elite displacement by replacing editorial gatekeepers and their chosen experts with aggregation rules decided by coders and developers.[39] It is these rules that now organize how knowledge is to be made publicly legible.[40] The average person must search the network of available material to generate an output that meets their expectations, as interpreted through the same vectoral and ordinalizing technologies we described in the context of consumer marketing and audience segmentation. In the process, the notion of a preexisting hierarchy of knowledge is displaced in favor of the ability of the network to generate a more precisely "relevant" answer, whether as a page of links or a summary paragraph of text.

When bad information propagates through search engines or media platforms, firms that make it their business to deliver relevant content fall back on an ostensibly laissez-faire attitude. They insist they are not (yet) liable for the content they produce. They are loath to tell the public what to trust. They warn that having platforms arbitrate truth claims is a dangerous move.[41] Less explicitly, they benefit financially from the ebb and flow of attention. They cannot of course escape it entirely. They find themselves hip-deep in the endless business of moderating and directing the gigantic flood of ever-renewing and often bad content. They are drawn into the task of rating webpages for quality, controlling bots, and removing the most offensive material. But much escapes scrutiny or does not seem to warrant it until after the content has already spread. The result is that the knowledge and information people have easy access to tends to be distributed according to popularity, market power, and estimated relevance to the individual—or, rather, that the mode of distribution is what now tends to count as knowledge. The very notion of epistemic authority has changed. There has been a shift in "the sense by which we take our bearings in the world."[42] In the process, the older knowledge monopolies of the media, professions, and sciences have taken an epistemic beating.[43]

This is the second step on the road to selfdom. When it comes to developing their beliefs and finding evidence to support them, people cultivate a "searching disposition" to explore the web of information available to them.[44] The authority of experts to dispense answers is increasingly outflanked and undermined by this disposition. Meanwhile, the obligation to search is both a kind of responsibility (this is the right way to get the information you need) and a necessity (it's not as if anyone else is there to look it up for you). In these circumstances it is understandable that critics—generally experts whose role and authority has been displaced—have been horrified at the outcomes. They emphasize the disastrous consequences of life in a "posttruth" world rife with echo chambers and empowering those who seek to exploit them. In such circumstances it is not so much that some benign common ground becomes hard to achieve but rather that the very idea of broad collective agreement about consensus reality threatens to become illegitimate. These changes in the sourcing and diffusion of information and ideas tend to exacerbate political polarization too. As search has become increasingly tied to advertising, and thus to knowing the user more intimately, it has in effect become more responsive to its knowledge of the searcher. The ability to produce results relevant to the wishes—and preferences—of users is not an intrinsically bad thing; doing so is what made modern search engines so effective in their early days. But the shift toward personalization, guided by the appetite to advertise, has happened while maintaining the original image of direct engagement with a collective or general stock of knowledge.

Francesca Tripodi has described how people approach search engines as truth finders designed to help them sift and sort the web's plentiful offerings into the believable and the deceptive.[45] As people do their research, they might even feel like good citizens doing their due diligence. After all, they are forming an opinion for themselves through a process of fact gathering and reflection. The difficulty is that the beliefs they bring to the search process itself, embedded in the vocabulary they use to consult the search engine, together with their whole search history, may yield results that conform to their already well-structured world. Moreover, beyond search the sophistication of "clickbait" continues to improve as platform owners learn what sorts of content produces the most engagement. The web is not a giant encyclopedia. Everyone participates in the making of its knowledge and reinforces its structure through the use they make of it. Rather than being a method for sifting and selecting on the basis of a general view of accuracy or truth, search becomes a system that learns to be relevant to particular types of users as they seek answers to the questions they have formulated.

We could simply stop here, having elaborated on these very real problems with this new order of knowledge, decrying the tendency toward polarization and post-truth personalization that the searching disposition tends to produce. But these same tendencies—specificity, relevance, participation, and engagement—are quite general.[46] They have greatly benefited the sciences and the professions too. The new knowledge regime is not some sort of rot that has taken hold among one group only. It is an epistemic order that has repositioned everyone. The fact is that experts themselves constantly cultivate, benefit from, and indeed enjoy the same searching disposition that they may worry is corrupting the less well informed. The character of scholarship and expert knowledge in general has been transformed in recent decades. It is far too easy to take for granted the massive, pervasive benefits of a connected global network of knowledge products and producers, traversable and accessible in real time. In the late 1990s, as the benefits of Google's model of search were becoming clear, an early meme invited people to consider "1950s Google." It was a picture postcard addressed to "Mountain

View, CA, USA" with a space to write your query and a polite note asking you to wait four to six weeks for a reply. To pick an illustration not entirely at random, by the early days of the COVID-19 pandemic a social scientist who wanted to understand the global behavioral response to lockdowns could sit at their kitchen counter and produce an analysis of what daily driving, walking, and transit patterns looked like in a thousand cities across the world over the previous six months. The data was condensed from pocket computers used by billions of people, drawing on positioning data from an orbiting family of what were once secret military satellites. A few million rows of it could be pulled down in a moment, courtesy of a national computer network originally designed by the government to be disaggregated and robust enough to survive a nuclear war. It could be processed using software originally written and supported by academics in their spare time, because they were convinced that sophisticated tools should be available to everyone for free—as if any of that were a reasonable thing to be able to do while stuck at home.

By the same token, the general capacity to search and quickly find good answers to highly particular questions has expanded beyond all recognition, whether one is asking about Python code or a medieval codex.[47] The same goes for the potential for making specialized connections or collaborative links in almost any field of research or creative activity. The impulse to search comes first and delivers benefits fast. Again, the gifts of the Maussian bargain persist to an astonishing degree, as semiorganized sociable sharing in a latently public space. A searching disposition is not simply the desire to look for and accept the first thing that confirms one's prejudices; it is also the tendency to search and connect across a network of knowledge without constraint, and to justifiably expect a reasonable degree of success. This disposition is embedded in the working lives of experts and scholars of all stripes. For all its problems, if you asked subject-matter experts whether they would go back to a predigital, prenetworked world of scholarship—one where the costs of search and connection in terms of time, money, usefulness, accuracy, and scope were to return to what they had been even as late as the early 1990s, the answer would overwhelmingly be "absolutely not."

The key point is the downward movement of these activities toward the individual, augmented by some device that connects to the world. Today everyone can, in their own mind, produce knowledge or "do research." Everyone can be their own expert. Everyone *should* be. Indeed, in a way everyone *must* be. Disintermediation means removing barriers and middle layers. It opens up parts of the world to direct contact, making them more amenable to investigation and action. But it also means that many activities or tasks tend to become less the purview of a specialist and more something people are expected to do for themselves with the assistance of some piece of technology. The phenomenon is quite general. Making a connection on the telephone once required an operator, a job long since eliminated by switched exchanges. Preparing correspondence was a job for the typing pool, but now even elite executives type their own emails. Finding a hotel required a travel agent, but now we simply search for one online. That last sort of activity is the most important and all-encompassing one. So many routine tasks involve finding things: a place to stay, and the way to get there; a book or article; a good or service; a piece of information. The expectation is that we will do it ourselves.

The proximity of networked and, increasingly, synthetic knowledge has transformed the way we approach the world—not only politically but also culturally. Search has become second nature. Soon, interrogating artificial agents will be too. That does not mean everyone will do it well, nor that the knowledge delivered by search engines or chatbots relieves people of the burdens of judgment and reflection. But much the same was true of newspapers, radio, and television. What it does mean, just as it did in the earlier regime, is that everyone is oriented to these activities. For better or for worse, it is through their arbitration that small and large conflicts are settled. They provide a technical framework and cultural script for how to be a member of society. Their moral valence is high. You *must* search.[48] It is a skill one ought to cultivate, a kind of civic expectation, even a species of professional responsibility—and one that pertains specifically to individuals. The irony is that the combination of personalization and auto-generated content has severely undermined the quality of search results, once the crown jewel of a service like Google, right at the time the searching disposition has properly taken hold. Crucially, as we saw in Chapter 5, the devices that enable all of this agency are not, in themselves, things we can easily break open and tinker with. Two forces pull in opposite directions: user agency is enabled, and required, in the sense that more and more powerful devices become increasingly personal and a searching disposition is the basic means of using them to navigate the world of knowledge and expertise. But the devices that make this possible themselves tend to become increasingly sealed off, opaque, and deficient.

The Self-Organization Man

The third step on the road to selfdom is a consequence of technologies of classification and self-classification. The ability, and subsequently the requirement, to locate oneself in a fine-grained way in particular classification situations affects the perception of one's own identity and of the space or landscape of identities in general. In the older era of mass politics and society, the effective analysis of social classification and its political dilemmas tended to come in two forms. For those who were named and recognized by broad social categories, the danger was that one's individuality might be subsumed by and dissolved into the crowd. The best-selling classics of mid-twentieth-century sociology repeatedly focused on the various forms of alienation or anomie associated with "man's" search for meaning and community in society.[49] The second kind of analysis, meanwhile, was the one that followed from not being recognized fully, or at all, and explored what it meant to be classified as less than a full person. The more radical critiques of the twentieth-century social order examined these marked or subaltern categories and types, often with a focus on the relationship between classification as an external social process, on the one hand, and the first-person consequences for experience and identity, on the other. We see this in W. E. B. Du Bois's naming and discussion of double consciousness, for instance, or in the painful self-awareness of a thinker like Frantz Fanon.[50]

In ordinal societies, by contrast, the flow of eigencapital into classification situations and the affordances of connective technologies yields a distinctive politics of self-location. Group-level categories and their intersections proliferate. Some classification situations may provide a basis for identity formation. The dilemma faced by the "authentic self" under such a system is not so much a matter of asserting one's identity in the face of some anonymous mass or of resisting subsumption by some overly broad social category. Rather, one is expected to explicitly locate oneself within a universe of highly differentiated, externalized, socially recognized categories. Aspects of experience, especially those that relate to the experience of oppression, become elements of identities that ought to be expressed, settled upon, and flagged. More generally, the redistribution of both status (in terms of "recognition") and resources along lines of social difference comes to be understood as a critical aspect of the quest for justice.[51] A distinctive form of microlegitimacy emerges from speaking *as a* member of some precisely defined category, while keeping the views of those who cannot claim membership at bay.

In this landscape, politics is about finding the right level of group aggregation. It is a little like conceptual debates in social theory about how many categories of social class there are. There is a constant downward pressure to disaggregate to the level of each unique individual. Classification situations are specific and typically not associated with identity categories. At the limit, the categories built up out of the fit between eigencapital and market opportunities may be strange or initially unrecognizable in terms of conventional social groups. Insofar as shared, socially recognizable groupings *do* emerge, they will tend to be very fine-grained, perhaps almost absurdly so from the perspective of "ordinary" social categories.

These combined pressures severely exacerbate the tendency of any democratic movement to subdivide into ever smaller grouplets. As we have argued, social classification and ranking is always moralized, tangled in a phenomenology of authenticity (for nominal classifications) and desert (for ordinal ones). A mode of social organization oriented to the precise classification of individuals not only provides grist for the mills of moral judgment but also allows those mills to grind exceedingly small. If these classifications can be mobilized through technology, this, in turn, provides efficient points of attack for those wishing to deliberately drive wedges between potential political allies.[52] The inexhaustible nuance of classification situations pushes right down to individuals, obscuring the central need of any kind of broad-based political movement to bracket the myriad particularities of its membership for the sake of a broader sense of belonging. The characteristic modes of failure here are, first, direct fragmentation into smaller and often ephemeral groups; second, the emergence of an internal hierarchy of classes based on some inevitably moralized criterion of authenticity or worthiness; and, third, the dogmatic assertion of some single dimension of identity as the only one that is truly real or politically relevant, with everything else relegated to some secondary status.

If the tendency to form "groups without people," or at least without many people, manifests most prominently on the Left, its most striking right-wing counterpart might be the tendency to reduce social categories to atomized mass politics or "people without groups." The best way to avoid the splintering of groups is for there to be only one group—the nation, usually—with leaders who not only embody and express its spirit but commune directly with their base, on social media. But this kind of populism is hard to sustain because, for the Right as much as the Left, the downward pressure in an ordinal society is fundamentally individualizing. So, in the most extreme cases, the current of political engagement runs entirely backward. Emotions are generated and tested online. People are amassed around issues and positions whose salience is inferred through social media: a strong response is reason enough to raise a topic's importance and further promote its visibility. Economic payoffs come through ad sales, as usual. But a populist movement organized this way, around and through social media, may also benefits at the ballot box.[53]

Populism is not native to the digital society, but the latter's characteristically flat, hyperreactive, and teeming knowledge economy certainly stimulates reactionary impulses, born out of opportunism and distrust.[54] In the rewiring of democratic politics by the tech industry, the citizen endowed with rights and a voice is valorized primarily as a potent object of market intervention. The agora overwhelms the polis. It is up to the individual to skillfully navigate the flood-tide of content.

There is a sort of elective affinity between the deployment of the ordinal society and the elevation of a radical, entrepreneurial kind of individualism in popular and sometimes scientific culture. A particularly relevant illustration, which extends a long line of neoliberal writings made for a mass public, is James Dale Davidson and William Rees-Mogg's *The Sovereign Individual*. Originally published in 1997, this book bore the subtitle *How to Survive and Thrive during the Collapse of the Welfare State*. It was reissued a few years later with the same title but a new subtitle, *Mastering the Transition to the Information Age*. The interchangeability of the subtitles gives a good indication of the substance of the argument. Davidson is an American investment adviser and writer. Rees-Mogg was a high-profile British Tory; at various stages of his life he was editor of the London *Times,* chairman of the British Arts Council, and a member of the BBC board of governors. The book is an account of large-scale social change, past and future. History, the authors argue, is driven by "megapolitical transformations"—that is, by shifts in the economic and political organization of society.[55] They see their present moment as on the edge of one such transformation, thanks to the information revolution. Though its content was very much individualist and right-wing, *The Sovereign*

Individual's argumentative form was somewhat Marxian in the sense that it posited emerging productive forces being repeatedly fettered by entrenched but outdated political and economic institutions. Just as the medieval fiefdoms and manors had inhibited the development of industrial capitalism, so too large capitalist corporations and the nation state were now blocking the emergence of the information-driven political order of the future.

The pendulum was about to swing back to the individual, however—or, rather, to a particular *kind* of individual. The key point about the emergence of the "sovereign individual" is that not everyone will be one. Instead a "cognitive elite" ambitious and able enough to lead the information revolution will reclaim the monopoly rents presently held by the state. These are the digital capitalists who will use technology to make production capital-intensive rather than labor-intensive, ending once and for all the exploitation of capital by labor and fatally undermining the political constituency for the state's provision of welfare. As for the sort of people who lack the talent to make a difference, the authors shed no tears: "New survival strategies for persons of lower intelligence will evolve, involving greater concentration on development of leisure skills, sports abilities, and crime, as well as service to the growing numbers of Sovereign Individuals as income inequality within jurisdictions rises."[56] Much like the leftist romantics, Davidson and Rees-Mogg believe the revolution in information technology means production will disaggregate, delocalize, and devolve. The required physical scale of production will fall sharply with advances in digitization.

Its operations will become more physically mobile. But this does not imply any sort of convivial post-Fordist utopia. Rather, we shall see the triumph of individual initiative and intelligence in a fully decentralized market with an absolutely minimal institutional infrastructure. Politics itself will also be transformed. The sort of mass democracy that characterized the twentieth century will give way to the "commercial sovereignty" of sovereign individuals who can negotiate their own tax treaties and their own access to public goods. The mobility of capital (and its individual owners) entails that if some jurisdiction fails to offer favorable terms to sovereign individuals, they will simply move elsewhere.

In its elitist and selective way, this vision is emancipatory in the sense that it sees individual talent under the present social order as highly constrained by the threat of coercion and violence, and of course repeatedly bled by the state and its tax collection and welfare-provision schemes. Echoing the likes of Ayn Rand, the idea is that talented individuals have for too long been stifled by the power of parasitic governments, expressed most recently in the egalitarianism of mass democracy. Now, at last, information technology will allow people to shake off their fetters, devolving sovereignty from states down to individuals—at least, sufficiently entrepreneurial and clever individuals. We can think of this sovereign individual as a "self-organization man," a sort of robustly active, definitely still very masculine alternative to the bland, lost, and enervated organization men of the 1950s.

The main thing in the way is the institution of money. This newly made world would need some means of exchange that enabled people to engage reliably in entrepreneurial transactions, but that circumvented the state and its monetary apparatus. If there could be some sort of denationalized cybermoney, Davidson and Rees-Mogg argued, some dependable private means of payment that would make transactions more difficult to regulate, then power would in effect be transferred from the sovereign state to the sovereign individual. Like all prognosticators, the authors were understandably short on details about how exactly this would be accomplished. But they were confident it would be. In this respect their anticipation of where things were going was quite striking.

As it happens, one of the people who came across *The Sovereign Individual*—and who came to see it as one of the most influential books they ever read—was a young Stanford University undergraduate turned entrepreneur named Peter Thiel. Of all the class of Web 2.0 billionaires, it is Thiel who most clearly and explicitly drew out and, at least to his own satisfaction, resolved the individualist dilemmas of information technology and the state. In his preface to the second edition of *The Sovereign Individual,* Thiel explicitly frames the core problem as a struggle between the individualism of liberty in democratic politics, on the one hand, and the individualism of freedom in the competitive market, on the other. For him, the only solution is not some sort of reconciliation between politics and the market, but simply a straightforward victory for the latter.

A vision of the future is not an analysis of how society actually works, let alone an accurate forecast of what is going to happen. Considered as political theory, Thiel's views have an all-encompassing character that most commentators would not be inclined to take all that seriously were it not for the fact that the person holding them is very rich indeed and has a strong taste for political intervention. Whether they are points of condensation for ideas already floating around in the ether, or proper originators of new theories which they attempt to enact, the influence of "practical men" and their particular visions of the world can be substantial. We have argued that, beginning with the general push for personalization, the overall tendency is toward a conception of the pure individual incorporating authenticity through authentication, personally validated expertise through search and broadcast, and, ultimately, the replacement of individual liberty within a polity by pure sovereignty within the market.

Again, movement in this direction is not some inevitable historical process. Nor is the individualist elitism of Peter Thiel any sort of necessary avatar of it. Still, insofar as it actually exists as a social form, it was assembled out of pieces made available by the development of the web since the late 1990s. In each case, the process was driven by delight, convenience, and a growing demand for authenticity in identification. Individuation reduced friction in a way that people enjoyed—when it worked. Targeted advertisements remain the subject of jokes, but accurate and relevant search results became accepted as a natural fact of life. Indeed, it is the tension between them that now seems strange, as recent experiments with search technologies have degraded their performance. Direct and immediate relevance is how people *want* things to work, whether for search or any other service. The tendency is thus to make things more and more granular, at least to the level of the individual, and perhaps even beyond when it comes to individual roles in different places and times. This produces a particular model of privacy, as each individual lives within their own world while being assisted by a service or a device that claims to know exactly who they are. Social pressures toward joint participation are reduced, as everyone gets an experience tailored to themselves alone. At the same time, with some exceptions, there is less and less anonymity with respect to the system as a whole.

Other forces have supported this increasingly tight link between participation and verification. For instance, Facebook implemented a policy of authentication for anyone who wants to place an ad in response to the 2018 public furor over ad-sponsored disinformation campaigns. In 2009 Twitter unveiled a system to verify the authenticity of "public interest" user accounts. It had a somewhat haphazard character. The criteria for becoming "verified" were always rather ad hoc, and processing applications became a chronic problem for the company. But this only served to make clear that a more consistent approach would be both much more useful and much trickier to get right.[57] After Elon Musk acquired the platform in 2022 the company began simply selling the verification mark, which missed the point of the practice entirely and only caused more problems.

While Twitter's shambolic trajectory is a high-profile and somewhat farcical example, the issue is quite general, and serious. The push for seamless and fully reliable verification and authentication is steady. Most recently, the largest platforms have begun implementing passkey-based successors to earlier password-based methods of access to services of all kinds. We can anticipate that demands for authentication will multiply for other reasons too. For instance, the diffusion of easy-to-use tools that allow people to generate text, images, code, or other outputs on demand put the relationship between authentication and participation under increased pressure in all kinds of ways, from telling whether someone "really" did the work they present as their own to establishing whether the person one is having an online conversation with is who they say they are or is even a person at all.

In each case, the authentic, empowered, and rigorously verified individual is at the core of the process. Since the first dot-com boom of the late 1990s, new technologies have repeatedly been pitched as the means of self-realization and reward through the market. It is the market that encourages and enables authentic self-expression; it is the market that eliminates bureaucratic hierarchies, be they governmental or corporate; it is the market that does away with needless managerial regulation; and it is the market that unseats undeserving, rent-seeking elites. Every fetter on personal freedom and every barrier to economic success is to be transcended by the power of technology to enable relations of exchange in their purest form. This is Marx's vision of postcapitalist utopia filtered through a YouTube channel and—explicitly, in Thiel's case—restricted to the talented few. The promise is not just a perfect individualization of exchange and its rewards but, at the limit and echoing Marx once more, the withering away of the state itself, at least with respect to its control of money. For its advocates, the road to selfdom is a sketch of historical development and a plan for the future. Its core elements are thought to be immanent in the technological developments that have driven online social organization since the 1990s, and especially in the past decade. One part grand vision, one part shared sensibility, and one part real methods, it has the ingredients for social organization. That is, it offers a basis for personal identity, a cultural model of the source of authority, and at least some means for coordinating both in practice. Meanwhile, though, the nation-state has been doing all of these things for a long time. It is unlikely to be simply swept away. What challenges does an ordinal society present to the state, and to the state's relationship to its citizens?

7

Ordinal Citizenship

PEOPLE ARE CREATED EQUAL. TALENTS AND VIRTUES SHOULD BE *recognized and rewarded. A society should value the right sort of things.* Modern conceptions of citizenship articulate and elaborate the practical consequences of ideas such as these. A core assumption of respectable social theory is that people are intrinsically equal in their personhood, though not necessarily in their talents. Individual citizenship is supposed to be one of the chief institutional guarantors of that equality. At the same time, huge inequalities in "outcomes" are easily observed. These inequalities might be understood and explained in terms of the functioning, whether benign or malign, of some overall social system. Or they might be taken to be simply the direct consequence of accumulated individual choices. Either way, justice tends to be conceived as a matter of mitigating whatever inequalities have arisen between individuals for bad reasons. This requires either adjusting how the system works, or making sure individuals who have suffered unfair outcomes are compensated to some degree.

In a different era, explaining and justifying the varied fates of individuals within society might have involved appealing to the will of God, or Providence, or some other external force. In the absence of such reason-givers, contemporary societies must face this challenge more directly, both in practice and in theory. Social-scientific research carefully documents inequalities—again, mostly conceived of as differences between nominally equal persons—in order to better critique or justify the status quo.[1] In politics, the resulting demands for remediation are carried on in terms of the idea of "social citizenship." As an idea, social citizenship posits nominally equal individuals as rights holders within a society that is systematically structured, rationally understandable, and practically governable. As a research enterprise, it entails the investigation of unfair inequalities among people in society. As a policy program, the remediation of these inequalities was an animating force in the domestic expansion of the state in the twentieth century. The institutionalization of social rights and their associated entitlement programs expressed the conviction that access to "the life of a civilized being" (to use T. H. Marshall's now quaint phrase) should not depend on wealth alone.[2] There is no question that the process of remediation was variously incomplete, inconsistent, and often stigmatizing. Still, the expansion of social citizenship did a great deal to mitigate the effects of sheer economic inequality in people's lives. The reliable provision of education, health care, housing, and social insurance became the government's main task. In return, the provision of a social safety net strengthened the claims of the state to demand sacrifices (such as military service) and duties (such as the payment of taxes) from the newly constituted citizenry.

Despite the widespread implementation of this bargain, social rights have remained conceptually suspect. Unlike civil and political rights, socioeconomic rights have had a tortuous relationship with liberal political theory. Liberalism's emphasis on contractual relations, possessive individualism, and negative freedoms left little room for anything but residual forms of solidarity.[3] For defenders of social citizenship as an idea, freedom would mean nothing if it boiled down to the freedom to live a wretched, inhuman life. Human autonomy was the capacity to act as a full member of one's society, and to participate in its politics. Thus, the argument went, social rights were essential to the concrete, practical achievement of that ideal.[4] Opponents insisted that such programs always amounted to an effort to impose a particular conception of the good on everyone, regardless of their preferences. This amounted to a kind of unjustifiable intervention to adjust the consequences of decisions and exchanges people had freely made, however detrimental.

As long as the state was taken to be the primary provider of social rights, the demands of individualist contractualism and inclusive solidarity seemed irreconcilable. But this assumption has gradually eroded. The politics of solidarity have shifted away from distributive justice and toward recognition and identity.[5] Consequently, the vocabulary of "citizenship" has escaped the confines of the state and diffused into many other economic and cultural domains. As before, the general demand is for the equal ability to participate in those activities that are essential to one's existence as a person in society. But what is and is not essential? On this question, liberal thought remains uncomfortable. One excuse for this awkwardness is that any universal or a priori definition of "the life of a civilized being" might force liberalism to confront its long history of exclusion.[6] A more palatable reason, harking back to the welfare debates of the 1970s, is that liberal theory should not concern itself with the problem of ends at all. Let people—via their collective struggles or private pursuits—define for themselves what is essential in their own lives. In this framework, the state's role is not to organize people's goals but to ensure that the market serves them well.

Today the language of citizenship is found across an increasingly wide range of institutions. Its scope has expanded but also thinned out. Rights claims have diversified as new freedoms are asserted or discovered.[7] Prefixes have multiplied accordingly: citizenship must be disaggregated into its economic, medical, biological, cultural, ecological and sexual dimensions, among others. Grassroots organizations, international financial institutions, central banks, and hedge funds advocate for "financial citizenship" as an aspect of social justice and a rational strategy for economic growth. Likewise, internet evangelists, education specialists, and tech companies have pitched the economic, political, and social benefits of online access, of bridging the "digital divide," as an essential component of citizenship in the information age. In spite of countless failures, the aspiration is relentless.[8]

In previous chapters we discussed how digital technologies have massively expanded and diversified the possibilities for sorting people into categories. We also showed that, in the technologists' political imaginary, the ideal members of an ordinal society are authentic, self-propelled, self-sovereign individuals who go about their business in a way that leaves measurable digital traces in their wake. What sort of citizens are these people? The original conception and extension of social rights thrived on a solidaristic foundation within a particular societal community. In effect it meant "the nation," however narrowly defined. By contrast, "ordinal citizenship" is a form of social inclusion that depends on the universal and precise measurement of imprecise ideals of intrinsic equality, personal merit, and social value.

The Problem of Equality

People are created equal. Casual observation suggests that, in terms of living conditions and material well-being, nothing could be less obviously true. To think clearly about how the response to this problem might be changing, it is useful to apprehend it "genealogically," by looking back at earlier inclusionary episodes that sought to mitigate deeply entrenched forms of social disadvantage.[9] Contemporary extensions of digitally based rights are presented as a liberal benefit that will help people help themselves. In a similar way, the extension of social rights in the late nineteenth and early twentieth centuries once affirmed that all lives should be guaranteed "a modicum of economic welfare and security." In particular, the expansion of educational opportunities supported the notion that everyone should have "the right to share to the full in the social heritage" of their country, in the words of T. H. Marshall.[10]

As Marshall himself was quick to point out, however, this institutional transformation also had a profound effect on the social structure. New rights created new divisions. Citizens were divided according to their ability to thrive in the new order. Following World War II, empirical studies by sociologists confirmed the point over and over again. First, those who relied on social services for their modicum of welfare suffered "psychological class discrimination."[11] Presumed to be lacking in intelligence, work-oriented values, or grit (the precise diagnosis and its label varied), they were treated as a morally inferior group. The administration of benefits was subjected to enhanced surveillance and coupled to work requirements.[12] Second, and by the same logic, the expansion of the right to an education also created a new axis of stratification. Daniel Bell wrote about "the codification of a new social order based, in principle, on the priority of educated talent."[13] Randall Collins warned of the advent of a "credential society."[14]

It soon became clear that, despite the shift in the basis of social status, these changes benefited the existing elite much more than the common mass. Education was both an effective social ladder and a conduit for the recycling of old inequalities across groups. In the United States, James Coleman concluded in 1966 that public schools were ineffective in reducing racial achievement gaps. In France, Pierre Bourdieu named a new form of capital, "cultural capital," through which the educated tended to reproduce themselves. In the newly expanded education system, it was the children of the bourgeoisie (as it was then called) who were being awarded the bulk of the new degrees and the better grades. Not only that, they also disproportionately earned the degrees that would lead to jobs that paid the most.[15] Rather than disappearing, economic and social differences were legitimated via the morally impeccable seal of a college diploma. Marshall had anticipated all of this when he characterized the fundamental dilemma of liberalism: "The right of the citizen in this process of selection and mobility is the right to equality of opportunity. Its aim is to eliminate hereditary privilege. In essence it is the equal right to display and develop differences, or inequalities; the equal right to be recognised as unequal."[16] Something like this diagnosis was repeatedly made. No one was as biting in his analysis of the new order as British sociologist and Labour Party intellectual Michael Young. In a satire published in 1958, he coined the term "meritocracy" and described its consequences as a cruel liberal fantasy. No matter how deep and how detailed the quantification of merit might become, Young predicted, those who dominated the game would be in a position to hoard resources, would come to concentrate political power, and would end up insisting that the excluded only had them-

selves to blame for their failures. In a substantially later re-
vision, written toward the end of his life, Young blasted
the sense of entitlement that a meritocratic system produced and predicted a populist revolt against it, born out
of resentment.[17] Today the verdict of sociologists on meritocracy is more widely shared than ever. In the United
States, especially, data on stalled intergenerational mobility
or widening health gaps between income groups show that
the country's social escalators no longer work.[18] Credential inflation is a well-recognized problem as many jobs demand a level of educational qualification decoupled from
any strictly skill-based prerequisites for tasks. Tales
of social closure, moral bankruptcy, and unfair advantage
fill podcast discussions, newspaper columns, and book-
shelves.[19] Most recently, and bearing out the core of Young's
analysis, educational attainment has begun to displace income as the primary axis of political division in Europe
and the United States.[20]

The inability of meritocratic institutions to deliver what
Daniel Bell called "equality of result" has sparked two main
reactions.[21] The first is arguments for compensation due to
historical disadvantage. These are institutionalized through
programs for diversity and inclusion that identify people
by their membership in underprivileged groups, such as
underrepresented minorities, or first-generation and low-
income students. (In the latter case, one's class position is
reconceptualized as a kind of personal identity, a sort of
left-leaning version of individual grit.) While these arguments and their institutional realizations fit comfortably

into an increasingly procedural, rule-governed work environment, they do not mesh as easily with ordinal technologies for sorting individuals. When adjustments for social disadvantage come into direct contact with ordinal technologies, conflict is almost guaranteed. Higher education, for instance, is full of examples of the "failed quantification" of race or social hardship, on the one hand, or the outright rejection of directly measuring performance through standardized tests, on the other.[22]

The second response has been to find new ways to measure what is valuable. If the old meritocracy has become moribund or easily gamed, perhaps a new one can replace it. Digital technologies allow for broader incorporation of people in economic or social terms while also expanding the possibilities for sorting and scoring them once they are incorporated. New metrics of merit have proliferated, from financial responsibility to social influence, from friendliness to punctuality, and from physical fitness to personal reliability. Organizations turn to building up and exploiting knowledge about their employees or clients in order to manage individual claims on resources and opportunities. Social inclusion goes beyond being nominally incorporated into these systems. One must then behave and perform according to their rules.

The Problem of Merit

People's talents and virtues should be recognized and rewarded. But there are consistent and legitimate complaints that the game is rigged. The problem of merit is about how to fairly or objectively measure and assess people's talent and reward their virtues. As we have just seen, this problem first presents itself within the reward structure of the education system. It extends to the assessment of merit among people out in the world, in both a negative way (e.g., in the realm of criminal justice) and a positive one (e.g., in the distribution of rewards in the economy). In an ordinal society, citizens should be assessed as individuals rather than as members of groups, and gauged not by their thoughts but by their actions. On its face, this seems an unlikely turn to make. Should we really expect interested parties to advocate for the objective, automated measurement of behavior, including their own? Notionally meritocratic institutions already tend to be captured by their elite members. What would those people have to gain from closer monitoring? By the same token, the failure of earlier schemes to protect marginalized and vulnerable citizens was, to critics, a feature rather than a bug. That is, the system worked to most people's disadvantage by design. Under those circumstances, why would a new scheme arise?

The irony is that the rise of ordinal citizenship is, at least in part, an unintended consequence of the elaboration of social citizenship itself, particularly in its universalistic aspirations. David Lyon makes the point,

> If government departments are to treat people equally, which is the starting point for the first of Marshall's rights, and from which other rights follow, then those people must be individually

identified. To exercise the right to vote, one's name must appear on the electoral roll; to claim welfare benefits, personal details must be documented. Thus as Nicholas Abercrombie et al. insist, the individuation that treats people in their own right, rather than merely as members of families or communities, means "freedom from specific constraints but also greater opportunities for surveillance and control on the part of a centralized state."[23]

The expansion of social rights turned out to have more than one cutting edge. It began with the struggle for substantive equality and the enlargement of positive freedoms for the individual, both with respect to the state and in the market. If the deployment of social citizenship increasingly brought the individual into view, individual pursuits were increasingly understood as matters of citizenship. The democratization of credit in postwar America, for instance, has many of the hallmarks of a hard-fought social right.[24] The slower but still undeniable drive toward the individualization of risk in insurance has the same character.[25] In both cases, as with more familiar demands for civil rights, people wanted to be seen and treated as individuals rather than merely as members of a class. But winning this right tended to come at the cost of control over how, and how much, one would be seen.

The shift from group category to individual behavior in the management of citizenship claims parallels a cultural movement in the discourse on citizenship, from status *back* to contract and from right *back* to privilege, which critics of neoliberalism have well documented.[26] After the 1970s, the individualizing logic of the market increasingly became the model for making social institutions more efficient, just as it had been offered as a solution to economic demands for inclusion. However threadbare it was in practice, the social safety net was seen by conservative critics as an unjustifiable benefit that encouraged people to live off of the state. That was to change in the name of personal responsibility. The moral crusade that accompanied the "great risk shift" of the 1980s and 1990s forced people to become more self-reliant—and more exposed—in domains as varied as education, credit, and welfare.[27] This shift also strengthened the conviction that success depends on grit and hard work, rather than on accidents of birth and broadly structural factors. Indeed, popular belief in self-reliance seems to have risen in step with income inequality, particularly among the working class in the Western world.[28]

But why did neoliberal citizenship become ordinalized? We should not underestimate the power of crisp, quantitative forms of valuation when considering the medium through which meritocratic ideas circulate. (After all, the original meritocratic ideal—which may not yet have been called that—developed in tandem with formal systems of evaluation, like school grades and standardized tests.)[29] Numbers seem more trustworthy. They make it easier to deal with the messiness of politics and social competition.[30] Indeed experimental evidence suggests that, relative to more narrative forms of valuation, scores or grades are more likely to be taken for granted, tend to reinforce the belief that people get what they deserve in life, and in general make people think better of the overall inequalities they observe.[31] Whatever the precise cause, the scoring of individual persons *appears* both less contentious and fairer.

In practice, the business of measuring and scoring citizens is anything but natural. Even with the best intentions, it requires considerable effort to get any kind of system up and running. When seeking to make predictions about individuals rather than groups, the more data one has the better. This is especially true for systems designed to predict relatively rare occurrences, such as crimes. System designers and operators always want more data, perhaps especially when the method of analysis is unreliable. In practice, organizations meet this hunger in all kinds of ways, including by inconspicuous tracking, by repurposing data held for other reasons, by forcing subjects into tedious record keeping, and by data-sharing agreements and commercial exchanges across organizations. This need for data in bulk is the reason training datasets used for predictive policing in New York City included rather low-level crimes, such as drinking in public or loitering; why risk-scoring models for child abuse in Pennsylvania enrolled data from public assistance systems; why failure to attend an appointment with an Australian welfare agency resulted in the suspension of benefit payments; or why British local councils paid commercial data firms to provide insights about the populations in their care.[32]

These processes are not particularly fair, either. One of the arguments for individual-level scoring technologies is that they give marginalized people the possibility of enjoying the benefits of modern citizenship while also weakening the consequences of being seen as the wrong kind of person. Indeed, the most significant moves toward individual-level scoring in the housing and credit markets were argued for on just these grounds, often by activists looking to dismantle earlier systems of straightforward group-based discrimination. But in practice, the social consequences of these methods are much more ambivalent. It is poor people—and racialized minorities especially—who find themselves repeatedly trapped in what Issa Kohler-Hausmann calls "Misdemeanorland." It is lower-income mothers who rely on public assistance to feed their children. It is foreign-born populations who are most likely to face difficulties meeting certain basic communicative or documentary expectations.[33] Should we be surprised that ordinal prediction schemes find that they are riskier?[34] By digging deeper into individual-level measures, by standardizing decision-making through increasingly detailed behavioral benchmarks, data collection ends up reconstituting, one tiny piece at a time, the ground truth of social structure.

It is not that the past was much better. Marshall saw modern citizenship as the outcome of a layered and gradually unfolding process of expanding rights, beginning with the development of civil rights from the eighteenth century onward, followed by political rights in the nineteenth century and social rights in the twentieth. But the expansion of citizenship was uneven and lopsided. States could always take away what they had given.

New citizenship demands could be resisted, even in the face of strong social pressure. Or states might simply refuse to apply formally codified rights in practice.[35] There were always categories of people who could not take their formal rights for granted, who had to press the legal system to be treated like everyone else to be given a fair chance—racial and sexual minorities, immigrants, or the disabled, among others.[36] The second half of the twentieth century was less about defining new substantive rights and more about extending already enumerated rights to previously excluded groups or guaranteeing their implementation for poorly served populations. This is what Judith Shklar, writing about the United States, termed "the quest for inclusion."[37]

The shift from codifying rights to equalizing them signaled the emergence of a more social-structural understanding of the pursuit and implications of citizenship, however. Enumerated rights are meaningless if institutions do not enforce them, or if they do not enforce them impartially.[38] The demand for inclusion is, at a minimum, about the right to have one's rights recognized and respected without selective privilege. The postwar elaboration of due process and antidiscrimination rules and policies comes out of that realization. Historically, the development of citizenship is often associated with the decline of criteria of gender, race, property, religion, ethnicity, caste, and more as core markers of the ability to vote, hold office, obtain insurance, credit, employment, get a higher education degree, use the internet, and so on. We have already suggested, the historical expansion of credit access in postwar America was justified as a benefit to marginalized groups.[39]

The same political rationale undergirds its expansion worldwide, to populations in poor countries.[40] Antidiscrimination laws, like the ones applying to credit markets, required that people be judged behind a veil of ignorance that specifically masked categorical differences. Organizations wanting to deliver a credit or loan decision had to comply with this demand too. Individual scoring systems were the solution. They promised to disentangle people considered as decision-makers and action-takers from people defined by ascribed social statuses. But as an exhaustive empirical literature shows, and as we have been arguing, the idea of a purely individual assessment of merit—something fully extricated from the broader social structure by way of more and more data—is a mirage. To the extent that social situations and thus social behaviors differ reliably across demographic categories, scores rooted in behavioral data will continue to differ reliably across these same categories.[41] Group-level differences that the law kicks out the door come back in through the window.

For instance, credit scores are built on top of detailed records about credit behavior: payments made, on time, on spending that did not exceed one's credit limit. Scoring agencies use no demographic information when calculating them. The closest thing to a standard demographic variable in the process is length of credit history, which is a good proxy for age. Information about salary, job title, employer, employment history, and place of residence are also excluded from consideration. Interest rates on particular credit cards, child support obligations, and rental agreement obligations are out-of-bounds too. The result is a score that *seems* stripped of all categorical markers, a pure measure of past behavior predictive of future credit risk. All misleading and discriminatory labels based on categorical differences, occupational status, income, or wealth have been removed, leaving only the choices people have made with whatever money they had.

The few empirical studies that have worked with proprietary credit data in the United States show that, even so, racial differences in credit behavior remain large. At practically every level of income, nonwhite people are more likely to pay only the minimum on a credit card bill, to pay a late fee, and to exceed their credit limit than nonwhite people. This results in much lower credit scores on average, everything else being equal. The introduction of machine learning plausibly aggravates this situation. As Barbara Underwood put it more than four decades ago, "a nonracial predictor that correlates highly with race [in this case a credit score] has some of the effects of selection based explicitly on race."[42] If credit scores are racialized in this way, nonwhite people will face adverse consequences when these scoring methods are used out in the world, which is exactly what we observe.[43]

When a battery of legal rules and computing technologies prevents group characteristics from directly determining outcomes, why does their effect remain so stubbornly persistent? The naive answer is simply to see this gap as a well-measured but problematic group behavior. A better answer is that rationalized measurement systems (such as credit scoring) necessarily come up short.[44] These methods cannot properly capture historical and

present-day patterns of exclusion and exploitation that
provide the raw material for people's experiences and
cultural formations. Scoring technologies appear to be especially well developed in places that have a history of legally enforced segregation, such as the United States and
South Africa.[45] In fact, we might turn the analytical logic
on its head and argue that an observed gap between
groups—an unexplained statistical "residual"—is in fact a
measure of advantages or disadvantages that have been
produced and reproduced over the very *longue durée*—a
kind of Solow residual for social inequalities.[46]

In such circumstances, embracing a logic of ordinalization is therefore misleading, even dangerous, for two reasons. First, the tools of measurement replace structure
with action. Everything that happens to people that might
lead them, for example, to make or miss a credit card payment is coded just in terms of its outcome, recorded only
as a behavior, and interpreted principally as an expression
of the decision-making abilities and financial virtue of the
individual consumer. The whole of social structure and circumstance is stuffed back into the channel labeled "individual choice." Anything from being preyed upon by
sketchy lenders to the good fortune of having a parent who
will quietly pay a bill on your behalf is recorded, in effect,
as a poor or wise decision by you personally. By appearing
as records of prior actions, scores seem to imply that
anyone who applies themselves can do well. Positions are
interpreted in a moralized way—as the fair and competitive outcome of prior good or bad individual actions
and decisions or, worse, as the product of some innate

"character." Everyone seems to get what they deserve. They ought to feel pride or shame accordingly.[47]

This is only partly a matter of the mechanics of data collection and the limits of what can be counted. Careful measurement and analysis is not impossible. Nor is it the case that experts are somehow too quick in their judgments or lazy in their assessments simply because their analysis is based on quantitative data. Indeed, and perhaps a little ironically, the dominant orientation of most quantitative social science in the wake of the "causal revolution" of the past two decades is now one of sharp skepticism at efforts to confidently state clear relationships of cause and effect. The bar is far higher than it used to be. Rather, the problem is with the practical application of analytical tools, and the tendency for interpretation to routinely outrun evidence. Efforts to compare and sort people, even just behaviorally, tend to produce assessments of moral desert and social desirability. Any priority order, any queue, any ranking system, tends to become imbued with value. Coupled with our ability to confidently tell stories about the categories we find in our data, the act of making some ordering ends up becoming, in Barry Schwartz's phrase, an "order of moral demand."[48] This is especially clear in the domain of credit and debt, which—as Friedrich Nietzsche remarked—is one of the most potent sites for the social distribution of feelings of superiority, moral desert, shame, and guilt.[49] The machinery of credit ratings and scores was built up to fairly assess merit on the basis of individual actions alone, rather than mere group membership. But in practice it became connected to the belief that scores represented the objective measurement of intrinsic character, and thus the conviction that the outcomes they determined were also well deserved.

What should the politics of ordinal citizenship be in conditions where history and social structure are rendered indistinct by the individualization of data and transformed into folktales of grit and hard work by the moralization of measurement? One solution, favored by policy advocates in general and economists in particular, is to educate the ordinal subject through literacy initiatives that teach people the "correct" behavior expected by scoring methods.[50] Alternatively, and diametrically opposed to this individualist solution, is the ambition to "correct" the algorithms instead by removing their categorical biases. Each approach builds on the social-scientific obsession with "the distinction between just and functional inequalities and unjust or power and ascription-ridden ones,"[51] just from opposite sides. While not without value, both may miss the deeper problem. Ordinal systems cannot really "adjust" or "correct" for an entire society and its past. These systems begin with a highly structured social world, they measure and score it at the level of individual behavior with the intention of making society go away, and then they face awkward problems when the original social facts reappear in the individual-level results. The repeated discovery and rediscovery of aspects of society writ large in the minutiae of data writ small produces reliably unproductive arguments. Properly evading these quagmires requires a more radical kind of politics, one which is vastly more challenging to implement than to insist upon.

The Problem of Value

When judging its citizens, a society should care about the right sort of things. The problem of value in an ordinal society is that the tools of ordinalization are always put to work in specific contexts. They are employed in the service of particular organizational objectives. In the market, and increasingly under the wing of the state, those objectives may not line up with what we might think of as personal merit or virtue in the ordinary sense of those words. In the context of market evaluations, in particular, this point is easy to miss. The language of markets—winners and losers, competition and striving, innovation and entrepreneurship—encourages us to think that success is substantively merited in some moral sense.[52] But this is an illusion. Friedrich Hayek dismisses it quickly in *The Constitution of Liberty*—the market is not rewarding you, it is optimizing itself: "The fact is, of course, that we do not wish people to earn a maximum of merit but to achieve a maximum of usefulness at a minimum of pain and sacrifice and therefore a minimum of merit."[53]

The data that powers evaluations of relative "merit" is put to use to optimize market value. We have seen in the previous section that, in ordinalized settings, what is measured is good behavior, not good intentions. But from the point of view of any particular market, what counts as *good* behavior is not a matter of morality at all. It is defined by what makes for a profitable sale. Poorly informed people may be the best customers. Weakness of the will may generate repeated sales. This is not simply a matter of there being "markets in vice," whatever one's conception of vice might be. It is also that a particular personal failing, some specific vulnerability, may be the most useful thing about you as far as the market is concerned. At its worst, this may mean evaluating someone's likelihood of being tempted by a rotten deal, or their willingness to accept a low salary, their measurable tendency to be easily confused, the risk that they will leave their company, or the chance that they will become a burden on social services. Even at its best, it means that people's movement up and down any ordinal scale of worth may have less to do with their own actions and more to do with shifts in whatever objective function the market is optimizing on given the circumstances. This is why, for instance, there is not just one credit score, but thousands, each tailored to the particular economic purpose it serves. Or why apartment rental companies may relax some tenant screening algorithm rules in periods of economic crisis.[54] Or, again, it is why many ordinal systems—such as ratings for online labor platforms—tend to better reward the people who produce value for them. Having a good credit score, for instance, depends first and foremost on actively using the credit system. Someone who has been careful not to accumulate a history of debt may look like a much poorer loan prospect than someone who has been juggling different credit lines for years without ever quite going under. Similarly, as of this writing the company TaskRabbit favors workers who complete more tasks over those who are careful to only take on tasks they can do well. Social media companies care best for their most active and connected users, whatever it is they may be doing. Those who rarely post, comment, click the Like button, or message others will see their occasional contribution disappear into the algorithmic void, ignored by the machine and by the public it tends to in real time.[55] The same will happen to those who are active but not liked enough by others.

Ordinal stratification is justified by a general ideology of merit and by the sense that what is being tracked looks something like a conventional picture of personal virtue. Yet scores or classifications are anchored by sharp differences in what is valuable in particular markets. People are pestered by ethical injunctions to self-optimize, self-appreciate, and self-care.[56] But the point of this ethical work is both increasingly obscure and subjectively pointless. The rules of the game are unclear, and they adjust dynamically, whether it is as a response to new information or to allow for the myriad of experiments always running in real time. As one of Veena Dubal's interviewees, a rideshare driver, puts it, gig work feels "like gambling. The house always wins!"[57] Similarly, Hatim Rahman's ethnography of a freelance work platform describes algorithmic management as an "invisible cage," where the criteria of control are illegible and fluctuate unpredictably.[58]

Whatever the faults of a system calibrated on a person's general merits may have been, a system calibrated on calculated estimates of someone's particular, local value to an organization or a third party is much harder to understand. The apparent capriciousness of the system is often hard to bear. According to a 2023 survey, two-thirds of California drivers working for ridesharing apps

Lyft and Uber (and a higher proportion of nonwhite drivers) have found themselves abruptly "deactivated" at least once from the app that provides their livelihood, in some cases permanently.[59]

Machine learning magnifies this problem. Rather than demanding specific kinds of inputs, data may be dredged to discover patterns with "virtually no pre-established conceptions" about its structure of meaning.[60] For instance, smart finance algorithms may "consider the speed at which you typed in your date of birth, how much battery power is left on your phone," and thousands of "weak features that correlate with creditworthiness."[61] Meaning is composed or engineered inductively, from within the pool of available data. It produces what Herbert Simon called a "synthetic" (rather than "artificial") construct. That is, it does not seek to replicate the structure of the world but instead generates its own way to see, understand, and value.[62] Think, for example, of how a chess engine like AlphaZero plays very differently from a human grand master. The machine's moves are bolder and more aggressive, its game is more open, and it is wildly more successful at anticipating its opponent's moves.[63] Chess enthusiasts have been eager to learn from its games, including by covertly using the new form of intelligence to win competitions.[64] But by the same token, AlphaZero's style remains somewhat alien. Like modern chess players, ordinary people find themselves poorly equipped to orient themselves toward the increasingly synthetic systems that intervene in their lives, let alone contest their decisions. They, too, have to cope with a new kind of feedback.

A chess engine is at least oriented toward the clear goal of winning a well-defined game. It cannot change the rules or designate some new end state that would count as a victory. Finding paths to generate new value or profit is a much more loosely defined sort of game that allows for substantially more experimentation. If new kinds of behavior are rewarded because they produce the right sort of value, participants are faced with the question of whether to accept the new surveillance and adapt to its standards. Some will flee if they are able. As Karen Levy reports, truck drivers have been threatening to exit the industry after the government required electronic logging devices (ELDs) in 2012. In practice, few have actually done so.[65] Resistance—voice—is a second possibility. The truckers made their dissatisfaction known, painted large "F-ELD" (Fuck Electronic Logging Devices) letters on their vehicles, and developed various strategies of coping and obfuscation.[66] But the small symbolic satisfactions they gain are, in Levy's words, "hollow victories." Labor rarely has the upper hand. *Les dés sont pipés.* Resentful loyalty is the more likely option. Absent institutional protections (and of course in this case it was the state that mandated the installation of ELDs in the first place), many workers will soon act on the incentives and sanctions of automated systems, finding some interstitial freedom and even subjective meaning—some sort of pride or contentment—in reclaiming the process for themselves. A growing body of research across industry settings shows that this process of subjective reappropriation often involves workers playing solitary "making out" games with themselves, where they obsessively track their interactions with others and their algorithmic rating.[67]

As they have spread through occupations, ordinal regimes have generated discontent and legal challenges, or provoked workarounds and organized resistance.[68] But their increasing ubiquity across all domains of life makes a unified challenge difficult to envision, let alone organize.[69] The result is a kind of universal personalization. Each and every person's value is determined by methods that are in one sense quite general but in another very specifically tailored.

Systematic outcomes look like the direct result of individual actions, actions are rewarded according to their market value, and value is expressed in ways that are experienced as a kind of personal virtue. Even if the criteria for being rewarded are strange and incomprehensible, there is a tendency for any system that produces a scheme of rewards or ranks, however perverse, to institutionalize itself as a value order and a basis for the attribution of personal merit. Scoring changes the intrinsic meaning of activities and the reasons why people pursue them, transforming them into so many metric-chasing games. On social media, the quest for virality displaces the enjoyment of genuine communication. The ambition to beat one's previous, metricized record drives the compulsion to exercise.[70] Optimization tends to reorganize moral intuitions by way of people's willingness to experience the positive, real-world outcomes associated with high scores as naturally deserved, as the consequence of being a good, reliable, popular, and trustworthy person.[71] It is tempting to say that, in a reversion to a much older, almost religious orientation to the mysteries of Divine Providence, the more opaque the evaluation process, the more willing people may be to believe that what is being recognized and rewarded is their own personal merits, their own worthy character.

Digital systems only know and manage fragments of ourselves, but they still maintain the cultural fiction of a knowable, purposeful, and agentic individual who can be measured, classified, and "civilized." This individual has little choice but to cultivate their digitally mediated, "dividually" managed and technologically assisted self. In practice, the political project to produce this fiction has taken many forms. One rests on straightforward coercion, whether by normative means (through social pressure) or physical ones (through restricted mobility). Such a framing was, for instance, explicit in China's original social credit system announcement. In the planning document released by the country's State Council in 2014, the measurement of individual or organizational "honesty" tied to multisectoral and cross-regional rewards and punishments systems would allow "the trustworthy to roam everywhere under heaven while making it hard for the discredited to take a single step."[72] (More prosaically, the system aims to regulate people's ability to move about and access various kinds of government-sponsored or market opportunities.) But this kind of design is not, and never was, the prerogative of nondemocratic regimes. Once institutionalized, the obligation to be seen, measured, and judged by some surveillance infrastructure may overflow its container and be put to all kinds of uses. Under the administration of President Donald Trump, for instance, the US Department of Homeland Security briefly used credit scores to help determine the eligibility of immigrants applying for a green card or US citizenship. The rationale behind the new policy was that a low credit score signals a risk of becoming a burden on the public purse in the future.

A different path, powered by behavioral economics and market design, rests on the use of choice architectures and incentives to govern individual and collective behavior.[73] In this approach, good citizenship rests primarily on institutional efforts to instill a disposition toward exposure as a natural, desirable state. These may include reporting suspicious behaviors through a website or sending pictures of uneven pavements or overwatered lawns to city officials. But it mostly being open to having one's financial, digital, or bodily activities nudged toward some institutionally desirable state by means of feedback or behavioral modification.[74] The price mechanism, rather than state coercion, is a central part of this loop. An ordinal citizen's personal goals might include walking a certain number of daily steps and hydrating regularly. A tracker can help them monitor these aims, while also reporting back so that their insurance risk may be assessed or priced more precisely. While driving to work they might agree to run an app on their phone that makes it clear to the insurer that they are not texting while driving. For this they might receive a small discount on their premium. When they get to work, they may be rated by customers. Their salary may depend on software running on their computer that breaks down their workflow, their communicative choices, or their connections to others. Other relevant measures that employers may look at include their estimated likelihood of quitting their job, or their cultural fit with the company. In each of these cases, they are priced not only according to their performance but also by their "willingness to accept." They may find it necessary to rely on paid services and ancillary applications to optimize themselves on multiple digital scales or to work around the devices that measure their daily moves. Sometimes the application that they depend upon for their livelihood, enjoy in their leisure time, or use to coordinate their romantic life will sell a "boost" yielding better connections, some new ability, or a higher chance to be noticed. While these "pay to win" schemes tend to be unpopular, they are also lucrative and thus not that uncommon.

Even with sophisticated props, metrics, and representations, informationally managed ordinal citizens might never fully come into view to themselves. As new streams of data come along, the machinery that could sustain such an effort has become opaque, amorphous, and unsettled. Perhaps in an effort to circumvent Goodhardt's law, the rules of ordinality change often.[75] Alternatively, they tend to shift because the actual magnitude of most of the effects tracked by these metrics is tiny. Many nudge-based measures and methods grew out of an influential generation of behavioral research that was often severely underpowered and at times plainly fraudulent.[76] The tendency of the ground to shift makes positions based on prior scores "algorithmically precarious" over the longer term, creating uncertainty about both the government of subjects and their self-conduct.[77] As the game of ordinal citizenship becomes increasingly hard to play, the technology hammers one last nail in the coffin of the liberal view of civic life. Why not give up on freedom altogether and outsource every action to a machine that claims to know you better than you know yourself?[78]

The desire to make such a vision a reality is quite persistent. In a video leaked to The Verge (a technology website), Nick Foster, the head of design at Google's moonshot unit, speculates about a world where people farm out all decision-making to digital devices. In this world Google seamlessly takes over, organizing your life and designing products "just for you" from a ledger of your past "actions, decisions, preferences, movement, and relationships." As the process goes on to include everyone across multiple generations, tools scan other people's ledgers to detect gaps in your data, use them to fill in those gaps, and thereby make your ledger "richer." In the final step, the ledger is given purpose as the algorithm works to reinforce those behavioral traits that it finds desirable at the level of the species, so that future generations can benefit from the behaviors and decisions of their predecessors.

As always with such flights of fancy, the gap between an executive's dreams and what can actually be put together as a working system is very wide indeed. The underlying impulse might be thought of as the desire to externalize aspects of morality in technology, the better to have it impose ends on ourselves and others.[79] Any particular application of such a scheme is likely to be severely imperfect. As Evgeny Morozov suggests, we might end up resembling "the confused analysts of the National Security Agency: unsure of the value of the data we generate, we will opt to store them for posterity. And, unsure of how to maximize that value, we will keep adding data streams in the vain hope that the value of our data portfolio (the sum total of our life) will rise."[80] Whether realized as a success on its own terms or experienced as a gigantic failure of implementation, this is probably not what Marshall had in mind when it came to each person "sharing to the full in the social heritage" of their country. But in the future this may well be the political horizon that sets bounds on how we think about that shared heritage.

Conclusion
The Unbearable Rightness of Being Ranked

WE BEGAN IN CALIFORNIA. AT THE OUTSET OF THIS BOOK, WE sketched the changing face of the Santa Clara Valley from its agricultural postwar origins to its suburbanized incarnation as Silicon Valley. We saw how this physical transformation was accompanied by another, less tangible, shift. The people living and working in the valley developed the tools and products that made possible our world of digital, distributed, self-modulating measurement and soft control. Once it got going, people quickly embraced it. *The ordinal society* is our name for that world. We have argued that it rests on a substrate of digital traces; that it began by exfiltrating human sociality by means of the gift; and that it now stratifies individuals through a myriad of differentiated methods of matching, scoring, and classification. Those methods have both a practical application and a moral valence. The ordinal society is both a means of social organization and a mode of first-person experience.

From the start, we have stressed the combination of generality and specificity that characterizes life in an ordinal society. Firms feel the general imperative to acquire and manage data, but they must also implement some specific software stack that may well be filled with bugs and incompatibilities, that will accumulate into technical debt, and that in time will become burdensome legacy code. Scoring methods and metrics are everywhere, but the classification situations they produce are local to the markets they are applied in. A searching disposition depends on a seething global network of information, but it is expressed in billions of individual queries and the choices that flow from them. In truth, this two-sidedness is a feature of any social form.[1] It is a mistake to think that just because it is pervasive, a mode of social organization is also therefore automatically "totalizing" in the sense of relentlessly subordinating every last shred of action and experience to a single template. Rather, social life tends to overflow the organizational and institutional matrix imposed on it, even when those institutions provide a powerful basis for coordination and control. People's experience does not quite fit the mold; ongoing situations are messy; circumstances require adjustment; events spin off in unexpected directions. The relevant question is, What are the criteria for legitimate action in any particular setting, what tools are at hand to engage in it, and who benefits from their use?

Social forms present different recipes for getting on with things, different tool kits for organizing action. The fulcrum of an ordinal society is the idea of coordination by ranking and matching, where rank is derived from the objective measurement of actual behavior and matching criteria depend on the purpose at hand. These methods are put to work within markets and organizations to sort and slot people into situations and positions. In practice, as we have repeatedly emphasized, this is a patchy process, typically adapted to circumstance, and often quite broken from a technical point of view. But efforts to do it are now pervasive thanks to the data-generating social substrate that produces the required material in volume and at speed. The promise of these tools is that they will be inclusive, objective, and efficient. They are pitched and sold to their users on that basis. They see every sparrow fall. They impassively record real actions. They never sleep. Most of all, they promise a form of justice, a kind of "actuarial fairness" in which rewards are carefully, individually metered thanks to the availability of data. These algorithmic intermediaries replace more conventionally solidaristic or universalist institutional classifications with an aesthetic of justified hierarchy. Rankings and ratings, and the associated matches that they enable, underpin an ordinal society's imagination. Their rightness feels hard to deny. The quantities they express rest on a foundation of personal decisions, of individual behaviors, of our own carefully recorded choices. The outputs they provide seem tailored to us, and people like us.

Ordinalization's Double Movement

In *Outline of a Theory of Practice,* and later in *Pascalian Meditations,* Pierre Bourdieu developed the concept of a "twofold truth," an idea meant to analytically hold together "the point of view of the agents who are caught up in the object and the point of view on this point of view, which the work of analysis enables one to reach." One way of understanding his point is to emphasize the tension between an individual and the "system" at large that organizes any particular person's life. A Marxian analysis, for example, might point to how the former unwittingly plays a role in the reproduction of the latter. Perhaps people derive some intrinsic satisfaction from doing even a "bad" job well, or take pleasure in the "minor privileges" they can seize upon in their workplace.[2] This will tend to mask, and thus render more effective, the wider exploitative system that contains these little games.[3] That, in Bourdieu's phrasing, would be a "twofold truth of labor."[4] We might see a similar sort of tension in people's use of digital tools. The convenience and affirmative pleasures of connectedness could, as a kind of side effect, functionally contribute to other ends, helping an organization exert control or a business make a profit.

A slightly different way to think about this twofold truth is to contrast a first-person perspective with a third-person one. There is the way things seem and feel to us from our own point of view, and there is the way they look from the outside. In the case of the gift, for instance, one side of a twofold truth might be found in the subjective perception of gift exchange as a spontaneous and free activity. Meanwhile, the other side could be seen in what, to an outside observer, looks to be a socially obligatory activity unfolding within a wider strategic social game. Who or what we take this "outside observer" to be is the beginning of a slew of chronic puzzles and arguments in social theory. The third-person point of view might be understood just as the perspective of a curious outsider. Or it might be an objective scientist, or a critical local in possession of a broader theoretical perspective. Or it might even be thought of as the very eye of God, or some other "view from nowhere."[5] Bourdieu's point is that this back-and-forth between the first- and third-person perspective is something that happens in practice all the time as people act and reflect on their actions. A great deal of ink has been spilled by social theorists wanting to reconcile or resolve this tension, either by eliminating one or other perspective for the purposes of making some analytical progress or by finding ways to keep both sides of the basic antinomy in view.

We can think of the rating and ranking that pervades ordinal societies in light of this tension. As a tool for doing things in the world, scores and grades have both a first-person and a third-person aspect. They are tremendously useful. They can help pick an employee, or a professor, or a restaurant, or an appliance. They provide information and order the world in a way that is easy to grasp and act on. They also have a curiously satisfying character. All of this is at its most straightforward when we are treating things instrumentally, as objects. From a first-person perspective, we generally prefer not to be subject to the power of these tools. Even here we tend not to want to reject them entirely. After all, we have come to expect and enjoy the personalization, safety, and convenience they bring. Moreover, the competition can be gratifying, like a somewhat challenging but enjoyable game. There is something thrilling about keeping track of oneself, all the more since the metrics have been designed to keep us hooked.[6] Still, we would prefer to be assessed according to the "right" method or using "worthwhile" criteria, that is, criteria that benefit us.[7]

The tension between feeling that a ranking is right and finding that it is unbearable runs deep. Consider, for example, the ranking of American universities and professional schools undertaken by *U.S. News and World Report* magazine. Wendy Espeland and Michael Sauder analyzed the dilemmas faced by the administrators in charge of the law schools ranked by the magazine. In this case, the world of legal academia—a profession twice over, embedded in academia, training lawyers—lost control over its ability to make authoritative judgments about quality and prestige. This is really quite strange, because professions are in large part defined by their legitimate claim to produce and certify authoritative knowledge in some domain. How, in the words of Bard College's president, Leon Botstein, did whole swaths of higher education end up "bamboozled by a third-rate news magazine. How could this happen?"[8]

In Espeland and Sauder's account, law school faculty heartily dislike the *U.S. News* rankings and complain at length about their negative effects. These range from additional performance pressures on administrators and faculty, to forced and perhaps wasteful changes in budgets, to a reformatting of the landscape of choice facing law school applicants, to significant consequences for the employment chances of law school graduates. But the attraction of the rankings to prospective law students is also perfectly apparent. What is of interest is how difficult they are to resist. The academic legal establishment did not so much fall into the trap of rankings as become entangled in them. Like a fly touched by the thread of a spider's web, they were at first only lightly caught up, but then found that each move they made in response only wound them in more tightly.[9]

What initially felt right to law school administrators about the rankings was that they expressed their sense of status in a visible and apparently objective way. But this visibility had a high price. A ranking system that people use and take seriously provides a link between the entities being ranked and their audiences, a link that is both seductive and coercive. Law schools were forced into a clear relationship with their peers—peers now publicly recognized as better or worse than them. In this way, a ranking is quite different from a threshold that any organization can meet or a certification that anyone can obtain—something that can be acquired without impugning the respectability of all the other players. By making comparison mandatory, rankings normalize competition. Moreover, they push people to compete on the dimensions that the ranking method values.

Late in 2022, several leading law schools did try to break the hold that *U.S. News* had on them. First one and then several others announced they would no longer be participating in the ranking process. Their efforts to break away were greeted with both praise and skepticism. In particular, critics complained that these schools wanted to have their cake and eat it too, believing they could remain prestigious while avoiding the useful, informative, and public discipline of a ranking system.[10] This dilemma, or moment of bad faith, is quite real. Law school faculty, deans, and administrators are long past the time of their lives when their individual performance is routinely assessed in terms of As or Bs, as magna or summa cum laude. But they still exercise that capacity for judgment over others every week of the semester. They believe in it. They are still committed to the view that they know and can assess quality when they see it, and they usually think they can reliably quantify it. They would just rather not be subject to that pressure themselves.

The point is quite general, and it extends far beyond the world of methodologically weak rankings carried out by a magazine. A whole class of firms are intermediators; they live by producing and publicizing rankings. The small-scale, brittle ranking of schools by a tiny number of experts is dwarfed in size by coarser review aggregators for things like restaurants and hotels, and outmatched in sophistication by automated rating systems that manage large workforces. The latter, for instance, increasingly take inspiration from the world of online games. Here large numbers of individuals or teams play against one another in a relatively clearly defined way that generates both tiers of users and leaderboards. These methods have their origin in the Elo ranking system developed by the physicist (and chess master) Arpad Elo, which was first used by the US Chess Federation in 1960. Elo-style ratings were subsequently adopted in many other games and sports as a way of ranking proficiency in head-to-head competitions where there can (and often must) be a winner and a loser. A significant generalization of the approach for competitive games with more than two players was developed by Microsoft in the early 2000s and patented under the name TrueSkill. It powers the leaderboards and tiered-ranking systems for many online games on the Xbox platform. A tool like this is a near perfect exemplar of the twofold character of an ordinalizing system. First, it efficiently identifies the best players and positions them on some leaderboard. Second, and no less important, categories or tiers of players naturally fall out of this ranking, allowing players to be effectively matched against one another in a manner commensurate with their demonstrated skills or record of prior successes.[11] The former gives individual players the prospect of a ladder that they might climb if they have the requisite skill and invest the needed time. But the latter also allows the majority of players to be comfortable within their tier, as they will be matched with opponents who are neither too difficult nor too easy for them.

Out in the world, methods that rank and match in order to stratify lie in between the clunky efforts of *U.S. News,* on the one side, and competitive online gaming in a wholly constructed environment, on the other. The former is, in effect, assembled by hand for about two hundred organizations every year or so. The latter constantly runs matching systems from moment to moment for millions of users across thousands of games. The ordinalizing tendency is to bring real-time ranking methods from the closed to the open world. In closed-world settings, the criteria for winning and losing are determined by designers and are fully tunable. Out in the more open, social world, success and failure are still definable, but the "games" being played are more diffuse and extended. Their stakes are also much higher. And, once again, what is especially powerful is the way that algorithmic ranking-and-matching systems bring order and discipline to social fields not just by producing groups and social strata though competition but also by setting the metrics through which competition is assessed and by rewarding and reinforcing the players who successfully compete on its terms.

Two-sided ranking schemes of the kind employed by Lyft or Uber have been one beachhead for transferring these methods. Thanks to smartphones, rating and matching on the basis of a "player's" demonstrated quality, skill, or success in this market is a practical aim. Much the same stratifying techniques used in the video game *Call of Duty* can be applied when it comes to calling not just a cab but a *good* cab. Dating apps have been a second point of entry. There the competition is for mates. The relevant ranking methods are direct, two-sided assessments of match quality or desirability. True to the principle that— just as in Google's PageRank—status is best conceived as the high regard of highly regarded others, dating apps may stratify users based on the interest their profile generates but weight those assignments by the scores of the people who express that interest. This, of course, immediately leads to the bleed-in of preference weighting based on the composition of the population. If the population of users is majority white, for example, and they tend to dismiss or give poor ratings to people of color because they do not want to date them, then in the aggregate there will be both severe homophily on match recommendations, on the one hand, and lower mean scores for nonwhite people, on the other.[12]

The people who run rating and matching systems of this sort are, by now, well aware of these kinds of problems. Players in different kinds of games (whether literal or social) can be assessed using different methods. Elo-style rankings are only the most straightforward type of stratifying device for the most direct kind of competition. The challenge is a dynamic one. Looking inward, so to speak, designers must try to understand the edge cases and failure modes that emerge from any ranking method when it works as designed. Meanwhile, looking outward, they find themselves trying to mitigate the overflow of preexisting social structure into their algorithmic scheme. One strategy is to look for other kinds of signal in the data over and above the obvious ones and to use those to tune the system. In a dating app, for example, this might be something like records of use patterns (such as how often you check the app) or more subtle features of your profile. How much do you write in your description? What kind of words are they? How many photos do you upload? What features do they have? Any such effort to wring a little more from the data will, in turn, be subject to the system being gamed or manipulated if users can figure out that this is what is happening. This back-and-forth amounts to a kind of multisided competition. The players are in a first-order competition with one another, searching for wins, but at least some of them are also in a second-order competition with the designers, searching for exploits.

Ordinalization's double movement is further propelled by this desire to be in the game and also outside it, to successfully rank and match while also finding ways to personally evade its bad consequences. There is a huge demand for a flow of crisp, actionable information in assessment and decision-making. Yet, few people and organizations want to be assessed on the basis of rapid, reductive, potentially biased or inaccurate methods—at least, not very often. Probably none want to be replaced. The usefulness of these methods, and their close connection to the inescapable act of judging one thing to be better than another, makes a *general* disdain for rankings hard to sustain in a full-throated way. More often, both the acceptance and the rejection of ranking remain acts of bad faith. Their acceptance is often mealymouthed, as when a university spokesperson says that while they are gratified to be ranked at the top, it is, the substantive goals or ideals of education that really matter. By the same token, their rejection often amounts to a kind of bastard solidarity. This can happen in either direction. One may experience the sort of sour grapes that come from knowing one has been branded a loser ("I don't care about your stupid ranking anyway"), or one may have some backdoor means to evade or reject the baleful, third-person eye of ordinalization.

The Will to Progress and the Will to Power

Bourdieu identifies his twofold truths primarily among the dominated segment of society. In the tradition of thinkers preoccupied with the failure of the working classes to properly grasp their own interests, he examines industrial workers who misrecognize their lot or Algerian peasants who misperceive the real meaning of social reciprocity. But misrecognition is not the sole domain of the destitute. The gap between objective situation and subjective understanding is hardly less insidious among the elite. Elites harbor a twofold truth of their own. At the top of society, the ambition to do well is closely intertwined with the insistence that one is also doing *good*.[13] Those who benefit from entrepreneurial success often also want to be hailed for their virtue. Fortunately for them, there is no shortage of complacent philosophers on hand to uphold the idea that "self-interest [is] indistinguishable from collective abundance."[14] In this moral universe, the creative destruction unleashed by technological advances is imagined not just as economic change but also as moral progress. Some of this flows from the "engineering" view of the world. As Fred Turner remarks, "the ethics of engineering is an ethics of 'does it work'? If you make something that works, you've done the ethical thing."[15] This kind of barebones ethics often blossoms in the most disruptive technological sectors, those that seek to devastate and reconfigure entire industries. It is especially easy to embrace given that many soi-disant disruptors lose a lot of money. If a company is bleeding capital, then what remains is the virtue that lies in what the product *does*.

But by itself this is rarely enough. Technology is endowed with other virtues too. It is somehow more democratic than democracy itself. It does not play favorites, it judges impartially, it is objective, and it works toward inclusiveness and equality. To be sure, this kind of ideological work is not unique to the tech sector. Corporations right across the economy partake in some version of it, in the same way that they also engage in philanthropy. But evangelizing talk of social progress through technological disruption, in particular, is often comically formulaic. In the TV show *Silicon Valley*, fictional software developers and venture capitalists reflexively mouth the platitude that their product, no matter how fatuous its purpose, is about "making the world a better place." Its satire hits close to home, as this refrain is just as pervasive in the real Silicon Valley. To the extent that moral commitment and passionate devotion are perceived as "feeling rules" that help foster social recognition and economic success, one must perform them. The fact that this kind of "emotional labor" may be genuine does not always help. Twitter offers countless examples of the performance going awry, of public self-regard collapsing into self-delusion and public ridicule.[16] The platform's distinctive visibility, combined with the bubble-like insulation of the most popular tech thought leaders, has tended to produce particularly acute cases. Think of venture capitalist Marc Andreessen posting that "thanks to Airbnb, now anyone with a house or apartment can offer a room for rent. Hence, income inequality reduced."[17] Or think of OpenAI CEO Sam Altman writing about his company's great promise of social equalization that "these tools will help us be more productive (can't wait to spend less time doing email!), healthier (AI [artificial intelligence] medical advisors for people who can't afford care), smarter (students using ChatGPT to learn), and more entertained (AI memes lolol)."[18] Or Twitter founder Jack Dorsey commenting after Elon Musk announced his plan to acquire the company, "In principle, I don't believe anyone should own or run Twitter. It wants to be a public good at a protocol level, not a company. Solving for the problem of it being a company however, Elon is the singular solution I trust. I trust his mission to extend the light of consciousness."[19] In each case, the blowback was predictable. Social media is a difficult, volatile place for anyone seeking approval and recognition, and billionaires are no exception.[20]

Philanthropy offers another, more indirect route to moral validation. Technology companies and executives, like their predecessors in the Gilded Age, have built empires of charity that annually pour billions of dollars into projects ranging from development to education to health care. At first blush, this burst of philanthropic activity among tech moguls must be understood in the context of the exponential rise of tech-related wealth and its attendant tax strategies.[21] But it is often more self-serving than this, both materially and psychologically. Many charitable projects aim to reorganize entire sectors in ways that strengthen the profile and perhaps the economic future of the company. The paradigmatic example is education, which has become "[a test bed] for a model of schooling that is rooted in the embedded technological knowledges, assumptions, and practices of corporate technology culture."[22] These interests advance by way of the Maussian bargain. Computers, learning management services, and apps are often offered as part of an explicit philanthropic gift to schools or simply given for free to teachers to generate word-of-mouth adoption.[23] Gifts are essential to construct what Juan del Nido calls the "gladiatorial truth" of technology, the idea that because the people (in this case, administrators, teachers, students, and parents) want it, they should have it.[24]

In this way the legitimation strategies of technologists are essentially populist. Their gifts, it is implied, work against established privilege and paternalistic, hidebound institutions. They act through and for the people, defending their freedom to choose, to search, and to express themselves. This, in turn, fosters healthy competition in every domain and, of course, a just distribution of rewards. In its strongest form, this view harkens back to the classically neoliberal position that markets are a model for the democratic process, more intrinsically democratic than the institutions of democracy itself. Ludwig von Mises, for instance, thought that the unique information-processing properties of markets made them better than democracy at delivering the right outcomes.[25] But the dual truth of this species of neoliberalism is that its principled celebration of market competition as an implicitly democratic mechanism gives rise to a practical fascination with winner-take-all outcomes.[26] The truth, brutally acknowledged by Mises, is that the market tends to reward those with more resources: "It is true, in the market the various consumers have not the same voting right. The rich cast more votes than the poorer citizens. But this inequality is itself the outcome of a previous voting process. To be rich, in a pure market economy, is the outcome of success in filling best the demands of the consumers. A wealthy man can preserve his wealth only by continuing to serve the consumers in the most efficient way."[27] The entrepreneurial class of Silicon Valley often expresses something like Mises's view, or an even coarser version of it. Succeeding in the market is much the same as contributing to the cause of social progress, and the former confirms one's authority to speak about the latter. The will to power uncomfortably sits on top of the will to progress.

Still, this sense of justified rewards does not do away with the desire to avoid being personally subject to the judgment of the market. For people accustomed to thinking they deserve their position at the top, the experience of being ranked can be all the more unbearable. Elon Musk's reported insistence that Twitter design an algorithmic bypass to ensure that *his own posts* would appear in a more favorable position is both ludicrous and telling.[28] The effort by social media platforms to sell social status itself, much as the king of France once sold titles of nobility, is the inevitable culmination of the tension between pure market power and the relentless force of ordinalization. Others, meanwhile, simply find ways to escape the world they have created. They retreat into personal spirituality and mindfulness, on the one hand, or try to buy out of the rules of the collective game, on the other.[29] Those at the very top hedge against the future by trying to build quite literal escape hatches that lead, according to taste, to a luxurious underground bunker, outer space, or New Zealand.[30]

The Twofold Truth of Social Science

Finally, we should turn the light back on ourselves. Social scientists, society's professional analysts, are no have been immune to self-deception than society's actors. They never have been. Back in the eighteenth century, the precursors of modern social science were "ideologues of progress," to use Krishan Kumar's phrase.[31] They, too, had vivid ideas about what the future would look like; they insisted on the connection between social change and moral progress; and they had strong views about the role of science and technology in this process. The French *philosophes* of the eighteenth and early nineteenth centuries—people like Turgot, Condorcet, and especially Saint-Simon—are particularly good examples. They gave us the modern use of words like *individualism, industrialism,* and *socialism.* Their successor and disciple Auguste Comte coined the word *sociology* (and, incidentally, also *altruism*) as he expounded his positivist religion of scientific humanism.

These thinkers were intoxicated at the prospect of the future. They also saw themselves as having scientifically discovered the stages that society would pass through to get there. They almost all thought that authority would soon be grounded in technical knowledge. Thus, they had fabulous plans for the future role of scientists, including what we would now call social scientists. They, too, wanted to eliminate politics from government and to replace it with rational administration by men of knowledge and expertise. Saint-Simon's version, or one of them, was named the Council of Newton. Comte's equivalent was to be called the Positive Occidental Committee. He said it would meet regularly in Paris and consist of eight Frenchmen, seven Englishmen, six Germans, five Italians, and four Spaniards. He designed a flag for it. These delusions became what Hayek disdainfully called "the religion of the engineers."[32] It reached its first high-water mark under the auspices of the state. The "high modernist" schemes associated with it were unprecedented in scope and, subsequently, became victims of the hubris they embodied.[33] Yet their residue is everywhere, from the Federal Reserve Board on down to comments on the Hacker News website insisting that software developers should not be fettered by ethical hand-wringing.

With the exception of elite economists, contemporary social scientists no longer expect to be technocratic high priests of a new society. These days, far from sitting on a Council of Newton, they—or *we*—spend time stuck on Zoom calls, pitching one another phrases coined to characterize the world we find ourselves in and our disaffection for it. This makes it easier for theorists to be justifiably skeptical of the happy talk and hype surrounding the social transformations that the commercial application of information technology has wrought over the past thirty years. Yet it also makes it easy to underestimate just how far we have come down the path that Comte and his ilk dreamed of walking.

The *philosophes* imagined a world where scientific knowledge would be deployed in the service of the rational administration of society by experts—which is to say, themselves. In the 1970s and 1980s, social network analysts tinkered with slow computers and trivially small datasets, dreaming of a world where the structure and flow of concrete social relations in real time might be captured in numerical form. Modern information technology opened up a new world of social data as both a blessing and a curse, an excess of information that was irresistible and frightening. By 2006, for example, Gueorgi Kossinets and Duncan Watts analyzed email communications using what was then an impressively large network dataset of forty-three thousand students, faculty, and staff at a university.[34] At around the same time, at the height of the so-called US war on terror, the public became aware that the National Security Agency (NSA) had assembled a gigantic database of telephone calls in the United States, with the assistance of most of the major telecommunications providers. It captured ties between people who phoned one other, ready to be analyzed for potential evidence of terrorist cells.

Any social scientist who works with quantitative data dreams of ideal datasets: the kind of things we would collect if money, time and ethics did not restrict us. These daydreams tend toward harmless megalomania, visions of maximally comprehensive data on the whole population of interest, in real time, with vast computing power to analyze it, and no constraints on updating or extending it. At the limit, even though we know it to be absurd, we picture something like Jorge Luis Borges's map, a perfect, one-to-one scale representation of the world. In this respect scientists and spies are not so different. The NSA's efforts to uncover the real structure of things is kin to what motivates many a social scientist. The little megalomaniac that lives inside anyone who collects data for a living ("More detail! More measures! More coverage!") thrills at the thought of what one could do at that scale. Think of the possibilities! The NSA was and is rather less constrained than the average researcher by money, personnel, or the law. The same goes for Google or Meta. To them, Borges's map is less a daydream than a design challenge.

The massive expansion in the availability of social data has not resulted in a correspondingly elevated status for social science as a whole. Instead technology firms increasingly dominate the production of social-scientific knowledge by way of their domination over the data economy. They often share in or reap the symbolic rewards. Some disciplinary social scientists do gain access to private treasure houses of information. Most find themselves very much on the outside. At a minimum, as the terms of the Maussian bargain are once more enforced, what previously was a free flow of data easily scraped from the web can suddenly disappear into walled gardens or behind an application programming interface (API) that is exorbitantly expensive to access. For those social scientists in a position to cooperate, the benefits can be handsome. That next grant from Google, that *Proceedings of the National Academy of Sciences* paper, that TED Talk may be theirs. For the others, the threat is one of obsolescence and exclusion from real intellectual action. And so social scientists face their own challenge of bad faith. Their historical position as social critics sits uncomfortably with their involvement in an academic game whose core institutions are increasingly oriented toward the market.[35]

To make things even more difficult, this challenge works from both the inside out and the outside in. Each new significant innovation presents new temptations and fears. At the end of November 2022, for instance, millions of people signed up to play with ChatGPT, a prototype large-language-model chatbot from OpenAI. Its simple interface made it easy for everyone to experiment, explore its limits, and share its output. It was shockingly good at taking a brief prompt and producing a plausible form letter, a mediocre essay, or some code that might or might not run as expected. You could make it write rap battles between real or imagined characters. As people considered its gifts, delight became mixed with anxiety in a familiar way. Could it invent a good joke? Could you make it say something obscene? Could you make it say something racist? What if small-time entrepreneurs used it to improve their communication with customers? What if enterprising hackers used it to write malicious code? What if undergraduates used it to write term papers? What if faculty used it to provide feedback? What if lawyers used it to replace paralegals? What if clients used it to replace lawyers? It was striking how many commentators expressed first-person or third-person anxieties about the prospects for gaming some familiar system of ranking or evaluation. Would ChatGPT render older modes of grading and assessment obsolete? Could it be exploited in a way that allowed people to pretend to be better than they "really" were? Meanwhile, consistent with the Maussian bargain, signing up to play with it meant you were providing data to OpenAI to help further tune the underlying models.

The buzz around ChatGPT contrasted sharply with events a few weeks earlier, when the crypto exchange FTX underwent perhaps the most outrageous collapse in the short history of digital capitalism. Spectacular as it was, FTX's fall was a painful reminder that the lure of the box of delights is first and foremost that of getting rich quick. In extreme cases, its dynamic boils down to utter reckless-ness and pure grift, but working out these goals through market modulation and financial abstraction is the normal state of things. Before its collapse, FTX was busy trying to get a new crypto derivatives trading process—one that bypassed the intermediation of brokers in favor of an au-tomated resolution mechanism—approved by US regula-tory authorities.[36] The firm's leaders were the children of prominent academics at the Massachusetts Institute of Technology's Economics Department and Stanford Law School. Its head, Sam Bankman-Fried, had set himself up as a ragged-trousered philanthropist of effective altruism—a well-funded intellectual movement spearheaded by moral philosophers in American, Australian, and British academia—and, in the process, charmed the guardians of funds like Sequoia Capital.

At the time of this writing, the venture capital appetite for crypto and Web3 has diminished. Sequoia Capital has turned its sights toward the crabgrass frontier of gen-erative artificial intelligence. The sector's capital needs are colossal. The financial and energy costs of data storage and processing for large models are exceedingly high, as is the legal exposure that comes with grabbing the world's stock of digital writing, images, and code.[37]

This quasi-academic homestead has quickly been taken over by a familiar handful of large, cash-rich corporations. OpenAI—the organization that originated ChatGPT, Codex, and DALL-E, among others—was established as a nonprofit research company in 2015 with a mission focused on "existential risk prevention."[38] As its products became more and more capable, the company became increasingly cagey about sharing its source code with the public, citing safety concerns. Access was moved to an API. In March 2019 OpenAI was officially reorganized as a capped-profit company, which allowed it to raise capital and offer stock options to employees. In 2020 it licensed the transformer language model GPT-3, its crown jewel, exclusively to Microsoft.[39] The arrival of ChatGPT and other large language models fuses many of the elements we have examined in this book: techno-optimism fueled by the easy availability of cash, Maussian bargains with users, a new data imperative for corporations, the consolidation of a crabgrass frontier dominated by a few power players, potentially vast financial applications, dilemmas of authenticity, merit, and value, with the whole thing tangled up in a paradoxical rhetoric of persons who are both individually sovereign and cybernetically supervised.

WE HAVE TRIED TO GRASP and critique the social form emerging in front of us. From a sociological point of view, capitalism's greatest systemic asset is its libidinal character, its ability to generate the "promise, constantly made explicit . . . , of a way to escape . . . dissatisfaction through either the accumulation of capital or the acquisition of the commodity."[40] Digital capitalism makes good on that promise. The acquisition process, often initiated with a gift, is easy and immediate. Its most direct implication, the possibility of sorting and thus of ordinalization, is deeply appealing. It equips organizations with the means to impose order and control, however flawed that may be. In the process it flatters and socializes people's disposition to compete.[41] Moved by a sense of obligation and inevitability, we have allowed it to dig deeper into our practices, our bodies, and our minds. The experience is totalizing: at once psychological, moral, and aesthetic.

The whole thing started innocuously. The computer geeks were likable. The World Wide Web was delightful, and harmless at first. But it was not immune to the arrival of capital, which often came with the blessing of the public and the state. As Tim Wu has observed, information and communication technologies tend to go through much the same economic cycle. Telephony, radio, television, film, and the web have all seen hobbies develop into industries, and industries into empires—until, that is, the state takes notice of their new scope.[42] Digital capitalism may be at such a crossroads, on the verge of a government-induced move to decentralize, most evidently in Europe and latterly in the United States, where courts and regulators have enacted new privacy rules and launched a flurry of antitrust actions. In China, the tech behemoths have been spectacularly chastised by the Chinese Communist Party's insistence on its juridical sovereignty over macrosocial coordination.[43]

The wheel may slow down and even stall for a while, but it never fully turns back. Particular information empires rise and then fall, but they do leave a lasting imprint on social life. The logic of layered sorting through personalization is by now built into economic infrastructures and social expectations. The advent of fine-grained, quantified personal data has propelled a rationalization of the social stratification process, and equipped it with a new kind of moral justification.[44] Even if, as companies, Meta fails or Uber is despised, no one wants an uncurated news feed or an unrated cab driver anymore. The instrumental rationality of technique has produced its own substantive rationality of deserved ends. It has also laid the foundations for its own backlash. Everywhere, algorithms are becoming a target for academic critique, legal complaint, and grassroots resistance. Entire disciplinary subfields have arisen to sustain these movements.[45] Meanwhile, alternatives to rationalized calculation are enjoying a revival. Under the banner of social justice, and in the name of excluded groups, progressive elites have rejected standardized testing and called for more informal and narrative modes of assessment once decried for being subjective and arbitrary. Critics of economic exploitation find themselves pining for the cash nexus and the anonymity built into it. Analysts of power and knowledge long for the certainties and security of respectable, credentialed expertise.[46]

What is it that they mourn? It is more than personal anxiety about a future that seems to escape their power and threatens to render them irrelevant. It is the unavoidable realization that the ordinal society is, as a mechanism of governance, a tangled and unfair mess. It is the sober acknowledgment that the proliferation of small-m meritocracies has installed a "hierarchical gaze" that sees social relations through the lens of quantified and ranked comparison, however ill conceived.[47] It is the sad recognition that any institution that strives for this kind of orderliness, with its ideology of clean measurement of differences and its monstrous technological affordances, has difficulty accommodating a community of equals. As the ordinal society extends its reach, the insistence on formal equality under the eye of the market eclipses the struggle for substantive equality in the shadow of the state. It blinds us to what we all share and chips away at solidaristic feelings and institutions. Public goods and collective goals are being dissolved in the acid bath of individualization and competition, leaving us increasingly alone in a hyperconnected world whose social ordering is precisely metered and, in its factitious way, inarguably "right." Life in the ordinal society may well be unbearable.

Notes

Introduction

1. Alexander R. Galloway, "Golden Age of Analog," *Critical Inquiry* 48, no. 2 (2022): 211–32.

2. Margaret O'Mara, *The Code: Silicon Valley and the Remaking of America.* (Penguin, 2019), 29.

3. Christophe Lécuyer, *Making Silicon Valley: Innovation and the Growth of High Tech, 1930–1970* (MIT Press, 2007), 13–52.

4. Vannevar Bush, *Science, the Endless Frontier: A Report to the President by Vannevar Bush, Director of the Office of Scientific Research and Development* (Office of Scientific Research and Development, July 1945).

5. Paul N. Edwards, *The Closed World: Computers and the Politics of Discourse in Cold War America* (MIT Press, 1996).

6. Steven Levy, *Hackers: Heroes of the Computer Revolution* (Anchor, 1984).

7. See, for example, the gradual shift in the importance of software in the National Aeronautics and Space Administration's Project Apollo during the 1960s, as discussed in David Mindell, *Digital Apollo: Human and Machine in Spaceflight* (MIT Press, 2011), esp. 145–180.

8. Eszter Hargittai, "Radio's Lessons for the Internet," *Communications of the ACM* 43, no. 1 (2000): 51–57.

9. Vannevar Bush, "As We May Think," *Atlantic Monthly*, July 1945, 101–108; Doug Englebart Institute, "Doug's Great Demo: 1968," web page, n.d., accessed October 6, 2022, https://dougengelbart.org /content/view/209/.

10. Richard Barbrook and Andy Cameron, "The Californian Ideology," *Science as Culture* 6, no. 1 (1996): 44–72; Manuel Castells, *The Rise of the*

Network Society (Wiley-Blackwell, 2009); Fred Turner, *From Counter-culture to Cyberculture: Stewart Brand, the Whole Earth Network, and the Rise of Digital Utopianism* (University of Chicago Press, 2006).

11. Kevin Driscoll, *The Modem World: A Prehistory of Social Media* (Yale University Press, 2022).

12. Howard Rheingold, *The Virtual Community: Homesteading on the Electronic Frontier* (Addison-Wesley, 1993).

13. Vincent Mosco, *The Digital Sublime: Myth, Power, and Cyberspace* (MIT Press, 2005), 3. Writing a few years after Mosco, Paul Dourish and Genevieve Bell, *Divining a Digital Future: Mess and Mythology in Ubiquitous Computing* (MIT Press, 2011), argued that by generating the myth that the future is "just around the corner" (they were studying the discourse about ubiquitous computing), the tech industry diverts attention from its present responsibilities—an argument that is now frequently taken up by present critics of AI.

14. Esther Dyson, George Gilder, George Keyworth, and Alvin Toffler, "Cyberspace and the American Dream: A Magna Carta for the Knowledge Age," Progress and Freedom Foundation, August 1994, http://www.pff.org/issues-pubs/futureinsights/fi1.2magnacarta.html.

15. John Perry Barlow, "A Declaration of the Independence of Cyberspace," Electronic Frontier Foundation, February 8, 1996, https://www.eff.org/cyberspace-independence; Langdon Winner, "Cyberlibertarian Myths and the Prospects for Community," *ACM SIGCAS Computers and Society* 27, no. 3 (1997): 14–19.

16. William Gibson, *Neuromancer* (Ace, 1984).

17. See Eric S. Raymond, *The Cathedral and the Bazaar: Musings on Linux and Open Source by an Accidental Revolutionary* (O'Reilly, 2001), particularly the title essay, 19–64, and "Homesteading the Noosphere," 65–112. For collections bringing together the debates of the time, see Chris DiBona, Sam Ockman, and Mark Stone, eds., *Open Sources: Voices from the Open Source Revolution* (O'Reilly, 1999); and Peter Ludlow, ed., *Crypto Anarchy, Cyberstates and Pirate Utopias* (MIT Press, 2001).

18. Kieran Healy and Alan Schussman, "The Ecology of Open Source Software Development" (research paper, January 14, 2003), arXiv, s://kieranhealy.org/files/papers/oss-activity.pdf.

19. Dan Schiller, *Crossed Wires: The Conflicted History of US Telecommunications, from the Post Office to the Internet* (Oxford University Press, 2023), 576.

20. Joseph Stiglitz, quoted in Gary Gerstle, *The Rise and Fall of the Neoliberal Order: America and the World in the Free Market Era* (Oxford University Press, 2022), 171.

21. Katherine Chen, *Enabling Creative Chaos: The Organization behind the Burning Man Event* (University of Chicago Press, 2009); Erik Davis, "Beyond Belief: The Cults of Burning Man," in *AfterBurn: Reflections on Burning Man,* ed. Lee Gilmore and Mark Van Proyen (University of New Mexico Press, 2005), 15–40; Fred Turner, "Burning Man at Google: A Cultural Infrastructure for New Media Production." *New Media and Society* 11, nos. 1–2 (2009): 73–94.

22. See Shoshana Zuboff, *The Age of Surveillance Capitalism: The Fight for a Human Future at the New Frontier of Power* (PublicAffairs, 2019), chapter 3.

23. Sergey Brin and Larry Page, quoted in Zuboff, *The Age of Surveillance Capitalism,* 71.

24. Clayton M. Christensen, *The Innovator's Dilemma: When New Technologies Cause Great Firms to Fail* (Harvard Business School Press, 1997); Antonio Garcia Martinez, *Chaos Monkeys: Obscene Fortunes and Random Failure in Silicon Valley* (HarperCollins, 2016); Anna Wiener, *Uncanny Valley: A Memoir* (Farrar, Straus and Giroux, 2020).

25. Chris Anderson (@chr1sa), Twitter, April 15, 2021, 10:45 a.m., https://twitter.com/chr1sa/status/1382706682304860166?lang=eng. The phrase "It is easier to ask for forgiveness than to ask for permission" has been attributed to Grace Hopper, although her intended meaning is generally assumed to be different than that celebrated by the tech industry today.

26. Evgeny Morozov, *To Save Everything, Click Here: The Folly of Technological Solutionism* (PublicAffairs, 2013).

27. Joseph A. Schumpeter, *Capitalism, Socialism, and Democracy* (Harper and Brothers, 1950).

28. Chris Herring, "The New Logics of Homeless Seclusion: Homeless Encampments in America's West Coast Cities," *City and Community* 13, no. 4 (2014): 285–309; Richard A. Walker, *Pictures of a Gone City: Tech and the Dark Side of Prosperity in the San Francisco Bay Area* (PM Press, 2018).

29. Sarah Bohn, Dean Bonner, Julien Lafortune, and Tess Thorman, *Income Inequality in California* (Public Policy Institute of California, December 2020), https://www.ppic.org/wp-content/uploads /incoming-inequality-and-economic-opportunity-in-california -december-2020.pdf; Estelle Sommelier and Mark Price, *The New Gilded Age: Income Inequality in the U.S. By State, Metropolitan Area, and County* (Economic Policy Institute, 2020).

30. On life in Silicon Valley, see Olivier Alexandre, *La tech: Quand la Silicon Valley refait le monde* (Seuil, 2023); Malcolm Harris, *Palo Alto: A History of California, Capitalism, and the World* (Little, Brown, 2023); and Wiener, *Uncanny Valley*.

31. Zeynep Tufekci, *Twitter and Tear Gas: The Power and Fragility of Networked Protest* (Yale University Press, 2017).

32. David Z. Morris, "The Rise of Cryptocurrency Ponzi Schemes," *Atlantic,* May 31, 2017, https://www.theatlantic.com/technology /archive/2017/05/cryptocurrency-ponzi-schemes/.

33. Mosco, *The Digital Sublime,* 20.

34. TCP/IP (Transmission Control Protocol / Internet Protocol) is the protocol specifying the system of packet switching that underpins orderly communication between computers on a network, whether locally or on the internet. SMTP (Simple Mail Transfer Protocol) is the protocol that specifies how email is relayed. HTTP (Hypertext Transfer Protocol) is the protocol for the presentation and transfer of documents and other media on the web.

35. Alexander R. Galloway, *Protocol: How Control Exists after Decentralization* (MIT Press, 2004), 3.

36. Kenneth Jackson, *Crabgrass Frontier: The Suburbanization of the United States* (Oxford University Press, 1985).

37. Incidentally, this vision tended to efface the conventional distinction between production and consumption, particularly in the sphere of

culture. As David Graeber, "Consumption," *Current Anthropology* 52, no. 4 (2011): 502, remarks in a more general context, "Any production not for the market is treated as a form of consumption, which has the incredibly reactionary political effect of treating almost every form of unalienated experience we do engage in as somehow a gift granted us by the captains of industry." The rapid rise of the language of "content" and "content providers" reflected this dilemma, as did the puzzle of how to "monetize" that content. The question of how to turn the flow of sociable, online creativity into a "real" economic activity was one of the early sources of puzzlement and skepticism about the web. We will examine this point at greater length in chapter 1.

38. Tim Wu, *The Master Switch: The Rise and Fall of Information Empires* (Alfred A. Knopf, 2010).

39. Moxie Marlinspike, "My First Impressions of Web3," blog post, January 7, 2022, https://moxie.org/2022/01/07/web3-first-impressions .html; Eric Lipton, Daisuke Wakabayashi, and Ephrat Livni, "Big Hires, Big Money and a D.C. Blitz: A Bold Plan to Dominate Crypto," *New York Times*, October 29, 2021, https://www.nytimes.com/2021/10/29 /us/politics/andreessen-horowitz-lobbying-cryptocurrency.html.

40. Barlow, "A Declaration."

41. Vili Lehdonvirta, *Cloud Empires: How Digital Platforms Are Overtaking the State and How We Can Regain Control* (MIT Press, 2022), 35–52.

42. Turner, *From Counterculture to Cyberculture.*

43. See, for example, Sergey Brin and Lawrence Page, "The Anatomy of a Large-Scale Hypertextual Web Search Engine," *Computer Networks and ISDN Systems* 30, nos. 1–7 (1998): 107–17.

44. Lawrence Page, Method for node ranking in a linked database, US patent 6,285,999, filed September 4, 2001. Cited prior work in the PageRank patent from bibliometrics and social network analysis includes Mark S. Mizruchi, Peter Mariolis, Michael Schwartz, and Beth Mintz, "Techniques for Disaggregating Centrality Scores in Social Networks," *Sociological Methodology* 16 (1986): 26; and Patrick Doreian, Vladimir Batagelj, and Anuška Ferligoj, "Partitioning Networks Based on Generalized Concepts of Equivalence," *Journal of Mathematical Sociology* 19, no. 1 (1994): 1–27. For some further sense of

the history and elements of these methods, see Stanley Wasserman and Katherine Faust, *Social Network Analysis: Methods and Applications* (Cambridge University Press, 1994), 199–214.

45. Amy N. Langville and Carl D. Meyer, "A Survey of Eigenvector Methods for Web Information Retrieval," *SIAM Review* 47, no. 1 (2005): 135–61.

46. "Soft city" is an image used to quite different ends by optimistic urban planners (see David Sim, *Soft City: Building Density for Everyday Life* [Island Press, 2019]; coolly postmodern chroniclers of the city's "signals, styles, systems of rapid, highly-conventionalised communication . . . amenable to a dazzling and libidinous variety of lives, dreams, interpretations" (Jonathan Raban, *Soft City* [Harvill, 1988], 9); and fearful prophets of dystopian surveillance (see Hariton Pushwagner, *Soft City* [New York Review Comics, 2016]). Each of these aspects is relevant here.

47. Kieran Healy, "The Performativity of Networks," *European Journal of Sociology / Archives Européennes de Sociologie* 56, no. 2 (2015): 175–205; Ori Schwarz, *Sociological Theory for Digital Society: The Codes That Bind Us Together* (Polity, 2021).

48. Gilles Deleuze, "Postscript on the Societies of Control," *October* 59 (1992): 6.

49. Nikolas Rose, *Powers of Freedom: Reframing Political Thought* (Cambridge University Press, 1999), 87.

50. Marc Andreessen, "Why Software Is Eating the World," *Andreessen Horowitz* (blog), August 20, 2011, https://a16z.com/2011/08/20/why -software-is-eating-the-world/.

51. Tom Simonite, "Nvidia CEO: Software Is Eating the World, but AI Is Going to Eat Software," *MIT Technology Review,* May 12, 2017, https://www.technologyreview.com/2017/05/12/151722/nvidia-ceo -software-is-eating-the-world-but-ai-is-going-to-eat-software/.

52. Richard Florida, *The Rise of the Creative Class* (Basic Books, 2002).

53. Jenna Burrell and Marion Fourcade, "The Society of Algorithms," *Annual Review of Sociology* 47, no. 1 (2021): 217.

54. Mark Chen, Jerry Tworek, Heewoo Jun, Qiming Yuan, Henrique Ponde de Oliveira Pinto, Jared Kaplan, Harri Edwards, et al., "Evalu-

ating Large Language Models Trained on Code" (research paper, July 14, 2021), arXiv, https://arxiv.org/pdf/2107.03374.

55. As Quinn Slobodian, *Crack-Up Capitalism: Market Radicals and the Dream of a World Without Democracy* (Metropolitan Books, 2023), 223, notes, "The cloud floats because the underclass holds it up." See also Aaron Benanav, *Automation and the Future of Work* (Verso, 2020); Tressie McMillan Cottom, "Where Platform Capitalism and Racial Capitalism Meet: The Sociology of Race and Racism in the Digital Society," *Sociology of Race and Ethnicity* 6, no. 4 (2020): 441–49; Mary Gray and Siddarth Suri, *Ghost Work: How to Stop Silicon Valley from Building a New Global Underclass* (Houghton Mifflin Harcourt, 2019); and Ricarda Hammer and Tina M. Park, "The Ghost in the Algorithm: Racial Colonial Capitalism and the Digital Age," in *Global Historical Sociology of Race and Racism*, ed. Alexandre I. R. White and Katrina Quisumbing King, Political Power and Social Theory 38 (Emerald, 2021), 221–49.

56. Kate Crawford, *Atlas of AI: Power, Politics, and the Planetary Costs of Artificial Intelligence* (Yale University Press, 2021); Nathan Ensmenger, "The Environmental History of Computing," *Technology and Culture* 59, no. 4, supplement (2018): S7–S33; Thomas S. Mullaney, Benjamin Peters, Mar Hicks and Kavita Philip, ed., *Your Computer Is on Fire* (MIT Press, 2021).

57. Safiya Umoja Noble, *Algorithms of Oppression: How Search Engines Reinforce Racism* (NYU Press, 2018); Latanya Sweeney, "Discrimination in Online Ad Delivery" (research paper, Harvard University, January 28, 2013), Data Privacy Lab, https://dataprivacylab.org/projects/onlineads/1071-1.pdf.

58. Rob Kitchin, "Thinking Critically about and Researching Algorithms," *Information, Communication and Society* 20, no. 1 (2017): 14–29.

59. Nick Seaver, "What Should an Anthropology of Algorithms Do?," *Cultural Anthropology* 33, no. 3 (2018): 375–85.

60. Jens Beckert, *Imagined Futures: Fictional Expectations and Capitalist Dynamics* (Harvard University Press, 2016).

61. F. A. Hayek, "Competition as a Discovery Procedure," *Quarterly Journal of Austrian Economics* 5, no. 3 (2002): 9–23; Evgeny Morozov, "Beyond Competition: Alternative Discovery Procedures and the

Postcapitalist Public Sphere" (online lecture, University of California–Berkeley, March 19, 2021), https://events.berkeley.edu/polisci/event/112651-beyond-competition-alternative-discovery.

62. Isaiah Berlin, "Two Concepts of Liberty," in *The Proper Study of Mankind: An Anthology of Essays,* ed. Henry Hardy and Roger Hausheer (Farrar, Straus and Giroux, 2000), 191–241.

63. Luc Boltanski and Eve Chiapello, *The New Spirit of Capitalism,* trans. Gregory Elliott (Verso, 2006); Castells, *The Rise of the Network Society;* Eran Fisher, *Media and New Capitalism in the Digital Age: The Spirit of Networks* (Palgrave Macmillan, 2010).

64. Daniel Bell, *The Cultural Contradictions of Capitalism* (Basic Books, 1976).

1. The Box of Delights

Epigraph: John Masefield, *The Box of Delights, or When the Wolves Were Running* (Heinemann, 1957), 177.

1. Howard Becker, cited in Rob Kitchin, *The Data Revolution: Big Data, Open Data, Data Infrastructures and Their Consequences* (Sage, 2014), 2.

2. B. J. Fogg, *Persuasive Technology: Using Computers to Change What We Think and Do* (Morgan Kaufmann, 2002). A more distant inspiration, mentioned by Shoshana Zuboff, is the behavioral engineering of Harvard psychologist BF Skinner. See Zuboff, *The Age of Surveillance Capitalism.*

3. Zuboff, *The Age of Surveillance Capitalism,* 140. See also Nick Couldry and Alison Powell, "Big Data from the Bottom Up," *Big Data and Society* 1, no. 2 (2014), https://doi.org/10.1177/205395171453927; Crawford, *Atlas of AI;* Carl Benedikt Frey, *The Technology Trap: Capital, Labor, and Power in the Age of Automation* (Princeton University Press, 2019); and Jathan Sadowski, *Too Smart: How Digital Capitalism Is Extracting Data, Controlling Our Lives, and Taking Over the World* (MIT Press, 2020).

4. Julie Cohen, *Between Truth and Power: The Legal Constructions of Informational Capitalism* (Oxford University Press, 2019); Nick Couldry and Ulises A. Mejias, *The Costs of Connection: How Data Is Colonizing Human Life and Appropriating It for Capitalism* (Stanford University Press, 2019).

5. Alexander R. Galloway, "Protocol," *Theory, Culture and Society* 23, nos. 2–3 (2006): 317–20. See also Bernard E. Harcourt, *Exposed: Desire and Disobedience in the Digital Age* (Harvard University Press, 2015).

6. Marcel Mauss, *The Gift: The Form and Reason for Exchange in Archaic Societies*, trans. W. D. Halls (W. W. Norton, 2000).

7. Pierre Bourdieu, *Outline of a Theory of Practice*, trans. Richard Nice (Cambridge University Press, 1977); Marcel Hénaff, "Mauss et l'invention de la réciprocité," *Revue du Mauss* 36, no. 2 (2010): 71–86; Mauss, *The Gift*.

8. Gabriel Rossman, "Obfuscatory Relational Work and Disreputable Exchange," *Sociological Theory* 32, no. 1 (2014): 43–63; Viviana Zelizer, *The Purchase of Intimacy* (Princeton University Press, 2005).

9. Bourdieu, *Outline of a Theory of Practice*.

10. James Carrier, "Gifts, Commodities, and Social Relations: A Maussian View of Exchange," *Sociological Forum* 6, no. 1 (1991): 19–37.

11. See Marion Fourcade and Daniel N. Kluttz, "A Maussian Bargain: Accumulation by Gift in the Digital Economy," *Big Data and Society* 7, no. 1 (2020), https://doi.org/10.1177/20539517198970.

12. Dave Elder-Vass, *Profit and Gift in the Digital Economy* (Cambridge University Press, 2016).

13. Erik Brynjolfsson, Avinash Collis, W. Erwin Diewert, Felix Eggers, and Kevin J. Fox, "GDP-B: Accounting for the Value of New and Free Goods in the Digital Economy" (NBER Working Paper 25695, National Bureau of Economic Research, March 2019), https://www.nber.org/papers/w25695.

14. Cohen, *Between Truth and Power*, 58. In 2016, a senior Facebook privacy officer expressed concern about "places where the draft [of Facebook's Data Protection Handbook] says that it is basically impossible for people to understand complex data flows and therefore consent is ultimately impossible" since "Facebook's data processing is complex and we rely on consent to justify it." Plaintiff's Corrected Brief in Support of Sanctions, in In re: Facebook Inc. Consumer Privacy User Profile Litigation, 18-MD-02843, September 15, 2022, Docket No. 1050-3, 32.

15. Howard Becker, *Artworlds* (University of California Press, 1984).

16. James Boyle, *Shamans, Software and Spleens: Law and the Construction of the Information Society* (Harvard University Press, 1997).

17. As Cohen, *Between Truth and Power,* 43, explains, "A dominant platform can reduce prices to one group—for example, book buyers or consumers of professional networking services—below marginal cost and still maintain its dominance by charging fees to some other group and a provider of free services to consumers can attain and maintain dominance by controlling access to the 'market for eyeballs.'" One important consequence is that this kind of market infrastructure is very hard to regulate: "because the economics of platforms permits so many different arrangements, pricing ceases to be a reliable sign of market power, and courts and regulators lose a previously reliable metric for determining whether power has been abused" (43).

18. Katharina Pistor, *The Code of Capital: How the Law Creates Wealth and Inequality* (Princeton University Press, 2019), 184.

19. Tim Sullivan, "Blitzscaling," *Harvard Business Review,* April 2016, 45–50.

20. See Thomas S. Mullaney, Benjamin Peters, Mar Hicks, and Kavita Philip, eds, *Your Computer Is on Fire* (MIT Press, 2021), particularly chapters by Nathan Ensmenger ("The Cloud is a Factory," 29–50), and Sarah T. Roberts, ("Your AI is Human," 51–70).

21. Jean-Charles Rochet and Jean Tirole, "Platform Competition in Two-Sided Markets," *Journal of the European Economic Association* 1, no. 4 (2003): 990–1029; Nick Srnicek, *Platform Capitalism* (Polity, 2017).

22. On programmed sociality, see Taina Bucher, *If . . . Then: Algorithmic Power and Politics* (Oxford University Press, 2018).

23. Mark Granovetter, "Economic Action and Social Structure: The Problem of Embeddedness," *American Journal of Sociology* 91 (1985): 485–510.

24. In economics, see Sanjeev Goyal, *Networks: An Economics Approach* (MIT Press, 2023); and Matthew O. Jackson, *Social and Economic Networks* (Princeton University Press, 2008). For sociology and other fields, see Craig M. Rawlings, Jeffrey A. Smith, James Moody, and Daniel A. McFarland, *Network Analysis: Integrating Social Network*

Theory, Method, and Application with R (Cambridge University Press, 2023).

25. Michael Gurevich, "The Social Structure of Acquaintanceship Networks" (PhD diss., Massachusetts Institute of Technology, 1961); Stanley Milgram, "The Small World Problem," *Psychology Today* 1, no. 1 (1967): 60–67; Jeffrey Travers and Stanley Milgram, "An Experimental Study of the Small World Problem," *Sociometry* 32, no. 4 (1969): 425–43.

26. Harrison C. White, Scott A. Boorman, and Ronald L. Breiger, "Social Structure from Multiple Networks I: Blockmodels of Roles and Positions," *American Journal of Sociology* 81, no. 4 (1976): 734.

27. Scott A. Boorman and Harrison C. White, "Social Structure from Multiple Networks II: Role Structures," *American Journal of Sociology* 81, no. 6 (1976): 1442.

28. Ronald L. Breiger, "The Duality of Persons and Groups," *Social Forces* 53, no. 2 (1974): 181–90; White, Boorman, and Breiger, "Social Structure from Multiple Networks I"; W. W. Zachary, "An Information Flow Model for Conflict and Fission in Small Groups," *Journal of Anthropological Research* 33 (1977): 452–73. The monks, debutantes, and karate club members are all from classic small-*n* datasets in the analysis of social networks.

29. Vivian Aplin-Brownlee, "Ethical Questions Arise from Computers Biting into Privacy: Computer Explosion Unearths New Questions of Ethics, Privacy," *Washington Post,* May 23, 1984.

30. Scott Boorman, quoted in Aplin-Brownlee, "Ethical Questions." This vision has by now been realized. See Sameer B. Srivivasta, Amir Goldberg, V. Govind Manian, and Christopher Potts, "Enculturation Trajectories: Language, Cultural Adaptation, and Individual Outcomes in Organizations," *Management Science* 64, no. 3 (2018): 1348–64.

31. Boorman, quoted in Aplin-Brownlee, "Ethical Questions."

32. Mosco, *The Digital Sublime.*

33. Gerald Berk and Annalee Saxenian, "Architectures of Participation," *Issues in Science and Technology* 38, no. 4 (2022): 62–69.

34. McKenzie Wark, *A Hacker Manifesto* (Harvard University Press, 2004).

35. Karl Marx, *Capital: A Critique of Political Economy*, vol. 1, trans. Ben Fowkes (Penguin Classics, 1992), 873–74.

36. Wark, *A Hacker Manifesto*.

37. Bucher, *If . . . Then*.

38. Leah Perlman, quoted in Julian Morgans, "The Inventor of the 'Like' Button Wants You to Stop Worrying about Likes," *Vice*, July 6, 2017, https://www.vice.com/en/article/mbag3a/the-inventor-of-the-like -button-wants-you-to-stop-worrying-about-likes.

39. Miriam E. Sweeney and Kelsea Whaley, "Technically White: Emoji Skin-Tone Modifiers as American Technoculture," *First Monday*, June 30, 2019, https://doi.org/10.5210/fm.v24i7.10060.

40. Lucy A. Suchman, *Plans and Situated Actions: The Problem of Human-Machine Communication* (Cambridge University Press, 1987).

41. Perlman, quoted in Morgans, "The Inventor of the 'Like' Button."

42. Tim Wu, *The Attention Merchants: The Epic Scramble to Get inside Our Heads* (Alfred A. Knopf, 2016).

43. As Katherine Losse, *The Boy Kings: A Journey into the Heart of the Social Network* (Free Press, 2012), 43, relates, "I shared my concerns with the bluntness of News Feed with Pasha [a coworker]—that it wasn't just telling me things quickly but telling me things I typically wouldn't know about—and she said she would get back to the engineers. None of the stories were removed. I wondered, then, if News Feed and the future of Facebook would be built on the model of how social cohesion works—what is comfortable and relevant to you and what isn't—or if it would be indifferent to etiquette and sensitivity. It turned out to be the latter, and I'm not sure Mark [Zuckerberg] knew the difference. To him and many of the engineers, it seemed, more data is always good, regardless of how you get it."

44. Emails between Facebook leaders uncovered by the British Parliament inquiry into the Cambridge Analytica privacy abuses confirm this. See, for example, Damian Collins, Note by Damian Collins MP, Chair of the DCMS Committee, Summary of Key Issues from the Six4Three Files, UK Parliament Digital, Culture, Media and Sports Committee, May 12, 2018, https://www.parliament.uk/globalassets/documents/commons

-committees/culture-media-and-sport/Note-by-Chair-and-selected
-documents-ordered-from-Six4Three.pdf, Exhibit 48: Mark Zuckerberg Email on Reciprocity and Data Value.

45. Fourcade and Kluttz, "A Maussian Bargain."

46. Michel Callon, "An Essay on Framing and Overflowing: Economic
Externalities Revisited by Sociology," *Sociological Review* 46, no. 1,
supplement (1998): 251.

2. The Data Imperative

Epigraph: Langdon Winner, *The Whale and the Reactor: A Search for Limits
in an Age of High Technology* (University of Chicago Press, 1986), 17.

1. Mark Andrejevic, *Infoglut: How Too Much Information Is Changing the
Way We Think and Know* (Routledge, 2013).

2. Lionel Robbins, *An Essay on the Nature and Significance of Economic
Science* (Macmillan, 1932).

3. Linsey McGoey, "Bataille and the Sociology of Abundance: Reassessing
Gifts, Debt and Economic Excess," *Theory, Culture and Society* 35, nos.
4–5 (2018): 69–91.

4. Georges Bataille, *The Accursed Share: An Essay on General Economy,*
vol. 1, *Consumption,* trans. Robert Hurley (Zone Books, 1991).

5. Maciej Cegłowski, "Haunted by Data," paper presented at the Strata +
Hadoop World conference, New York City, October 1, 2015, *Idle Worlds*
(blog), https://idlewords.com/talks/haunted_by_data.htm. See also
Andrejevic, *Infoglut.*

6. Robyn Caplan and danah boyd, "Isomorphism through Algorithms:
Institutional Dependencies in the Case of Facebook," *Big Data and
Society* 5, no. 1 (2018), https://doi.org/10.1177/2053951718757253.

7. Jack Goody, *The Logic of Writing and the Organization of Society*
(Cambridge University Press, 1986); Michael Mann, *The Sources of
Social Power,* vol. 1, *A History of Power from the Beginning to A.D. 1760*
(Cambridge University Press, 1986).

8. William Deringer, *Calculated Values: Finance, Politics, and the
Quantitative Age* (Harvard University Press, 2018), ix.

9. Theodore M. Porter, *Trust in Numbers: The Pursuit of Objectivity in Science and Public Life* (Princeton University Press, 1996). See also Rebecca Jean Emigh, Dylan Riley, and Patricia Ahmed, *Antecedents of Censuses from Medieval to Nation States: How Societies and States Count* (Palgrave Macmillan, 2015); Wendy Nelson Espeland and Mitchell L. Stevens, "A Sociology of Quantification," *European Journal of Sociology/Archives Européennes de Sociologie* 49, no. 3 (2008): 401–36; and Andrea Mennicken and Wendy Nelson Espeland, "What's New with Numbers? Sociological Approaches to the Study of Quantification," *Annual Review of Sociology* 45 (2019): 223–45.

10. According to James Beniger, *The Control Revolution: Technological and Economic Origins of the Information Society* (Harvard University Press, 1989), vi, 7, the technologies developed during the so-called control revolution (between the 1830s and the 1920s, roughly) are "photography and telegraphy (1830s), rotary power printing (1840s), the typewriter (1860s), transatlantic cables (1866), telephone (1876), motion pictures (1894), wireless telegraphy (1895), magnetic tape recording (1899), radio (1906) and television (1923)."

11. Max Weber, "Bureaucracy," in *From Max Weber: Essays in Sociology,* ed. and trans. Hans H. Gerth and C. Wright Mills (Oxford University Press, 1958), 196–244.

12. Craig Robertson, *The Filing Cabinet: A Vertical History of Information* (University of Minnesota Press, 2021).

13. Dan Bouk, "The History and Political Economy of Personal Data over the Last Two Centuries in Three Acts," *Osiris* 32, no. 1 (2017): 94.

14. Bruce Carruthers, *The Economy of Promises: Trust, Power, and Credit in America* (Princeton University Press, 2022).

15. Bruce G. Carruthers, "From Uncertainty toward Risk: The Case of Credit Ratings," *Socio-economic Review* 11, no. 3 (2013): 533.

16. As James Scott, *Seeing Like a State: How Certain Schemes to Improve the Human Condition Have Failed* (Yale University Press, 1999), argues at length, making things visible and understandable in their detail— "legibility"—was the most distinctive modernist aspiration of this new kind of organization.

17. Beniger, *The Control Revolution*, 422.

18. Dan Bouk, *How Our Days Became Numbered: Risk and the Rise of the Statistical Individual* (University of Chicago Press, 2015); Viviana Zelizer, *Morals and Markets: The Development of Life Insurance in the United States* (Columbia University Press, 1979).

19. See, for example, John Carson, *The Measure of Merit: Talents, Intelligence, and Inequality in the French and American Republics, 1750–1940* (Princeton University Press, 2006).

20. Laurence Barry, "Insurance, Big Data and Changing Conceptions of Fairness," *European Journal of Sociology / Archives Européennes de Sociologie* 61, no. 2 (2020): 159–84.

21. Sarah Igo, *The Averaged American: Surveys, Citizens, and the Making of a Mass Public* (Harvard University Press, 2007); Sarah Igo, *The Known Citizen: A History of Privacy in Modern America* (Harvard University Press, 2018).

22. Caitlin Rosenthal, *Accounting for Slavery: Masters and Management* (Harvard University Press, 2018); Meredith Whittaker, "Origin Stories: Plantations, Computers, and Industrial Control," *Logic(s)*, no. 19, https://logicmag.io/supa-dupa-skies/origin-stories-plantations-computers-and-industrial-control/; Elton Mayo, *The Human Problems of an Industrial Civilization* (Macmillan, 1933); Frederick Winslow Taylor, *The Principles of Scientific Management* (Harper and Brothers, 1911). See also Stephen P. Meyer III, *The Five Dollar Day: Labor Management and Social Control in the Ford Motor Company, 1908–1921* (SUNY Press, 1981).

23. David F. Noble, *America by Design: Science, Technology, and the Rise of Corporate Capitalism* (Alfred A. Knopf, 1977).

24. Christine von Oertzen, "Machineries of Data Power: Manual versus Mechanical Census Compilation in Nineteenth-Century Europe," *Osiris* 32, no. 1 (2017): 129–50.

25. Jon Agar, *The Government Machine: A Revolutionary History of the Computer* (MIT Press, 2003); Edwin Black, *IBM and the Holocaust: The Strategic Alliance between Nazi Germany and America's Most Powerful Corporation* (Crown, 2001).

26. Louis Hyman, "Temps, Consultants, and the Rise of the Precarious Economy," *Hedgehog Review* 18, no. 1 (2016): 17–32. Meanwhile, workplaces were becoming more and more institutionalized—that is, more and more subject to the elaboration of policies, regulations, and procedures. The nascent quasi-profession of human resource management increasingly formalized detailed standards for "best practices" and monitored compliance with the general requirements of the law. See, for example, Frank Dobbin, *Inventing Equal Opportunity* (Princeton University Press, 2009).

27. Ensmenger, "The Environmental History of Computing," S13.

28. Jon Agar, "What Difference Did Computers Make?," *Social Studies of Science* 36, no. 6 (2006): 869–907.

29. Chris Wiggins and Matthew L. Jones, *How Data Happened: A History from the Age of Reason to the Age of Algorithms* (W. W. Norton, 2023), chapter 8.

30. On the concept of "data double," see Dan Bouk, "The National Data Center and the Rise of the Data Double," *Historical Studies in the Natural Sciences* 48, no. 5 (2018): 627–36; Kevin D. Haggerty and Richard V. Ericson, "The Surveillant Assemblage," *British Journal of Sociology* 51, no. 4 (2000): 605–22.

31. As Zuboff, *The Age of Surveillance Capitalism*, 69–70, notes,

> In addition to key words, each Google search query produces a wake of collateral data such as the number and pattern of search terms, how a query is phrased, spelling, punctuation, dwell times, click patterns, and location. Early on, these behavioral by-products were haphazardly stored and operationally ignored. Amit Patel, a young Stanford graduate student with special interest in "data mining," is frequently credited with the groundbreaking insight into the significance of Google's accidental data caches. His work with these data logs persuaded him that detailed stories about each user—thoughts, feelings, interests— could be constructed from the wake of unstructured signals that trailed every online action. These data, he concluded, actually provided a "broad sensor of human behavior" and could be put to immediate use in realizing cofounder Larry Page's dream of Search as a comprehensive artificial intelligence. Google's engineers soon grasped that the

continuous flows of collateral behavioral data could turn the search engine into a recursive learning system that constantly improved search results and spurred product innovations such as spell check, translation, and voice recognition. . . . What had been regarded as waste material—"data exhaust" spewed into Google's servers during the combustive action of Search—was quickly reimagined as a critical element in the transformation of Google's search engine into a reflexive process of continuous learning and improvement.

32. Evgeny Morozov makes this point in his critique of Zuboff: Morozov, "Capitalism's New Clothes," *Baffler*, February 4, 2019, https://thebaffler.com/latest/capitalisms-new-clothes-morozov.

33. Peter L. Berger and Thomas Luckmann, *The Social Construction of Reality: A Treatise in the Sociology of Knowledge* (Anchor, 1967); John W. Meyer and Brian Rowan, "Institutionalized Organizations: Formal Structure as Myth and Ceremony," *American Journal of Sociology* 83, no. 2 (1977): 340–63.

34. Cohen, *Between Truth and Power*; Margaret Jane Radin, *Boilerplate: The Fine Print, Vanishing Rights, and the Rule of Law* (Princeton University Press, 2013). See also Amy Kapczynski, "The Law of Informational Capitalism," *Yale Law Journal* 129, no. 5 (2020): 1460–515.

35. Paul J. DiMaggio and Walter W. Powell, "The Iron Cage Revisited: Institutional Isomorphism and Collective Rationality in Organizational Fields," *American Sociological Review* 48 (1983): 147–60. See also David Graeber, *Bullshit Jobs: A Theory* (Simon and Schuster, 2019).

36. Max Weber, "Science as a Vocation," in *From Max Weber*, 137.

37. Kitchin, *The Data Revolution*, 8.

38. Gérard Noiriel, *L'identification: Genèse d'un travail d'état* (Belin, 2007). See also David Lyon, *Identifying Citizens: ID Cards as Surveillance* (Polity, 2009).

39. Igo, *The Known Citizen*.

40. Fred Block and Matthew Keller, *State of Innovation: The U.S. Government's Role in Technology Development* (Routledge, 2016); Nathan Newman, *Net Loss: Internet Prophets, Private Profits and the Costs to Community* (Pennsylvania State University Press, 2002).

41. Keith Breckenridge, *Biometric State: The Global Politics of Identification and Surveillance in South Africa, 1850 to the Present* (Cambridge University Press, 2014); Lyon, *Identifying Citizens.*

42. Kean Birch, D. T. Cochrane, and Callum Ward, "Data as Asset? The Measurement, Governance, and Valuation of Digital Personal Data by Big Tech," *Big Data and Society* 8, no. 1 (2021), https://doi.org/10.1177/20539517211017308.

43. Oscar Gandy Jr., *The Panoptic Sort: A Political Economy of Personal Information* (Westview, 1993); Josh Lauer, *Creditworthy: A History of Consumer Surveillance and Financial Identity in America* (Columbia University Press, 2017).

44. Justin Sherman, "Data Brokers and Sensitive Data on U.S. Individuals: Threats to American Civil Rights, National Security, and Democracy" (research paper, Duke Sanford Cyber Policy Program, August 2021), https://techpolicy.sanford.duke.edu/wp-content/uploads/sites/4/2021/08/Data-Brokers-and-Sensitive-Data-on-US-Individuals-Sherman-2021.pdf.

45. Tactical Tech, "The Dating Brokers: An Autopsy of Online Love," October 31, 2018, https://tacticaltech.org/news/dating-brokers/. The brokers' business model is under increasing pressure from regulators (especially in Europe), from companies that rely on advertising and tracking (in the United States), and sometimes from the state wanting to assume the role of data broker itself (in China).

46. Sam Biddle, "ICE Searched LexisNexis Database over 1 Million Times in Just Seven Months," Intercept, June 9, 2022, https://theintercept.com/2022/06/09/ice-lexisnexis-mass-surveillances/; Sam Biddle, "LexisNexis to Provide Giant Database of Personal Information to ICE," Intercept, April 2, 2021, https://theintercept.com/2021/04/02/ice-database-surveillance-lexisnexis/. The enormously important role of private contracts with police, border, intelligence, and military agencies in the development and deployment of surveillance and security technologies, in the United States and elsewhere (e.g., Israel), merits its own treatment. Many of these technologies are often repurposed for commercial use. See for instance Nitsan Chorev, "The Political Economy of Surveillance-for-Hire: Military Capitalism in

Israel and Intelligence Commercialization Worldwide" (working paper, Brown University, October 2023).

47. This lore goes back to the earliest days of large-scale software development. See, most famously, Fred Brooks, *The Mythical Man Month: Essays on Software Engineering* (Addison Wesley, 1975).

48. Matthew J. Salganik, *Bit by Bit: Social Research in the Digital Age* (Princeton University Press, 2018), 13–40.

49. Frank Pasquale, *The Black Box Society: The Secret Algorithms That Control Money and Information* (Harvard University Press, 2015), 8.

50. Meredith Broussard, *Artificial Unintelligence: How Computers Misunderstand the World* (MIT Press, 2018); Hannah Fry, *Hello World: Being Human in the Age of Algorithms* (W. W. Norton, 2018); Arvind Narayanan and Sayash Kapoor, "Introducing the AI Snake Oil Book Project," AI Snake Oil, August 25, 2022, https://www.aisnakeoil.com/p/introducing-the-ai-snake-oil-book; Benjamin Recht, "Reflections on Random Kitchen Sinks," *arg min blog*, December 5, 2017, https://www.argmin.net/2017/12/05/kitchen-sinks/.

51. François Chollet and J. J. Allaire, *Deep Learning with R* (Manning, 2018), 5.

52. Jenna Burrell, "How the Machine 'Thinks': Understanding Opacity in Machine Learning Algorithms," *Big Data and Society* 3, no. 1 (2016), https://doi.org/10.1177/2053951715622512.

53. W. N. Venables and B. D. Ripley, *Modern Applied Statistics with S* (Springer, 2002), 342. Logistic regression is the variety of linear model where the outcome of interest can take one of two values only (yes or no, true or false, success or failure, present or absent, and so on).

54. The most significant early success was in image recognition as applied US postal codes on handwritten envelopes. See Yann LeCun, Léon Bottou, Yoshua Bengio, and Patrick Haffner, "Gradient-Based Learning Applied to Document Recognition," *Proceedings of the IEEE* 86, no. 11 (1998): 2278–324. Their main competitors were kernel-based methods, especially support vector machines. These had, at the time, the twin advantages of being better grounded analytically and more interpretable

in use. See Corinna Cortes and Vladimir Vapnik, "Support-Vector Networks," *Machine Learning* 20, no. 3 (1995): 273–97.

55. As Ian Goodfellow, Yoshua Bengio, and Aaron Courville, *Deep Learning* (MIT Press, 2016), 223, note, "Rather than being viewed as an unreliable technology that must be supported by other techniques, gradient-based learning in feedforward networks has been viewed since 2012 as a powerful technology that can be applied to many other machine learning tasks. In 2006, the community used unsupervised learning to support supervised learning, and now, ironically, it is more common to use supervised learning to support unsupervised learning."

56. For an introductory overview to deep-learning approaches, see Chollet and Allaire, *Deep Learning with R;* and Gareth James Daniela Witten, Trevor Hastie, and Robert Tibshirani, *An Introduction to Statistical Learning with Applications in R* (Springer, 2021), especially chapter 10. James and colleagues also provide an accessible tour of machine-learning methods more generally. For a useful discussion contrasting classical linear modeling and machine-learning approaches from the point of view of social science research, see Julien Boelaert and Étienne Ollion, "The Great Regression," *Revue Française de Sociologie* 59, no. 3 (2018): 475–506.

57. Crawford, *Atlas of AI,* 93.

58. As Michel Foucault, *Discipline and Punish: The Birth of the Prison,* trans. Alan Sheridan (Vintage, 1995), 228, asks, "Is it surprising that the cellular prison, with its regular chronologies, forced labor, authorities of surveillance and registration, its experts in normality, who continue and multiply the functions of the judge, should have become the modern instrument of penalty? Is it surprising that prisons resemble factories, schools, barracks, hospitals, which all resemble prisons?" See also Mark Andrejevic, *Automated Media* (Routledge, 2019), 53.

59. Max Kuhn and Kjell Johnson, *Feature Engineering and Selection* (CRC Press, 2020).

60. Norms and expectations for how, exactly, to go about this methodologically have shifted substantially over the past fifteen years across the social sciences. Many once standard approaches are now seen as

unacceptably complacent about causal identification and incorrect on the details of model fitting. See, for example, Andrew Gelman, Jennifer Hill, and Aki Vehtari, *Regression and Other Stories* (Cambridge University Press, 2021); Richard McElreath, *Statistical Rethinking: A Bayesian Course with Examples in R and Stan* (Chapman and Hall / CRC, 2020); and Judea Pearl, Madelyn Glymour, and Nicholas P. Jewell, *Causal Inference in Statistics: A Primer* (Wiley, 2016).

61. Barbara Kiviat, "The Moral Limits of Predictive Practices: The Case of Credit-Based Insurance Scores," *American Sociological Review* 84, no. 6 (2019): 1134–58; Barbara Kiviat, "Which Data Fairly Differentiate? American Views on the Use of Personal Data in Two Market Settings," *Sociological Science* 8 (2021): 26–47.

62. Inioluwa Deborah Raji, Emily M. Bender, Amandalynne Paullada, Emily Denton, and Alex Hanna, "AI and the Everything in the Whole Wide World Benchmark" (research paper, November 26, 2021), arXiv, https://arxiv.org/abs/2111.15366.

63. Virginia Eubanks, *Automating Inequality: How High-Tech Tools Profile, Police, and Punish the Poor* (St. Martin's, 2017), 129.

64. Stuart Russell, *Human Compatible: Artificial Intelligence and the Problem of Control* (Viking, 2019).

65. Zahira Jaser, Dimitra Petrakaki, Rachel Starr, and Ernesto Oyarbide-Magaña, "Where Automated Job Interviews Fall Short," *Harvard Business Review,* January 27, 2022, https://hbr.org/2022/01/where-automated-job-interviews-fall-short; Luke Stark and Jevan Hutson, "Physiognomic Artificial Intelligence," *Fordham Intellectual Property, Media and Entertainment Law Journal* 32, no. 4 (2022): 922.

66. Recht, "Reflections on Random Kitchen Sinks."

67. Tyler Vigen, *Spurious Correlations* (Hachette, 2015).

68. A particularly elegant example is Stephan Valavanis, *Econometrics: An Introduction to Maximum-Likelihood Methods* (McGraw-Hill, 1959), 83: "Econometric theory is like an exquisitely balanced French recipe, spelling out precisely with how many turns to mix the sauce, how many carats of spice to add, and for how many milliseconds to bake the mixture at exactly 474 degrees of temperature. But when the statistical

cook turns to raw materials, he finds that hearts of cactus fruit are unavailable, so he substitutes chunks of cantaloupe; where the recipe calls for vermicelli he uses shredded wheat; and he substitutes green garment die for curry, ping-pong balls for turtles eggs, and for Chalifougnac vintage 1883, a can of turpentine."

69. Ruth Schwartz Cowan, "Francis Galton's Statistical Ideas: The Influence of Eugenics," *Isis* 63, no. 4 (1972): 509–28; Thomas C. Leonard, "Retrospectives: Eugenics and Economics in the Progressive Era," *Journal of Economic Perspectives* 19, no. 4 (2005): 207–24; Edmund Ramsden, "Confronting the Stigma of Eugenics: Genetics, Demography and the Problems of Population," *Social Studies of Science* 39, no. 6 (2009): 853–84; Richard A. Soloway, *Demography and Degeneration: Eugenics and the Declining Birthrate in Twentieth-Century Britain* (University of North Carolina Press, 1995).

3. Classification Situations

1. Caleb Richard Scoville, "A 'Stupid Little Fish': Science, Law and the Politics of Environmental Decline in California" (PhD diss., University of California–Berkeley, 2020).

2. Berger and Luckmann, *The Social Construction of Reality*, 1–128.

3. Paul Starr, *Entrenchment: Wealth, Power, and the Constitution of Democratic Societies* (Yale University Press, 2019).

4. Geoffrey C. Bowker and Susan Leigh Star, *Sorting Things Out: Classification and Its Consequences* (MIT Press, 2000); Paul Starr, "Social Categories and Claims in the Liberal State," *Social Research* 59, no. 2 (1992): 263–95.

5. Ian Hacking, *The Social Construction of What?* (Harvard University Press, 1999), 104.

6. Nancy Fraser, "From Redistribution to Recognition? Dilemmas of Justice in a 'Post-Socialist' Age," *New Left Review*, August 1, 1995, 68–93; Charles Taylor, "The Politics of Recognition," in *Multiculturalism: Examining the Politics of Recognition*, ed. Amy Gutmann (Princeton University Press, 1994), 25–73.

7. Haggerty and Ericson, "The Surveillant Assemblage"; Felix Stalder and
    David Lyon, "Electronic Identity Cards and Social Classification," in
    Surveillance as Social Sorting: Privacy, Risk, and Digital Discrimination,
    ed. David Lyon (Psychology Press, 2003), 77–93.

8. Gandy, *The Panoptic Sort,* 15.

9. Gandy, *The Panoptic Sort,* 1.

10. Nick Seaver, *Computing Taste: Algorithms and the Makers of Music
    Recommendation* (University of Chicago Press, 2022).

11. Marion Fourcade and Kieran Healy, "Classification Situations: Life-
    Chances in the Neoliberal Era," *Accounting, Organizations and Society*
    38, no. 8 (2013): 559–72.

12. Miller McPherson, "An Ecology of Affiliation," *American Sociological
    Review* 48 (1983): 519–32; J. Miller McPherson, Lynn Smith-Lovin, and
    James M. Cook, "Birds of a Feather: Homophily in Social Networks,"
    Annual Review of Sociology 27 (2001): 415–44.

13. Douglas Heaven, "Why Deep-Learning AIs Are So Easy to Fool,"
    Nature 574, no. 7777 (2019): 163–66; Kashmir Hill, "Wrongfully
    Accused by an Algorithm," *New York Times,* June 24, 2020.

14. Ruha Benjamin, *Race after Technology: Abolitionist Tools for the New
    Jim Code* (Polity, 2019); Noble, *Algorithms of Oppression.*

15. Milagros Miceli, Tianling Yang, Adriana Alvarado Garcia, Julian
    Posada, Sonja Mei Wang, Marc Pohl, and Alex Hanna, "Documenting
    Data Production Processes: A Participatory Approach for Data Work"
    (research paper, July 11, 2022), arXiv, https://arxiv.org/abs/2207
    .04958.

16. Joy Buolamwini and Timnit Gebru, "Gender Shades: Intersectional
    Accuracy Disparities in Commercial Gender Classification," *Proceed-
    ings of Machine Learning Research* 81 (2018): 1–15; Jeffrey Dastin,
    "Amazon Scraps Secret AI Recruiting Tool That Showed Bias against
    Women," Reuters, October 10, 2018, https://www.reuters.com/article
    /us-amazon-com-jobs-automation-insight/amazon-scraps-secret-ai
    -recruiting-tool-that-showed-bias-against-women-idUSKCN1MK08G.

17. Indeed, Amazon used an automated process to fire underperforming
    workers. See Spencer Soper, "Fired by Bot at Amazon: 'It's You against

the Machine'," Bloomberg.com, June 28, 2021, https://www.bloomberg
.com/news/features/2021-06-28/fired-by-bot-amazon-turns-to
-machine-managers-and-workers-are-losing-out.

18. Philip Cimiano, Christian Chiarcos, John P. McCrae, and Jorge Gracia,
Linguistic Linked Data: Representation, Generation and Applications
(Springer, 2020); Brent Hecht and Darren Gergle, "The Tower of Babel
Meets Web 2.0: User-Generated Content and Its Applications in a
Multilingual Context," in *Proceedings of the SIGCHI Conference on
Human Factors in Computing Systems* (Association for Computing
Machinery, 2010), 291–300.

19. Eubanks, *Automating Inequality*.

20. Larissa MacFarquhar, "The Separation: When Should a Child Be
Removed from His Home?," *New Yorker*, August 7, 2017, 36–47.

21. John R. Zech, Marcus A. Badgeley, Manway Liu, Anthony B. Costa,
Joseph J. Titano, and Eric Karl Oermann, "Variable Generalization
Performance of a Deep Learning Model to Detect Pneumonia in Chest
Radiographs: A Cross-sectional Study," *PLOS Medicine* 15, no. 11
(2018): e1002683. For a similar kind of problem, where a model to
detect malignant skin lesions learned that pictures of malignant
lesions were more likely to come with a ruler, which doctors used to
assess whether a lesion had grown over time, see Akhila Narla, Brett
Kuprel, Kavita Sarin, Roberto A. Novoa, and Justin Ko, "Automated
Classification of Skin Lesions: From Pixels to Practice," *Journal of
Investigative Dermatology* 138, no. 10 (2018): 2108–10.

22. Robert Geirhos, Jörn-Henrik Jacobsen, Claudio Michaelis, Richard
Zemel, Wieland Brendel, Matthias Bethge, and Felix A. Wichmann,
"Shortcut Learning in Deep Neural Networks," *Nature Machine
Intelligence* 2, no. 11 (2020): 665–73.

23. Louise Amoore, *Cloud Ethics: Algorithms and the Attributes of
Ourselves and Others* (Duke University Press, 2020).

24. Louise Amoore, "The Deep Border," *Political Geography*, November 25,
2021, https://www.sciencedirect.com/science/article/pii
/S0962629821002079; John Cheney-Lippold, "Jus Algoritmi: How the
National Security Agency Remade Citizenship," *International Journal
of Communication* 10 (2016): 1721–42. See also Joel R. Reidenberg, "Lex

Informatica: The Formulation of Information Policy Rules through Technology," *Texas Law Review* 76, no. 3 (1997–98): 553–94.

25. Amoore, *Cloud Ethics*; John Cheney-Lippold, *We Are Data: Algorithms and the Making of Our Digital Selves* (NYU Press, 2018).

26. In an earlier version of this argument, we used the term *ubercapital*. We explain here why we think *eigencapital* better captures what we mean. Marion Fourcade and Kieran Healy, "Seeing Like a Market," *Socio-economic Review* 15, no. 1 (2017): 9–29.

27. Lewis Namier, quoted in Alan Bennett, *Writing Home* (Picador, 2003), 486–87.

28. In German, *eigencapital* is a financial term that refers to equity, or any capital raised through selling shares.

29. Pierre Bourdieu, "Les trois états du capital culturel," *Actes de La Recherche En Sciences Sociales* 30 (1979): 3–6.

30. Barry Schwartz, "Waiting, Exchange, and Power: The Distribution of Time in Social Systems," *American Journal of Sociology* 79, no. 4 (1974): 841.

31. Thorstein Veblen, *The Theory of the Leisure Class,* ed. Martha Banta (Oxford University Press, 2009).

32. Kunal Sawarkar, "How to Subjectively Route Incoming Calls by Predicting Their Importance," *Medium,* July 14, 2020, https://medium .com/inside-machine-learning/how-to-subjectively-route-calls-by -predicting-incoming-call-importance-1146da95338e.

33. Jordan Brensinger, "Data Work: The Nature and Implications of Managing Personal Information in Everyday Life" (presentation, Center for the Study of Social Difference, Columbia University, September 23, 2020).

34. Jennifer Streaks, "The Financial Literacy App Teaching Kids about Credit," *Forbes,* September 18, 2020, https://www.forbes.com/sites /forbestheculture/2020/09/18/the-financial-literacy-app-teaching -kids-about-credit/.

35. For a discussion of the moral economy of data in a different context (the protection of privacy), see Janet Vertesi, Jofish Kaye, Samantha N.

Jarosewski, Vera D. Khovanskaya, and Jenna Song, "Data Narratives: Uncovering Tensions in Personal Data Management," in *Proceedings of the 19th ACM Conference on Computer-Supported Cooperative Work and Social Computing, CSCW 2016* (Association for Computing Machinery, 2016), 478–90. On "machine socialization," see Massimo Airoldi, *Machine Habitus: Toward a Sociology of Algorithms* (Polity, 2022).

36. Shazeda Ahmed, "State-Firm Co-production of China's Social Credit System" (PhD diss., University of California–Berkeley, 2022); Chuncheng Liu, "Governing Everything: The Sociopolitical Life of a Social Credit System in China" (PhD diss., University of California–San Diego, 2023).

37. Shazeda Ahmed, "The Messy Truth about Social Credit," *Logic,* May 1, 2019, https://logicmag.io/china/the-messy-truth-about-social-credit/; Severin Engelmann, Mo Chen, Lorenz Dang, and Jens Grossklags, "Blacklists and Redlists in the Chinese Social Credit System: Diversity, Flexibility, and Comprehensiveness," in *Proceedings of the 2021 AAAI/ACM Conference on AI, Ethics, and Society* (Association for Computing Machinery, 2021), 78–88; Simina Mistreanu, "Life inside China's Social Credit Laboratory," *Foreign Policy,* April 3, 2018, https://foreignpolicy.com/2018/04/03/life-inside-chinas-social-credit-laboratory/.

38. Dev Lewis, "Separating Myth from Reality: How China's Social Credit System Uses Public Data for Social Governance," in *The AI Powered State: China's Approach to Public Sector Innovation,* comp. Hessy Elliot (Nesta, 2020), 43–50.

39. Liav Orgad and Wessel Reijers, "How to Make the Perfect Citizen—Lessons from China's Social Credit System," *Vanderbilt Journal of Transnational Law* 54, no. 5 (2021): 1087–121.

40. In the summer of 2022, the *New York Times* used a trove of leaked documents from the Chinese AI firm Megvii to report on the proposed deployment of tools to prevent both traditional and algorithmic classes of people from moving about their country, province, or district. Those flagged for suspicious behavior included "local petitioners" who had made various complaints to their local authorities; stigmatized groups such as the mentally ill, migrants, or people infected with HIV; and individuals who frequented closely monitored locations. See Paul

Mozur, Muyi Xiao, and John Liu, "'An Invisible Cage': How China Is Policing the Future," *New York Times,* June 26, 2022.

41. This is the general problem of "commensuration" well known to sociologists. See Wendy Nelson Espeland and Mitchell L. Stevens, "Commensuration as a Social Process," *Annual Review of Sociology* 24, no. 1 (1998): 313–43.

42. Barbara Kiviat, "Going against the Record: How Algorithms Shape the Way Landlords Make Exceptions for Bad Background Checks" (colloquium, Social Science Department, University of California–Berkeley, January 30, 2023); Akos Rona-Tas, "The Off-Label Use of Consumer Credit Ratings," *Historical Social Research / Historische Sozialforschung* 42 (2017): 52–76; Eva Rosen, Philip M. E. Garboden, and Jennifer E. Cossyleon, "Racial Discrimination in Housing: How Landlords Use Algorithms and Home Visits to Screen Tenants," *American Sociological Review* 86, no. 5 (2021): 787–822; Julien Migozzi, "The Good, the Bad and the Tenant: Rental Platforms Renewing Racial Capitalism in the Post-Apartheid Housing Market," *Environment and Planning D: Society and Space* (2023), https://doi.org/10.1177/02637758231195962.

43. Alya Guseva and Akos Rona-Tas, "Uncertainty, Risk, and Trust: Russian and American Credit Card Markets Compared," *American Sociological Review* 66, no. 5 (2001): 623–46.

44. See Sarabjit Singh Bajeva, Anish Das Sarma, and Nilesh Dalvi, Determining trustworthiness and compatibility of a person, US patent 10,169,708 B2, filed January 1, 2019.

45. Fourcade and Healy, "Classification Situations"; Marx, *Capital.*

4. The Great Unbundling

Epigraph: Jim Barksdale, quoted in Justin Fox, "How to Succeed in Business by Bundling—and Unbundling," *Harvard Business Review,* June 24, 2014, https://hbr.org/2014/06/how-to-succeed-in-business-by -bundling-and-unbundling.

1. Adam Smith [George J. Goodman], *The Money Game* (Vintage, 1976).

2. Juan Pablo Pardo-Guerra, *Automating Finance: Infrastructures, Engineers, and the Making of Electronic Markets* (Cambridge

University Press, 2019); Caitlin Zaloom, *Out of the Pits: Traders and Technology from Chicago to London* (University of Chicago Press, 2006), 137.

3. Donald MacKenzie, "How Algorithms Interact: Goffman's 'Interaction Order' in Automated Trading," *Theory, Culture and Society* 36, no. 2 (2019): 39–59.

4. Josh Lauer, "Plastic Surveillance: Payment Cards and the History of Transactional Data, 1888 to Present," *Big Data and Society* 7, no. 1 (2020), https://doi.org/10.1177/2053951720907632. See also Gandy, *The Panoptic Sort;* and Lauer, *Creditworthy.*

5. Lauer, "Plastic Surveillance.".

6. American Express advertisement, quoted in Dan Schiller, *How to Think about Information* (University of Illinois Press, 2006), 3.

7. Lauer, "Plastic Surveillance."

8. See Sadowski, *Too Smart.*

9. Marshall McLuhan anticipated this shift in his 1958 classic *Understanding Media: The Extensions of Man* (MIT Press, 1994), 137: "As work is replaced by the sheer movement of information, money as a store of work merges with the informational forms of credit and credit card. From coin to paper currency, and from currency to credit card there is a steady progression toward commercial exchange as the movement of information itself."

10. This is a matter of discovery rather than calculation. Hayek's point is that the price system *reveals* all this information, not simply that it aggregates some huge but already available pile of data in a way that a central planner with a very fast computer could, in principle, replicate. This idea was subsequently made more precise by Leonid Hurwicz, leading to the literature on "incentive compatible" market mechanisms. See Leonid Hurwicz, "On Informationally Decentralized Systems," in *Decision and Organization: A Volume in Honor of Jacob Marschak,* ed. C. B. McGuire and Roy Radner (North Holland, 1972), 297–336.

11. F. A. Hayek, "The Use of Knowledge in Society," *American Economic Review* 35, no. 4 (1945): 519–30. Hayek's formulation of the "knowledge problem," incidentally, was largely derived from Ludwig von Mises and widely shared by Austrian economists, philosophers, and

sociologists, including Alfred Schutz. See Christian Knudsen, "Alfred Schutz, Austrian Economists and the Knowledge Problem," *Rationality and Society* 16, no. 1 (2004): 45–89.

12. The literature on this topic is enormous. By way of illustration, see Theodore C. Bestor, *Tsukiji: The Fish Market at the Center of the World* (University of California Press, 2004); Clifford Geertz, "The Bazaar Economy: Information and Search in Peasant Marketing," *American Economic Review* 68, no. 2 (1978): 28–32; Robert Jensen, "The Digital Provide: Information (Technology), Market Performance, and Welfare in the South Indian Fisheries Sector," *Quarterly Journal of Economics* 122, no. 3 (2007): 879–924; and Alan P. Kirman, "The Economy as an Interactive System," in *The Economy as an Evolving Complex System II,* ed. W. Brian Arthur, Steven N. Durlauf, and David A. Lane (CRC Press, 1997).

13. Morozov acknowledges, however, that even for Hayek a market system does not rely solely on prices because people will "acquire other forms of information" that are also relevant to the competitive process. See Evgeny Morozov, "Digital Socialism? The Calculation Debate in the Age of Big Data," *New Left Review* 116–117 (2019): 33–67.

14. Jim Farber, "Bespoke This, Bespoke That. Enough Already." *New York Times,* August 8, 2016.

15. Viktor Mayer-Schönberger and Thomas Ramge, *Reinventing Capitalism in the Age of Big Data* (Basic Books, 2018).

16. Zuboff, *The Age of Surveillance Capitalism.*

17. The technology sector has been one of the most concentrated in a heavily concentrated economy, even before the onset of the COVID-19 pandemic. See Thomas Philippon, *The Great Reversal: How America Gave Up on Free Markets* (Belknap Press, 2019); and Joseph E. Stiglitz, "Market Concentration Is Threatening the US Economy," *Project Syndicate,* March 11, 2019, https://www.project-syndicate.org /commentary/united-states-economy-rising-market-power-by-joseph -e-stiglitz-2019-03?barrier=accesspaylog.

18. Cédric Durand, *Techno-féodalisme: Critique de l'économie numérique* (La Découverte, 2020); Yanis Varoufakis, *Technofeudalism: What Killed Capitalism* (London: Penguin, 2023). For a critique of the concept, see Evgeny Morozov, "Critique of Techno-Feudal Reason," *New Left Review* 133–134 (2022): 89–126; and, for Durand's response,

see Cédric Durand, "Scouting Capital's Frontiers," *New Left Review* 136 (2022): 29–39.

19. Diane Coyle writes: "If [platforms] are not huge, they are usually dead. These are the basics of digital platform economics and it makes the way that markets operate different from the mental model in economics." Coyle, *Cogs and Monsters: What Economics Is, and What It Should Be* (Princeton University Press, 2021), 176.

20. David O. Sacks and Peter A. Thiel, *The Diversity Myth: Multiculturalism and the Politics of Intolerance at Stanford* (Independent Institute, 1996); Peter Thiel and Blake Masters, *Zero to One: Notes on Startups, or How to Build the Future* (Currency, 2014).

21. Peter Thiel, "Competition Is for Losers," *Wall Street Journal*, September 12, 2014.

22. Schumpeter, *Capitalism, Socialism, and Democracy*. For an eminently readable summary of the neo-Schumpeterian literature in economics, see Paul M. Romer, "The Origins of Endogenous Growth," *Journal of Economic Perspectives* 8, no. 1 (1994): 3–22. See also David Warsh, *Knowledge and the Wealth of Nations: A Story of Economic Discovery* (W. W. Norton, 2006).

23. Paul A. Baran and Paul M. Sweezy, *Monopoly Capitalism: An Essay on the American Economic and Social Order* (Monthly Review Press, 1966); Joan Robinson, *The Economics of Imperfect Competition* (Macmillan, 1961).

24. Although that theorization came late, after major antitrust law legislation was passed in the United States, it is an important tenet of the economics canon today. See Anne Mayhew, "How American Economists Came to Love the Sherman Antitrust Act," *History of Political Economy* 30, supplement (1998): 179–201.

25. Arindrajit Dube, Jeff Jacobs, Suresh Naidu, and Siddharth Suri, "Monopsony in Online Labor Markets," *American Economic Review: Insights* 2, no. 1 (2020): 33–46.

26. As Mayer-Schönberger and Ramge, *Reinventing Capitalism*, 163, note, "The scale effect lowers the cost, the network effect expands utility, and the feedback effect improves the product."

27. Evgeny Morozov, "Socialize the Data Centres!," *New Left Review* 91 (2015): 56. See also Tejas N. Narechania, "Machine Learning as Natural Monopoly," *Iowa Law Review* 107 (2022): 1543–614.

28. Coyle, *Cogs and Monsters;* Srnicek, *Platform Capitalism.*

29. Lina M. Khan, "Amazon's Antitrust Paradox," *Yale Law Journal* 126, no. 3 (2016–2017): 710–805; Moira Weigel, "Amazon's Trickle-Down Monopoly: Third-Party Sellers and the Transformation of Small Business" (research paper, Data & Society Research Institute, 2023), https://papers.ssrn.com/sol3/papers.cfm?abstract_id=4317167.

30. Leon Yin and Adrianne Jeffries, "How We Analyzed Amazon's Treatment of Its Brands in Search Results," The Markup, October 14, 2021, https://themarkup.org/amazons-advantage/2021/10/14/how-we -analyzed-amazons-treatment-of-its-brands-in-search-results.

31. Dina Srinivasan, "Why Google Dominates Advertising Markets," *Stanford Technology Law Review* 24 (2020–2021): 55; U.S. et al. v. Google LLC, No. 1-23-CV-00018 (E.D.Va., 2023), "Complaint," September 15, 2022, Docket No. 1.

32. Cory Doctorow, "The 'Enshittification' of TikTok," *Wired,* January 23, 2023, https://www.wired.com/story/tiktok-platforms-cory-doctorow/, colloquially calls this process—a straightforward consequence of the search for monopolistic profits—"platform enshittification": "Surpluses are first directed to users; then, once they're locked in, surpluses go to suppliers; then once they're locked in, the surplus is handed to shareholders and the platform becomes a useless pile of shit." For a presentation of the same ideas, see Rebecca Giblin and Cory Doctorow, *Chokepoint Capitalism: How Big Tech and Big Content Captured Creative Labor Markets and How We'll Win Them Back* (Beacon Press, 2022). For earlier statements, see Wu, *The Master Switch;* and Durand, *Techno-féodalisme.*

33. Martin Chorzempa, "China's Campaign to Regulate Big Tech Is More Than Just Retaliation," *Nikkei Asia,* August 3, 2021, https://asia.nikkei .com/Opinion/China-s-campaign-to-regulate-Big-Tech-is-more-than -just-retaliation.

34. Deleuze, "Postscript on the Societies of Control."

35. Mark E. Bergen, Shantanu Dutta, James Guszcza, and Mark J. Zbaracki, "How AI Can Help Companies Set Prices More Ethically," *Harvard Business Review,* March 26, 2021, https://hbr.org/2021/03/how-ai-can-help-companies-set-prices-more-ethically.

36. Heather Vogell, "Rent Going Up? One Company's Algorithm Could Be Why," ProPublica, October 15, 2022, https://www.propublica.org/article/yieldstar-rent-increase-realpage-rent.

37. Dirk Bergemann, Benjamin Brooks, and Stephen Morris, "The Limits of Price Discrimination," *American Economic Review* 105, no. 3 (2015): 921–57.

38. Liran Einav, Mark Jenkins, and Jonathan Levin, "Contract Pricing in Consumer Credit Markets," *Econometrica* 80, no. 4 (2012): 1387–432; Hong Ru and Antoinette Schoar, "Do Credit Card Companies Screen for Behavioural Biases?" (BIS Working Paper No. 814, Bank for International Settlements, Basel, Switzerland, February 12, 2020), https://www.bis.org/publ/work842.htm; Ryan Calo, "Digital Market Manipulation," *George Washington Law Review* 82, no. 4 (2013–2014): 995–1051.

39. In the domain of credit, see, for example, Mehrsa Baradaran, *The Color of Money: Black Banks and the Racial Wealth Gap* (Belknap Press, 2019); Rachel Dwyer, "Credit, Debt, and Inequality," *Annual Review of Sociology* 44 (2018): 237–61; David M. P. Freund, *Colored Property: State Policy and White Racial Politics in Suburban America* (University of Chicago Press, 2007); Louise Seamster and Raphael Charron-Chénier, "Predatory Inclusion and Education Debt: Rethinking the Racial Wealth Gap," *Social Currents* 4, no. 3 (2017), 199–207; Keeanga-Yamahtta Taylor, *Race for Profit: How Banks and the Real Estate Industry Undermined Black Homeownership* (University of North Carolina Press, 2019).

40. Ifeoma Ajunwa, *The Quantified Worker: Law and Technology in the Modern Workplace* (Cambridge University Press, 2023); Brishen Rogers, *Data and Democracy at Work: Advanced Information Technologies, Labor Law, and the New Working Class* (MIT Press, 2023).

41. See, for instance, the description of Google's "People's Operations" in ShinJoung Yeo, *Behind the Search Box: Google and the Global Internet Industry* (University of Illinois Press, 2023), 131–35.

42. Veena Dubal, "On Algorithmic Wage Discrimination," (research paper, University of California–San Francisco, January 19, 2023), https://papers.ssrn.com/sol3/papers.cfm?abstract_id=4331080; Katherine C. Kellogg, Melissa A. Valentine, and Angéle Christin, "Algorithms at Work: The New Contested Terrain of Control," *Academy of Management Annals* 14, no. 1 (2020): 366–410; Karen E. C. Levy, "The Contexts of Control: Information, Power, and Truck-Driving Work," *Information Society* 31, no. 2 (2015): 160–74; Madison Van Oort, "The Emotional Labor of Surveillance: Digital Control in Fast Fashion Retail," *Critical Sociology* 45, nos. 7–8 (2019): 1167–79.

43. Katharina Pistor, "Rule by Data: The End of Markets? The Market as a Legal Construct," *Law and Contemporary Problems* 83, no. 2 (2020): 101–24.

44. Matthew Ponsford, "iBuyer Beware," *MIT Technology Review*, April 13, 2022, 68–76.

45. See Jathan Sadowski, "The Internet of Landlords: Digital Platforms and New Mechanisms of Rentier Capitalism," *Antipode* 52, no. 2 (2020): 562–80; Kean Birch, "Technoscience Rent: Toward a Theory of Rentiership for Technoscientific Capitalism," *Science, Technology, and Human Values* 45, no. 1 (2020): 3–33.

46. As Chris Jay Hoofnagle, Aniket Kesari, and Aaron Perzanowski, "The Tethered Economy," *George Washington Law Review* 87, no. 4 (2019): 785, define it, tethering is a "strategy of maintaining an ongoing connection between a consumer good and its seller that often renders that good in some way dependent on the seller for its ordinary operation. Such products present as physical goods but often function as vessels for the delivery of services."

47. See Kelly Bronson and Irena Knezevic, "Big Data in Food and Agriculture," *Big Data and Society* 3, no. 1 (2016), https://doi.org/10.1177/2053951716648174; and Nick Srnicek, "The Challenges of Platform Capitalism: Understanding the Logic of a New Business Model," *Juncture* 23, no. 4 (2017): 254–57.

48. Adam Clark Estes, "We're One Step Closer to Self-Farming Farms," Vox, January 8, 2022, https://www.vox.com/recode/2022/1/8/22872749/john-deere-self-driving-tractor-autonomous-farming.

49. Peter Waldman and Lydia Mulvany, "Farmers Fight John Deere over Who Gets to Fix an $800,000 Tractor," *Bloomberg Businessweek,* March 5, 2020, https://www.bloomberg.com/news/features/2020-03 -05/farmers-fight-john-deere-over-who-gets-to-fix-an-800-000 -tractor#xj4y7vzkg.

50. Technology companies, Apple first among them, lobbied heavily against state right to repair bills. Apple changed their position on this issue in 2023.

51. Greta R. Krippner, "The Financialization of the American Economy," *Socio-economic Review* 3, no. 2 (2005): 173–208.

52. Lee Hawkins Jr., "Outside Audit: Guess Why GM Is More Bank Than Car Maker?," *Wall Street Journal,* May 5, 2004.

53. Jesse Newman and Bob Tita, "America's Farmers Turn to Bank of John Deere," *Wall Street Journal,* July 18, 2017.

54. Federal Trade Commission, *FTC Policy Statement on Enforcement Related to Gig Work* (Washington, DC, Federal Trade Commission, September 15, 2022), 3.

55. Caitlin Harrington, "Workers Are Trading Staggering Amounts of Data for 'Payday Loans,'" *Wired,* March 23, 2022, https://www.wired.com /story/payday-loan-data/.

56. Jaeah Lee, "Repo Madness," *Mother Jones,* March / April 2016, 50–51. Note that kill switches have police uses, too, which further multiply their adverse effects on already vulnerable populations.

57. Laurence Barry and Arthur Charpentier, "Personalization as a Promise: Can Big Data Change the Practice of Insurance?," *Big Data and Society* 7, no. 1 (2020), https://doi.org/10.1177/2053951720935143; Ramnath Balasubramanian, Ari Libarikian, and Doug McElhaney, "Insurance 2030—The Impact of AI on the Future of Insurance," McKinsey & Company, March 12, 2021, https://www.mckinsey.com /industries/financial-services/our-insights/insurance-2030-the -impact-of-ai-on-the-future-of-insurance; Jathan Sadowski, "Total Life Insurance: Logics of Anticipatory Control and Actuarial Gover- nance in Insurance Technology," *Social Studies of Science* (2023), https://doi.org/10.1177/03063127231186437.

58. And even there, wide differences remain in various social groups' exposure to car-related risks *posed by others,* from accidents to thefts.

59. Friedrich August von Hayek, "The Pretence of Knowledge," *American Economic Review* 79, no. 6 (1989): 3-7.

60. The passage in Michael C. Jensen and William H. Meckling, "Theory of the Firm: Managerial Behavior, Agency Costs and Ownership Structure," *Journal of Financial Economics* 3, no. 4 (1976): 113, reads in full, "the private corporation or firm is simply one form of a legal fiction which serves as a nexus for contracting relationships and which is also characterized by the existence of divisible residual claims on the assets and cash flows of the organization which can generally be sold without permission of the other contracting individuals."

61. For a related concept in the case of cryptocurrency markets, see Koray Çalışkan, "Platform Works as Stack Economization: Cryptocurrency Markets and Exchanges in Perspective," *Sociologica* 14, no. 3 (2020): 115-42.

5. Layered Financialization

1. Krippner, "The Financialization of the American Economy," 5. See also Giovanni Arrighi, *The Long Twentieth Century: Money, Power and the Origins of Our Times* (Verso, 2010).

2. The relevant sectoral category is traditionally "finance, insurance and real estate" (FIRE).

3. Michel Feher, *Rated Agency: Investee Politics in a Speculative Age,* trans. Gregory Elliott (Zone Books, 2018); Kean Birch and Fabian Muniesa, *Assetization* (MIT Press, 2020); Luc Boltanski and Arnaud Esquerre, *Enrichment: A Critique of Commodities* (Polity, 2020); Ivan Ascher, *Portfolio Society: On the Capitalist Mode of Prediction* (Zone Books, 2016).

4. Tobias A. Huber and Didier Sornette, "Boom, Bust, and Bitcoin: Bitcoin-Bubbles as Innovation Accelerators," *Journal of Economic Issues* 56, no. 1 (2022): 113-36; William H. Janeway, *Doing Capitalism in the Innovation Economy: Reconfiguring the Three-Player Game between Markets, Speculators and the State* (Cambridge University Press, 2018).

5. Michel Callon, "Introduction: The Embeddedness of Economic Markets in Economics," *Sociological Review* 46, no. 1, supplement (1998): 1–57; Bruce G. Carruthers and Arthur L. Stinchcombe, "The Social Structure of Liquidity: Flexibility, Markets, and States," *Theory and Society* 28, no. 3 (1999): 353–82.

6. Boltanski and Esquerre, *Enrichment.* See also Bernard E. Harcourt, *The Illusion of Free Markets: Punishment and the Myth of Natural Order* (Harvard University Press, 2011).

7. Classic studies include William Cronon, *Nature's Metropolis: Chicago and the Great West* (W. W. Norton, 1991); and Marie-France Garcia-Parpet, "The Social Construction of a Perfect Market: The Strawberry Auction at Fontaines-en-Sologne," in *Do Economists Make Markets? On the Performativity of Economics,* ed. Donald MacKenzie, Fabian Muniesa, and Lucia Siu (Princeton University Press, 2008), 20–53.

8. Boltanski and Esquerre, *Enrichment.*

9. Rogers Brubaker, *Hyperconnectivity and Its Discontents* (Polity, 2022).

10. Veena Dubal, "Digital Piecework," *Dissent,* Fall 2020, 37–44.

11. Schwarz, *Sociological Theory for Digital Society.*

12. Tim Hwang, *Subprime Attention Crisis: Advertising and the Time Bomb at the Heart of the Internet* (FSG Originals, 2020); Kevin Mellet and Thomas Beauvisage, "Cookie Monsters: Anatomy of a Digital Market Infrastructure," *Consumption Markets and Culture* 23, no. 2 (2020): 110–29; Hal R. Varian "Online Ad Auctions," *American Economic Review* 99, no. 2 (2009): 430–34.

13. On the convergence between market finance, automation, and the datafication of ocean freight, see Miriam Posner, "Ghost Ships," *Logic(s),* December 21, 2022, https://logicmag.io/pivot/ghost-ships/.

14. Robinhood, "How Robinhood Makes Money," web page, n.d., accessed November 1, 2020, https://robinhood.com/us/en/support/articles /how-robinhood-makes-money/.

15. The key point is that if you invest in some shares and your investment goes bad, you can lose whatever amount it was that you put down. If your position on some highly leveraged options goes bad, however, you can lose everything you have.

16. Spencer Jakab, *The Revolution That Wasn't: GameStop, Reddit, and the Fleecing of Small Investors* (Portfolio, 2022).

17. On the social psychology of day traders in the pre-Robinhood era, see Alex Preda, *Noise: Living and Trading in Electronic Finance* (University of Chicago Press, 2017).

18. Koray Çalışkan, "Data Money: The Socio-technical Infrastructure of Cryptocurrency Blockchains," *Economy and Society* 49, no. 4 (2020): 540–61. Çalışkan defines data money as "the first money that is created . . . by people who use scientific and designerly competences and without the contribution of banks and states" (543). For a clear and useful presentation of blockchain technologies, see Primavera De Filippi and Aaron Wright, *Blockchain and the Law: The Rule of Code* (Harvard University Press, 2018).

19. Karin Knorr Cetina and Urs Bruegger, "Global Microstructures: The Virtual Societies of Financial Markets," *American Journal of Sociology* 107, no. 4 (2002): 905–50; Pardo-Guerra, *Automating Finance*.

20. On the importance of narrative to economics and finance, see Beckert, *Imagined Futures;* Alex Preda, *The Spectacle of Expertise: Why Financial Analysts Perform in the Media* (Columbia University Press, 2023); Robert J. Shiller, *Narrative Economics: How Stories Go Viral and Drive Major Economic Events* (Princeton University Press, 2019); and Nigel Thrift, "'It's the Romance, Not the Finance, That Makes the Business Worth Pursuing': Disclosing a New Market Culture," *Economy and Society* 30, no. 4 (2001): 412–32.

21. For the longer history of "digital cash" and public key cryptography, see Finn Brunton, *Digital Cash: The Unknown History of the Anarchists, Utopians, and Technologists Who Created Cryptocurrency* (Princeton University Press, 2019).

22. Igor Makarov and Antoinette Schoar, "Blockchain Analysis of the Bitcoin Market" (NBER Working Paper 29396, National Bureau of Economic Research, October 2021), https://www.nber.org/papers/w29396.

23. Geoffrey Ingham, *The Nature of Money* (Polity, 2004).

24. Stefan Eich, "Old Utopias, New Tax Havens: The Politics of Bitcoin in Historical Perspective," in *Regulating Blockchain: Techno-social and*

Legal Challenges, ed. Philipp Hacker, Ioannis Lianos, Georgios Dimitropoulos, and Stefan Eich (Oxford University Press, 2019), 85–98. Adam Tooze, "Chartbook Newsletter #15: Talking (and Reading) about Bitcoin," Chartbook, March 3, 2021, https://adamtooze .substack.com/p/chartbook-newsletter-15, is rather more blunt: "To paraphrase [Antonio] Gramsci, crypto is the morbid symptom of an interregnum, an interregnum in which the gold standard is dead but a fully political money that dares to speak its name has not yet been born. Crypto is the libertarian spawn of neoliberalism's ultimately doomed effort to depoliticize money."

25. Vitalik Buterin, *Proof of Stake: The Making of Ethereum and the Philosophy of Blockchains,* ed. Nathan Schneider (Seven Stories Press, 2022).

26. David Golumbia, *The Politics of Bitcoin: Software as Right-Wing Extremism* (University of Minnesota Press, 2016).

27. Kyle Chayka, "The Promise of DAOs, the Latest Craze in Crypto," *New Yorker,* January 28, 2022, https://www.newyorker.com/culture/infinite -scroll/the-promise-of-daos-the-latest-craze-in-crypto; Nathan Schneider, *Everything for Everyone: The Radical Tradition That Is Shaping the Next Economy* (Bold Type Books, 2018).

28. "The Charm of Cryptocurrencies for White Supremacists," *Economist,* February 5, 2022.

29. Pistor, *The Code of Capital.*

30. Andrejevic, *Infoglut,* 63.

31. Laura Bear, "Speculation: A Political Economy of Technologies of Imagination," *Economy and Society* 49, no. 1 (2020): 1–15; Feher, *Rated Agency;* Aris Komporozos-Athanasiou, *Speculative Communities: Living with Uncertainty in a Financialized World* (University of Chicago Press, 2022).

32. Dan Davies, *Lying for Money: How Legendary Frauds Reveal the Workings of Our World* (Scribner, 2021); Matthew Levine, "The Stability of Algorithmic Stablecoins," Bloomberg, April 19, 2022, https://www .bloomberg.com/opinion/articles/2022-04-19/the-stability-of-algorithmic -stablecoins.

33. Robert Z. Aliber and Charles P. Kindleberger, *Manias, Panics, and Crashes: A History of Financial Crises,* 7th ed. (Palgrave Macmillan, 2015).

34. Donald MacKenzie, *An Engine, Not a Camera: How Financial Models Shape Markets* (MIT Press, 2006); Robert J. Shiller, *Irrational Exuberance*, 3rd ed. (Princeton University Press, 2016); Susan Strange, *Casino Capitalism* (Manchester University Press, 2015).

35. From that point of view, the politics of crypto very much resembles Friedrich Hayek's views on the benefits of a competitive system of private monies. There is one key difference, however. As Stefan Eich, "Old Utopias," shows, Hayek mostly imagined a system of competing bank-issued currencies. Writing after the 2008 financial crisis, Satoshi Nakamoto's ambition was instead to bypass both the state and the banking system, since neither could be trusted. Hence the rhetorical emphasis on bitcoin as a "trustless" infrastructure. F. A. Hayek, *Denationalisation of Money: An Analysis of the Theory and Practice of Concurrent Currencies* (Institute of Economic Affairs, 1977).

36. Nathan Schneider, "Cryptoeconomics as a Limitation on Governance," OSF, August 22, 2021, 3, https://osf.io/dzasq/?view_only=a10581ae9a8 04aa197ac39ebbba05766.

37. Jimmy Wales, "'You Can't Ban Blockchain. It's Math': A Talk with Jimmy Wales," interview by Catherine Ross, Cointelegraph, June 11, 2018, https://cointelegraph.com/news/you-can-t-ban-blockchain-it-s -math-a-talk-with-jimmy-wales.

38. Lana Swartz, "What Was Bitcoin, What Will It Be? The Techno-economic Imaginaries of a New Money Technology," *Cultural Studies* 32, no. 4 (2018): 623.

39. Christian Borch, *Social Avalanche: Crowds, Cities and Financial Markets* (Cambridge University Press, 2020). See also John Maynard Keynes, *The General Theory of Employment, Interest, and Money* (Harcourt Brace, 1936); André Orléan, *Le pouvoir de la finance* (Odile Jacob, 1999); Shiller, *Irrational Exuberance;* and Charles W. Smith, *The Mind of the Market: A Study of Stock Market Philosophies, Their Uses, and Their Implications* (Rowman and Littlefield, 1981).

40. Trevor Jackson, "The Crypto Crisis," *Dissent* online, August 8, 2022, https://www.dissentmagazine.org/online_articles/the-crypto-crisis/.

41. Lynette Shaw, "The Inevitable Sociality of Money: The Primacy of Practical Affirmation over Conceptual Consensus in the Construction of Bitcoin's Economic Value," *Socio-economic Review* 21, no. 1 (2023): 51–78.

42. The company Larva Labs gave nine thousand of its ten thousand minted CryptoPunks for free (with the exception of so-called gas fees, or the fees for minting them, which were around eleven cents apiece at the time). The founders kept the remaining one thousand Crypto-Punks, hoping the price would go up, which it did for a time, before crashing.

43. Evgeny Morozov, "Web3: A Map in Search of Territory," Crypto Syllabus, January 13, 2022, https://the-crypto-syllabus.com/web3-a -map-in-search-of-territory/.

44. Paul Kiernan, "Crypto Legislation Could Undermine Market Regulations, Gensler Says," *Wall Street Journal,* June 14, 2022.

45. Pistor, *The Code of Capital.*

46. The 2022 complaint in Underwood v. Coinbase, 21 Civ. (PAE 2022), argues,

> Other digital assets are similar to traditional securities in that they represent one's investment in a project that is to be undertaken with the funds raised through the sale of the tokens. Like traditional securities, investors purchase these tokens with the hope that their value will increase as the issuer that created the token uses its managerial efforts to create some use—typically described to investors in a "whitepaper"—that will give the token value. This similarity with traditional securities is enhanced by the fact that these tokens are offered to the public in an Initial Coin Offering ("ICO") that is modeled on the IPO of a traditional security.

See also Securities and Exchange Commission v. Binance Holdings Limited, No. 1:23-cv-01599 (2023); and Securities and Exchange Commission v. Coinbase, Inc,1:23-cv-4738 (2023).

47. Eric Lipton and David Yaffe-Bellany, "Crypto Industry Helps Write, and Pass, Its Own Agenda in State Capitols," *New York Times,* April 10, 2022; "Crypto Lobbying Is Going Ballistic," *Economist,* December 7, 2021.

48. Peter Thiel, "PayPal Co-founder Peter Thiel—Bitcoin Keynote—Bitcoin 2022 Conference," video, 26:21, YouTube, https://www.youtube .com/watch?v=ko6K82pXcPA.

49. Jackson, "The Crypto Crisis."

50. Tabby Kinder and Richard Waters, "Peter Thiel's Fund Wound Down 8-Year Bitcoin Bet before Market Crash," *Financial Times*, January 18, 2023. As Jackson, "The Crypto Crisis," notes, familiar scams include wash trades, where "traders anonymously buy and sell NFTs and coins to themselves, to drive prices up" and pump and dump, where new entrants are attracted to the market so they can absorb the incumbents' overvalued holdings before the burst of the bubble.

51. Ian Bogost, "The Internet Is Just Investment Banking Now," *Atlantic*, February 4, 2022, https://www.theatlantic.com/technology/archive /2022/02/future-internet-blockchain-investment-banking/621480/. For the term *hyperfinancialization,* see Stephen Diehl, "Web3 Is Bullshit," blog post, December 4, 2021, https://www.stephendiehl.com /blog/web3-bullshit.html.

52. Rex Woodbury, "What Happens When You're the Investment," *Atlantic*, November 29, 2021, https://www.theatlantic.com/ideas /archive/2021/11/financialization-everything-investment-system -token/620804/.

53. An example would be the replacement of the state by the crypto network. See Balaji Srinivasan, *The Network State: How to Start a New Country* (1729, 2022).

6. The Road to Selfdom

1. Marshall Berman, *The Politics of Authenticity: Radical Individualism and the Emergence of Modern Society* (Atheneum, 1972), ix–x.

2. Zuboff, *The Age of Surveillance Capitalism.* The literature on privacy is enormous; see especially Danielle Citron, *The Fight for Privacy: Protecting Dignity, Identity, and Love in the Digital Age* (W. W. Norton, 2022); Helen Nissenbaum, *Privacy in Context: Technology, Policy, and the Integrity of Social Life, Privacy in Context* (Stanford University Press, 2009); Pasquale, *The Black Box Society*; Daniel J. Solove, *Understanding Privacy* (Harvard University Press, 2008); Ari Ezra Waldman, *Industry Unbound: The Inside Story of Privacy, Data, and Corporate Power* (Cambridge University Press, 2021); and Ari Ezra Waldman, *Privacy as Trust: Information Privacy for an Information Age* (Cambridge University Press, 2018).

3. Igo, *The Known Citizen;* Waldman, *Industry Unbound.*

4. See, e.g., Erving Goffman, *The Presentation of Self in Everyday Life* (Anchor, 1959); and Jean-Paul Sartre, *Being and Nothingness: An Essay in Phenomenological Ontology,* trans. Sarah Richmond (Routledge, 2018).

5. Gina Neff and Dawn Nafus, *Self-Tracking* (MIT Press, 2016).

6. Nora A. Draper and Joseph Turow, "The Corporate Cultivation of Digital Resignation," *New Media and Society* 21, no. 8 (2019): 1824–39.

7. Rogers Brubaker, "Digital Hyperconnectivity and the Self," *Theory and Society* 49, no. 5 (2020): 771–801; Harcourt, *Exposed;* Schwarz, *Sociological Theory for Digital Society.*

8. Breckenridge, *Biometric State;* Jordan Brensinger and Gil Eyal, "The Sociology of Personal Identification," *Sociological Theory* 39, no. 4 (2021): 265–92.

9. Sherry Turkle, *Life on the Screen: Identity in the Age of the Internet* (Simon and Schuster, 1997).

10. Sheera Frenkel and Cecilia Kang, *An Ugly Truth: Inside Facebook's Battle for Domination* (HarperCollins, 2021), traces the original idea to Mark Zuckerberg's high school years at the prestigious boarding school Phillips Exeter Academy, where he had first come into contact with an online student directory. Zuckerberg formally developed Facebook while he was a student at Harvard University as a place where students could "waste time" and freely share loads of information with each other (and, incidentally, the site manager and engineers).

11. Amelia Lester, "Show Your Best Face," *Harvard Crimson,* February 17, 2004.

12. Charlie Cheever, quoted in Alexis C. Madrigal, "Before It Conquered the World, Facebook Conquered Harvard," *Atlantic,* February 4, 2019, https://www.theatlantic.com/technology/archive/2019/02/and-then -there-was-thefacebookcom/582004/.

13. Madrigal, "Before It Conquered the World."

14. Alice E. Marwick and danah boyd, "I Tweet Honestly, I Tweet Passionately: Twitter Users, Context Collapse, and the Imagined Audience," *New Media and Society* 13, no. 1 (2011): 114–33.

15. Lyon, *Identifying Citizens;* John C. Torpey, *The Invention of the Passport: Surveillance, Citizenship and the State* (Cambridge University Press, 2018); Tabby Kinder, "Worldcoin's Premise Is a Disturbing One." *Financial Times,* July 31, 2023, https://www.ft.com/content/59b09c99 -2c46-4d23-b861-5d520a85162c.

16. David Lyon, *The Electronic Eye: The Rise of Surveillance Society* (University of Minnesota Press, 1994); Joseph Turow, *The Voice Catchers: How Marketers Listen In to Exploit Your Feelings, Your Privacy, and Your Wallet* (Yale University Press, 2021).

17. "The telos of practices of personal identification is not one way toward a future of precise identifiability. There is of course also pressure in the other direction, toward a degree of imprecision and anonymity." Brensinger and Eyal, "The Sociology of Personal Identification," 572.

18. Finn Brunton and Helen Nissenbaum, *Obfuscation: A User's Guide for Privacy and Protest* (MIT Press, 2015); Francis Tseng, "Monkey-wrenching the Machine," *Logic(s),* December 1, 2017, https://logicmag .io/justice/monkeywrenching-the-machine/.

19. Sarah K. Cowan, "Secrets and Misperceptions: The Creation of Self-Fulfilling Illusions," *Sociological Science* 1, no. 26 (2014): 466–92.

20. Pasquale, *The Black Box Society.*

21. Harcourt, *Exposed.*

22. David Lyon, *The Culture of Surveillance: Watching as a Way of Life* (Polity, 2018), 14.

23. Sartre, *Being and Nothingness.*

24. Alice E. Marwick, *The Private Is Political: Networked Privacy and Social Media* (Yale University Press, 2023).

25. Sarah Brayne, *Predict and Surveil: Data, Discretion, and the Future of Policing* (Oxford University Press, 2020), 37–55.

26. Forrest Stuart, *Ballad of the Bullet: Gangs, Drill Music, and the Power of Online Infamy* (Princeton University Press, 2020); Marwick, *The Private Is Political,* 6. On the practice of Black online identity more generally, see André Brock Jr., *Distributed Blackness: African American Cybercultures* (New York University Press, 2020).

27. An example is businesses that operate on both sides of the reputation market, trashing people's online reputations so they can make money from repairing them. See Aaron Krolik and Kashmir Hill, "The Slander Industry," *New York Times,* April 24, 2021.

28. European Parliament, General Data Protection Regulation (GDPR), Eur-Lex, April 27, 2016, https://eur-lex.europa.eu/legal-content/EN /TXT/?uri=celex%3A32016R0679; see especially Article 17, "Right to Erasure (Right to Be Forgotten)."

29. Abigail C. Saguy, *Come Out, Come Out, Whoever You Are* (Oxford University Press, 2020).

30. Hill, "Wrongfully Accused by an Algorithm." This of course extends to the ability of private companies to surveil government leaders (as was the case with the Israeli firm NSO), which gives them considerable political power. See Chorev, "The Political Economy of Surveillance-for-Hire."

31. Ivan Illich, *Deschooling Society* (Harper and Row, 1971), 93.

32. Marshall McLuhan, "Living in an Acoustic World" (lecture, University of South Florida, 1970), https://marshallmcluhanspeaks.com/lectures -panels/living-in-an-acoustic-world.

33. William Davies, "The Problem of Trust in the Digital Public Sphere" (lecture, University of California–Berkeley Social Science Matrix, February 24, 2022), https://matrix.berkeley.edu/research-article/the -problem-of-trust-in-the-digital-public-sphere/.

34. Hwang, *Subprime Attention Crisis;* Wu, *The Attention Merchants.*

35. Andrejevic, *Infoglut,* 128.

36. In "On Television" (1952), an acerbic W. E. B. Du Bois writes: "I can think of splendid entertainment and education through television, but it will never come so long as the main object of television is, as it seems to be now, the entertainment of stupid people and the making of profits by almost compulsory methods of sales promotion." *The Complete Works of W. E. B. DuBois,* vol. 4, *Writings by Du Bois in Periodicals Edited by Others,* ed. Herbert Aptheker. (Kraus-Thompson, 1982), chapter 54.

37. Wendy Brown, *Undoing the Demos: Neoliberalism's Stealth Revolution* (Zone Books, 2017); Jen Schradie, *The Revolution That Wasn't: How*

Digital Activism Favors Conservatives (Harvard University Press, 2019); Astra Taylor, *The People's Platform: Taking Back Power and Culture in the Digital Age* (Henry Holt, 2014). Brown discusses the pivotal role of the US Supreme Court's *Citizens United* decision, which prohibited restrictions in political spending by corporations.

38. Zuboff, *The Age of Surveillance Capitalism.*

39. Angèle Christin, *Metrics at Work: Journalism and the Contested Meaning of Algorithms* (Princeton University Press, 2020).

40. Burrell and Fourcade, "The Society of Algorithms"; William Davies, "Elite Power under Advanced Neoliberalism," *Theory, Culture and Society* 34, nos. 5-6 (2017): 227-50; Henry Farrell and Marion Fourcade, "The Moral Economy of High-Tech Modernism," *Daedalus* 152, no. 1 (2023): 225-35.

41. In the deregulatory fever of the 1990s, the US Congress helpfully backed these positions as the debate over the future of the telecommunications industry unfolded. See Cohen, *Between Truth and Power;* and Gerstle, *The Rise and Fall of the Neoliberal Order,* 165-73.

42. Hannah Arendt, *Between Past and Future* (Penguin, 2006), 252.

43. Gil Eyal, *The Crisis of Expertise* (Polity, 2019).

44. Andrejevic, *Automated Media;* Marion Fourcade and Fleur Johns, "Loops, Ladders and Links: The Recursivity of Social and Machine Learning," *Theory and Society* 49, no. 5 (2020): 803-32.

45. Francesca Bolla Tripodi, *The Propagandists' Playbook: How Conservative Elites Manipulate Search and Threaten Democracy* (Yale University Press, 2022).

46. Chris Bail, *Breaking the Social Media Prism: How to Make Our Platforms Less Polarizing* (Princeton University Press, 2021).

47. Daniel Steven Griffin, "Situating Web Searching in Data Engineering: Admissions, Extensions, Repairs, and Ownership" (PhD diss., University of California–Berkeley, 2022).

48. David Weinberger, *Too Big to Know: Rethinking Knowledge Now That the Facts Aren't the Facts, Experts Are Everywhere, and the Smartest Person in the Room Is the Room* (Basic Books, 2012).

49. C. Wright Mills, *White Collar* (Oxford University Press, 1951); David Reisman, Nathan Glaser, and Reuel Denney, *The Lonely Crowd: A Study of the Changing American Character* (Yale University Press, 2001); William H. Whyte, *The Organization Man* (Simon and Schuster, 1956).

50. W. E. B. Du Bois, *The Souls of Black Folk: With "The Talented Tenth" and "The Souls of White Folk"* (Penguin, 1996); Frantz Fanon, *Black Skin, White Masks* (Grove Weidenfeld, 1991).

51. Axel Honneth, *The Struggle for Recognition: The Moral Grammar of Social Conflicts* (Polity, 1995); Keeanga-Yamahtta Taylor, ed., *How We Get Free: Black Feminism and the Combahee River Collective* (Haymarket Books, 2012); Iris Marion Young, *Justice and the Politics of Difference* (Princeton University Press, 1990).

52. Brian Judge, "The Birth of Identity Biopolitics: How Social Media Serves Antiliberal Populism," *New Media and Society* (2022), https://doi.org/10.1177/14614448221099587.

53. A good example is the Italian Movimento Cinque Stelle (Five Star Movement, or M5S). See Giuliano da Empoli, *Les ingénieurs du chaos* (Paris: Lattes, 2019). See also Paolo Gerbaudo, "Social Media and Populism: An Elective Affinity?," *Media, Culture and Society* 40, no. 5 (2018): 745–53.

54. Rogers Brubaker, *Hyperconnectivity and Its Discontents* (Polity, 2022).

55. James Dale Davidson and William Rees-Mogg. *The Sovereign Individual: Mastering the Transition to the Information Age* (Touchstone, 1999).

56. Davidson and Rees-Mogg, *The Sovereign Individual*, 256.

57. Alison Hearn, "Verified: Self-Presentation, Identity Management, and Selfhood in the Age of Big Data," *Popular Communication* 15, no. 2 (2017): 62–77.

7. Ordinal Citizenship

1. John Meyer, "The Evolution of Modern Stratification Systems," in *Social Stratification,* ed. David B. Grusky (Westview, 2000), 881–90.

2. T. H. Marshall, *Citizenship and Social Class, and Other Essays* (Cambridge University Press, 1950), 11.

3. For C. B. MacPherson, *possessive individualism* is the "conception of the individual as essentially the proprietor of his own person or capacities, owing nothing to society for them. The individual was seen neither as a moral whole, nor as part of a larger social whole, but as an owner of himself." MacPherson, *The Political Theory of Possessive Individualism: Hobbes to Locke* (Oxford University Press, 1962), 3.

4. Margaret R. Somers, *Genealogies of Citizenship: Markets, Statelessness, and the Right to Have Rights* (Cambridge University Press, 2008).

5. Fraser, "From Redistribution to Recognition?"; Christian Joppke, "Transformation of Citizenship: Status, Rights, Identity," *Citizenship Studies* 11, no. 1 (2007): 37–48.

6. Evelyn Glenn, "Citizenship and Inequality: Historical and Global Perspectives," *Social Problems* 47, no. 1 (2000): 1–20; Uday S. Mehta, "Liberal Strategies of Exclusion," *Politics and Society* 18, no. 4 (1990): 427–54.

7. Irene Bloemraad, "Theorising the Power of Citizenship as Claims-Making," *Journal of Ethnic and Migration Studies* 44, no. 1 (2018): 4–26; Christian Joppke, "The Inevitable Lightening of Citizenship," *European Journal of Sociology / Archives Européennes de Sociologie* 51, no. 1 (2010): 9–32; Will Kymlicka and Wayne Norman, "Return of the Citizen: A Survey of Recent Work on Citizenship Theory," *Ethics* 104, no. 2 (1994): 352–81; Angus Stewart, "Two Conceptions of Citizenship," *British Journal of Sociology* 46, no. 1 (1995): 63–78.

8. On failures, see Morgan G. Ames, *The Charisma Machine: The Life, Death, and Legacy of One Laptop per Child* (MIT Press, 2019); and Daniel Greene, *The Promise of Access: Technology, Inequality, and the Political Economy of Hope* (MIT Press, 2021).

9. Somers, *Genealogies of Citizenship.*

10. Marshall, *Citizenship and Social Class,* 11.

11. Marshall, *Citizenship and Social Class,* 55.

12. Margaret R. Somers and Fred Block, "From Poverty to Perversity: Ideas, Markets, and Institutions over 200 Years of Welfare Debate," *American Sociological Review* 70, no. 2 (2005): 260–87.

13. Daniel Bell, "Meritocracy and Equality," *Public Interest,* Autumn 1972, 41.

14. Randall Collins, *The Credential Society: An Historical Sociology of Education and Stratification* (Columbia University Press, 2019).

15. Pierre Bourdieu, "Cultural Reproduction and Social Reproduction," in *Knowledge, Education, and Cultural Change: Papers in the Sociology of Education,* ed. Richard Brown (Taylor and Francis, 1973), 71–84; Pierre Bourdieu and Jean-Claude Passeron, *Reproduction in Education, Society and Culture,* trans. Richard Nice (Sage, 1977); James S. Coleman, *Equality of Educational Opportunity (Summary Report),* vol. 1 (US Department of Health, Education, and Welfare, Office of Education, 1966).

16. Marshall, *Citizenship and Social Class,* 65.

17. Michael Young, *The Rise of the Meritocracy* (Routledge, 2017).

18. Raj Chetty, David Grusky, Maximilian Hell, Nathaniel Hendren, Robert Manduca, and Jimmy Narang, "The Fading American Dream: Trends in Absolute Income Mobility since 1940," *Science* 356, no. 6336 (2017): 398–406; Frederick J. Zimmerman and Nathaniel W. Anderson, "Trends in Health Equity in the United States by Race / Ethnicity, Sex, and Income, 1993–2017," *JAMA Network Open* 2, no. 6 (2019): e196386.

19. Daniel Markovits, *The Meritocracy Trap: How America's Foundational Myth Feeds Inequality, Dismantles the Middle Class, and Devours the Elite* (Penguin, 2019).

20. Thomas Piketty, *Capital and Ideology* (Belknap Press, 2020).

21. Bell, "Meritocracy and Equality," 40.

22. Daniel Hirschman, Ellen Berrey, and Fiona Rose-Greenland, "Dequantifying Diversity: Affirmative Action and Admissions at the University of Michigan," *Theory and Society* 45, no. 3 (2016): 265–301.

23. Lyon, *Electronic Eye,* 32, 33; Nicholas Abercrombie, Stephen Hill, and Bryan S. Turner, *Sovereign Individuals of Capitalism* (Allen and Unwin, 1986).

24. Marion Fourcade, "Ordinal Citizenship," *British Journal of Sociology* 72, no. 2 (2021): 154–73; Greta R. Krippner, "Democracy of Credit: Ownership and the Politics of Credit Access in Late Twentieth-Century America," *American Journal of Sociology* 123, no. 1 (2017): 1–47.

25. Greta R. Krippner and Daniel Hirschman, "The Person of the Category: The Pricing of Risk and the Politics of Classification in

Insurance and Credit," *Theory and Society* 51, no. 5 (2022): 685–727; Greta R. Krippner, "Unmasked: A History of the Individualization of Risk," *Sociological Theory* 41, no. 2 (2023): 83–104.

26. Christian Joppke, "From Liberal to Neoliberal Citizenship: A Commentary on Marion Fourcade," *British Journal of Sociology* 72, no. 2 (2021): 181–89; Margaret R. Somers, "Dedemocratizing Citizenship: How Neoliberalism Used Market Justice to Move from Welfare Queening to Authoritarianism in 25 Short Years," *Citizenship Studies* 26, nos. 4–5 (2022): 661–74.

27. Jacob S. Hacker, *The Great Risk Shift: The New Economic Insecurity and the Decline of the American Dream,* 2nd ed. (Oxford University Press, 2019).

28. Jonathan J. B. Mijs and Mike Savage, "Meritocracy, Elitism and Inequality," *Political Quarterly* 91, no. 2 (2020): 397–404.

29. Nicholas Lemann, *The Big Test: The Secret History of the American Meritocracy* (Macmillan, 2000).

30. Porter, *Trust in Numbers.*

31. Fabien Accominotti and Daniel Tadmon, "How the Reification of Merit Breeds Inequality: Theory and Experimental Evidence" (Working Paper 42, International Inequalities Institute, London School of Economics and Political Science, March 2020), https://core.ac.uk /download/pdf/293753365.pdf.

32. Eubanks, *Automating Inequality;* Luke Henriques-Gomes, "Welfare Suspensions Increase by 40% under New Compliance Regime," *Guardian,* February 19, 2019; Hettie O'Brien, "Revealed: How Citizen-Scoring Algorithms Are Being Used by Local Government in the UK," *New Statesman,* July 15, 2019; Cathy O'Neil, *Weapons of Math Destruction: How Big Data Increases Inequality and Threatens Democracy* (Crown, 2016).

33. Linsey Nicole Edwards, "Time and Efficacy: Neighborhoods, Temporal Constraints, and the Persistence of Poverty" (PhD diss., Princeton University, 2018); Issa Kohler-Hausmann, *Misdemeanorland: Criminal Courts and Social Control in an Age of Broken Windows Policing* (Princeton University Press, 2018); Loïc Wacquant, *Punishing the Poor: The Neoliberal Government of Social Insecurity* (Duke University Press, 2009).

34. In 2021, the city of Rotterdam accidentally leaked training data for its 315-variable welfare fraud detection system to a team of data journalists. For the previous four years, the city had used a machine learning model to generate risk scores for thirty thousand benefit recipients in the city. The top 10 percent in this ranking were automatically selected for investigation. It turned out that being a woman, having children, or not speaking Dutch well all increased fraud risk. See Justin-Casimir Braun, Eva Constantaras, Htet Aung, Gabriel Geiger, Dhruv Mehrotra, and Daniel Howden, "Suspicion Machines Methodology," Lighthouse Reports, March 6, 2023, https://www.lighthousereports.com/suspicion -machines-methodology.

35. Shamus Khan, "States against Citizens: On the (Limited) Value of Market Citizenship," *British Journal of Sociology* 72, no. 2 (2021): 190–95.

36. John Skrentny, *The Minority Rights Revolution* (Belknap Press, 2004).

37. Judith N. Shklar, *American Citizenship: The Quest for Inclusion* (Harvard University Press, 1991).

38. As Margaret Somers, "Margaret Somers in Conversation with Daniel Hirschman," *Sociologica* 16, no. 1 (2022): 159, asserts, "however much we conceive ourselves as 'rights-bearers,' from a sociological perspective rights are not individual possessions. . . . Rights are better understood as the subject positions we occupy temporarily in shifting institutional and social arrangements."

39. Elisabeth Anderson, "Experts, Ideas, and Policy Change: The Russell Sage Foundation and Small Loan Reform, 1909–1941," *Theory and Society* 37, no. 3 (2008): 271–310; Carruthers, *The Economy of Promises*; Mark Kear, "Governing Homo Subprimicus: Beyond Financial Citizenship, Exclusion, and Rights," *Antipode* 45, no. 4 (2013): 926–46; Krippner, "Democracy of Credit"; Chloe N. Thurston, *At the Boundaries of Homeownership: Credit, Discrimination, and the American State* (Cambridge University Press, 2018); Gunnar Trumbull, "Credit Access and Social Welfare: The Rise of Consumer Lending in the United States and France," *Politics and Society* 40, no. 1 (2012): 9–34.

40. Daniela Gabor and Sally Brooks, "The Digital Revolution in Financial Inclusion: International Development in the Fintech Era," *New Political Economy* 22, no. 4 (2017): 423–36.

41. Solon Barocas, Moritz Hardt, and Arvind Narayanan, *Fairness and Machine Learning,* Fairmlbook.org, 2019, https://fairmlbook.org/.

42. Bernard E. Harcourt, "Risk as a Proxy for Race: The Dangers of Risk Assessment," *Federal Sentencing Reporter* 27, no. 4 (2015): 237–43; Barbara D. Underwood, "Law and the Crystal Ball: Predicting Behavior with Statistical Inference and Individualized Judgment," *Yale Law Journal* 88, no. 7 (1979): 1408.

43. Solon Barocas and Andrew D. Selbst, "Big Data's Disparate Impact," *California Law Review* 104, no. 3 (2016): 671–732; Board of Governors of the Federal Reserve System, *Report to the Congress on Credit Scoring and Its Effects on the Availability and Affordability of Credit* (Federal Reserve System, August 2007); Andreas Fuster, Paul Goldsmith-Pinkham, Tarun Ramadorai, and Ansgar Walther, "Predictably Unequal? The Effects of Machine Learning on Credit Markets," *Journal of Finance* 77, no. 1 (2022): 5–47; Davon Nicholas Norris, "How All Data Became Credit Data: The Logic of Scoring and the Limits to Racial Inclusion in an Algorithmic Age" (PhD diss., Ohio State University, 2022).

44. Ellis P. Monk, "Inequality without Groups: Contemporary Theories of Categories, Intersectional Typicality, and the Disaggregation of Difference," *Sociological Theory* 40, no. 1 (2022): 3–27.

45. Benjamin, *Race after Technology*; Simone Browne, *Dark Matters: On the Surveillance of Blackness* (Duke University Press, 2015); Julien Migozzi, "Apartheid by Algorithm," *Logic(s),* August 22, 2022, https://logicmag.io/home/apartheid-by-algorithm/.

46. Orlando Patterson, "Culture and Continuity: Causal Structures in Socio-cultural Persistence," in *Matters of Culture: Cultural Sociology in Practice,* ed. Roger Friedland and John Mohr (Cambridge University Press, 2004), 71–109. We emphasize that "residual" here is purely a statistical concept. The analogy comes from the concept of the residual in theories of economic growth, which refers to the portion of economic growth that cannot be attributed to the growth in production factors (capital and labor). Classically, Robert Solow interpreted it as being the effect of technological change. See Robert Solow, "Technical Change and the Aggregate Production Function," *Review of Economics and Statistics* 39, no. 3 (1957): 312–20. In our case, the

residual refers to group differences that are the compounded result of these groups' entire (relational) history. It manifests as a persistent gap that no assortment of individualized measures, no matter how precise, can manage to erase.

47. It is in the less solidaritistic societies, such as the United States, that people tend to blame themselves more for their failure to succeed. See Victor Tan Chen, *Cut Loose: Jobless and Hopeless in an Unfair Economy* (University of California Press, 2015); Ofer Sharone, *Flawed System / Flawed Self: Job Searching and Unemployment Experiences* (University of Chicago Press, 2013); and Cathy O'Neil, *The Shame Machine: Who Profits in the New Age of Humiliation* (Crown, 2022).

48. Barry Schwartz, "Queues, Priorities, and Social Process," *Social Psychology* 41, no. 1 (1978): 3–12.

49. Friedrich Nietzsche, *On the Genealogy of Morals,* ed. Robert C. Holub, trans. Michael A. Scarpitti (Penguin Classics, 2014).

50. This is a common option in the financial domain. See Kear, "Governing Homo Subprimicus"; Jeanne Lazarus, "Financial Literacy Education: A Questionable Answer to the Financialization of Everyday Life," in *The Routledge International Handbook of Financialization,* ed. Philip Mader, Daniel Mertens, and Natascha van der Zwan (Routledge, 2020), 390–99; and Frederick F. Wherry, Kristin S. Seefeldt, and Anthony S. Alvarez, *Credit Where It's Due: Rethinking Financial Citizenship* (Russell Sage Foundation, 2019).

51. Meyer, "The Evolution of Modern Stratification Systems," 889.

52. On the notion that metrics foster competition, see David Beer, *Metric Power* (Palgrave Macmillan, 2016); and Wendy Nelson Espeland and Michael Sauder, *Engines of Anxiety: Academic Rankings, Reputation, and Accountability* (Russell Sage Foundation, 2016).

53. Friedrich A. Hayek, *The Constitution of Liberty* (University of Chicago Press, 1978), 96.

54. Kiviat, "Going against the Record."

55. Taina Bucher, "Want to Be on the Top? Algorithmic Power and the Threat of Invisibility on Facebook," *New Media and Society* 14, no. 7 (2012): 1164–80; TaskRabbit Support. "Elite Status Overview," October

9, 2023, https://support.taskrabbit.com/hc/en-us/articles/179584422 41933-Elite-Status-Overview.

56. Feher, *Rated Agency;* Steffen Mau, *The Metric Society: On the Quantification of the Social* (Polity, 2019); Malte Ziewitz, "Rethinking Gaming: The Ethical Work of Optimization in Web Search Engines," *Social Studies of Science* 49, no. 5 (2019): 707–31.

57. Dubal, "On Algorithmic Wage Discrimination," 40.

58. Hatim A. Rahman, "The Invisible Cage: Workers' Reactivity to Opaque Algorithmic Evaluations," *Administrative Science Quarterly* 66, no. 4 (2021): 945–88.

59. Brian Merchant, "Uber and Lyft's 'Deactivation' Policy Is Dehumanizing and Unfair. It Must End," *Los Angeles Times,* February 28, 2023.

60. Boelaert and Ollion, "The Great Regression." See also Chris Anderson, "The End of Theory: The Data Deluge Makes the Scientific Method Obsolete," *Wired,* June 23, 2008, https://www.wired.com/2008/06/pb -theory/.

61. Kai-Fu Lee, *AI Superpowers: China, Silicon Valley, and the New World Order* (Harper Business, 2018), 113.

62. Herbert A. Simon, *The Sciences of the Artificial* (MIT Press, 2019).

63. James Somers, "How the Artificial Intelligence Program AlphaZero Mastered Its Games," *New Yorker,* December 28, 2018, https://www .newyorker.com/science/elements/how-the-artificial-intelligence -program-alphazero-mastered-its-games.

64. Carlie Porterfield, "Grandmaster at Center of Chess World Scandal Likely Cheated More Than 100 Times, Investigation Finds," *Forbes,* October 4, 2022, https://www.forbes.com/sites/carlieporterfield/2022 /10/04/grandmaster-at-center-of-chess-world-scandal-likely-cheated -more-than-100-times-investigation-finds/?sh=6fd6d6f6681e.

65. Karen Levy, *Data Driven: Truckers, Technology, and the New Workplace Surveillance* (Princeton University Press, 2022).

66. See Madison Van Oort, *Worn Out: How Retailers Surveil and Exploit Workers in the Digital Age and How Workers Are Fighting Back* (MIT Press, 2023), which reports similar strategies in the fast fashion business.

67. Lindsey D. Cameron, "Making Out While Driving: Relational and Efficiency Games in the Gig Economy," *Organization Science* 33, no. 1 (2022): 231–52; Sophia Galière, "When Food-Delivery Platform Workers Consent to Algorithmic Management: A Foucauldian Perspective," *New Technology, Work and Employment* 35, no. 3 (2020): 357–70; Mark Kear, "Playing the Credit Score Game: Algorithms, 'Positive' Data and the Personification of Financial Objects," *Economy and Society* 46, nos. 3–4 (2017): 346–68. The three-pronged conceptual scheme (exit, voice, loyalty) is from Albert O. Hirschman, *Exit, Voice, and Loyalty: Responses to Decline in Firms, Organizations, and States* (Harvard University Press, 1970).

68. Feher, *Rated Agency*; Lilly C. Irani and M. Six Silberman, "Turkopticon: Interrupting Worker Invisibility in Amazon Mechanical Turk," in *CHI '13: Proceedings of the SIGCHI Conference on Human Factors in Computing Systems* (Association for Computing Machinery, 2013), 611–20; Brian Merchant, *Blood in the Machine: The Origins of the Rebellion against Big Tech* (Little, Brown, 2023); O'Neil, *Weapons of Math Destruction*.

69. Tung-Hui Hu, *Digital Lethargy: Dispatches from an Age of Disconnection* (MIT Press, 2022).

70. C. Thi Nguyen, "How Twitter Gamifies Communication," in *Applied Epistemology*, ed. Jennifer Lackey (Oxford University Press, 2021), 410–36; Natasha Dow Schüll, "Data for Life: Wearable Technology and the Design of Self-Care," *BioSocieties* 11, no. 3 (2016): 317–33.

71. Amoore, *Cloud Ethics*.

72. State Council of China, "State Council's Notice on the Issuance of the Outline of the Construction Plan for the Social Credit System," June 14, 2014, http://www.gov.cn/zhengce/content/2014-06/27/content_8913 .htm; Kai Strittmatter, *We Have Been Harmonized: Life in China's Surveillance State* (Custom House, 2020).

73. Carliss Y. Baldwin and Kim B. Clark, *Design Rules: The Power of Modularity* (MIT Press, 2000); Rose, *Powers of Freedom*.

74. Schüll, "Data for Life"; Zuboff, *The Age of Surveillance Capitalism*.

75. Originally formulated by British economist Charles Goodhardt in the context of monetary policy and generalized as Goodhardt's law, the

adage states that "when a measure becomes a target, it ceases to be a good measure." See Marilyn Strathern, "'Improving Ratings': Audit in the British University System," *European Review* 5, no. 3 (1997): 308.

76. Open Science Collaboration, "Estimating the Reproducibility of Psychological Science," *Science* 349 (2015): aac4716; "Retraction for Shu et al., Signing at the Beginning Makes Ethics Salient and Decreases Dishonest Self-Reports in Comparison to Signing at the End," *Proceedings of the National Academy of Sciences* 118 no. 38 (2021): e2115397118; "Retraction of Gino et al. (2020)," *Journal of Personality and Social Psychology* 125, no. 3 (2023): 648.

77. Brooke Erin Duffy, Annika Pinch, Shruti Sannon, and Megan Sawey, "The Nested Precarities of Creative Labor on Social Media," *Social Media and Society* 7, no. 2 (2021), https://doi.org/10.1177/20563051211021368.

78. This is what Brubaker, *Hyperconnectivity and Its Discontents,* 147, calls the "post-neoliberal self," or the "self governed not in and through its choices, but in and through automated procedures that make choice unnecessary or impossible." See also Hu, *Digital Lethargy.*

79. Bruno Latour and Couze Venn, "Morality and Technology," *Theory, Culture and Society* 19, nos. 5–6 (2002): 247–60.

80. Evgeny Morozov, "Silicon Valley Is Turning Our Lives into an Asset Class," *Financial Times,* March 13, 2014.

Conclusion

1. Georg Simmel, "How Is Society Possible?," trans. Kurt H. Wolff, in *Georg Simmel on Individuality and Social Forms,* ed. Donald N. Levine (University of Chicago Press, 1971), 6–22.

2. Pierre Bourdieu, *Pascalian Meditations,* trans. Richard Nice (Stanford University Press, 2000), 198–205.

3. Michael Burawoy, *Manufacturing Consent: Changes in the Labor Process under Monopoly Capitalism* (University of Chicago Press, 1982).

4. Bourdieu, *Pascalian Meditations,* 202.

5. Thomas Nagel, *The View from Nowhere* (Oxford University Press, 1986).

6. Nicholas Carr, *The Shallows: What the Internet Is Doing to Our Brains* (W. W. Norton, 2010); Nitsan Chorev, "The Virus and the Vessel, or: How We Learned to Stop Worrying and Love Surveillance," *Socio-economic Review* 19, no. 4 (2021): 1497–513; Marion Fourcade, "The Fly and the Cookie: Alignment and Unhingement in 21st-Century Capitalism," *Socio-economic Review* 15, no. 3 (2017): 661–78; Mau, *The Metric Society;* Nguyen, "How Twitter Gamifies Communication"; Natasha Dow Schüll, *Addiction by Design: Machine Gambling in Las Vegas* (Princeton University Press, 2012).

7. Marion Fourcade, "The Unbearable Rightness of Being Ranked," *British Journal of Sociology* 72, no. 2 (March 2021): 203–6.

8. Espeland and Sauder, *Engines of Anxiety,* 1.

9. In British academia, where departmental excellence rankings have been implemented since the 1980s, administrators and faculty alike understand them as an acceptable and legitimate game that is part and parcel of the academic vocation. As Juan Pablo Pardo-Guerra, *The Quantified Scholar: How Research Evaluations Transformed the British Social Sciences* (Columbia University Press, 2022), 5, notes, "If quantification holds a strong grip over the work of British academics—and those elsewhere exposed to the countless metrics of modern scholarly work—it is because scholars collectively come to accept and reproduce cultures of repute, overwork, and sacrifice connected to the ideals of research in science."

10. Anemona Hartocollis and Eliza Fawcett, "As More Top Law Schools Boycott Rankings, Others Say They Can't Afford to Leave," *New York Times,* November 18, 2022.

11. Ralf Herbrich, Tom Minka, and Thore Graepel, "TrueSkill(TM): A Bayesian Skill Rating System," in *Advances in Neural Information Processing Systems,* vol. 20, ed. John C. Platt, Daphne Koller, Yoram Singer, and Sam T. Roweis, (MIT Press, 2007), 569–76.

12. Marie Bergström, *The New Laws of Love: Online Dating and the Privatization of Intimacy* (John Wiley and Sons, 2021); Elizabeth E. Bruch and M. E. J. Newman, "Aspirational Pursuit of Mates in Online Dating Markets," *Science Advances* 4, no. 8 (2018): eaap9815.

13. Marion Fourcade, "The Will to Progress and the Twofold Truth of Capital," in *Destabilizing Orders—Understanding the Consequences of Neoliberalism; Proceedings of the MaxPo Fifth-Anniversary Conference, Paris, January 12–13, 2018,* ed. Jenny Andersson and Olivier Godechot (Max Planck Sciences Po Center on Coping with Instability in Market Societies, 2018), 92–96.

14. Linsey McGoey, "Philanthrocapitalism and Its Critics," *Poetics* 40, no. 2 (2012): 185–99.

15. Fred Turner, "Don't Be Evil: Fred Turner on Utopias, Frontiers, and Brogrammers," *Logic(s),* December 1, 2017, https://logicmag.io/justice/fred-turner-dont-be-evil/.

16. Steven Shapin, *The Scientific Life: A Moral History of a Late Modern Vocation* (University of Chicago Press, 2008), 294. On the concepts of "feeling rules" and "emotional labor," see Arlie Russell Hochschild, *Managed Heart: Commercialization of Human Feeling* (University of California Press, 1983).

17. Marc Andreessen, quoted in Alessandra Stanley, "Silicon Valley's New Philanthropy," *New York Times,* October 31, 2015.

18. Sam Altman (@sama), Twitter February 19, 2023, 8:00 p.m., https://twitter.com/sama/status/1627110889508978688?lang=en.

19. Jack Dorsey (@jack), Twitter, April 25, 2022, 10:03 p.m., https://twitter.com/jack/status/1518772756069773313?lang=en.

20. Brooke Erin Duffy, *(Not) Getting Paid to Do What You Love: Gender and Aspirational Labor in the Social Media Economy* (Yale University Press, 2022); Rebecca Lewis and Angèle Christin, "Platform Drama: Cancel Culture, Celebrity, and the Struggle for Accountability on YouTube," *New Media and Society* 24, no. 7 (2022): 1632–56; O'Neil, *The Shame Machine.*

21. Jesse Eisinger, "How Mark Zuckerberg's Altruism Helps Himself," *New York Times,* December 3, 2015.

22. Ben Williamson, "Silicon Startup Schools: Technocracy, Algorithmic Imaginaries and Venture Philanthropy in Corporate Education Reform," *Critical Studies in Education* 59, no. 2 (2018): 219.

23. Marion Fourcade, "The Great Online Migration: COVID and the Platformization of American Public Schools," in *Pandemic Exposures:*

Economy and Society in the Time of Coronavirus, ed. Didier Fassin and Marion Fourcade (HAU Books, 2021), 345–67.

24. Juan Manuel del Nido, *Taxis vs. Uber: Courts, Markets, and Technology in Buenos Aires* (Stanford University Press, 2021).

25. For Mises, spending and voting are both ways of choosing freely between available alternatives, but the former compels beneficial adjustments that the latter can afford to ignore. As Mises, *Human Action: A Treatise on Economics* (Ludwig Von Mises Institute, 1998), 271, notes,

> With every penny spent the consumers determine the direction of all production processes and the minutest details of the organization of all business activities. This state of affairs has been described by calling the market a democracy in which every penny spent gives the right to cast a ballot. It would be more correct to say that a democratic constitution is a scheme to assign to the citizens in the conduct of government the same supremacy the market economy gives them in their capacity as consumers. However, the comparison is imperfect. In the political democracy only the votes cast for the majority candidate or the majority plan are effective in shaping the course of affairs. The votes polled by the minority do not directly influence politics. But on the market no vote is cast in vain. Every penny spent has the power to work upon the production process.

The reference in Mises's text ("calling the market a democracy in which every penny spent gives the right to cast a ballot") is to Frank Albert Fetter, *The Principles of Economics: With Applications to Practical Problems* (Century, 1911).

26. Brown, *Undoing the Demos;* Rob Van Horn, "Reinventing Monopoly and the Role of Corporations: The Roots of Chicago Law and Economics," in *The Road from Mont-Pèlerin: The Making of the Neoliberal Thought Collective,* ed. Philip Mirowski and Dieter Plehwe (Harvard University Press, 2009), 204–37.

27. Mises, *Human Action.*

28. Casey Newton, "Yes, Elon Musk Created a Special System for Showing You All His Tweets First," *The Verge,* February 15, 2023, https://www.theverge.com/2023/2/14/23600358/elon-musk-tweets-algorithm-changes-twitter.

29. Carolyn Chen, *Work Pray Code: When Work Becomes Religion in Silicon Valley* (Princeton University Press, 2022).

30. Raymond Craib, *Adventure Capitalism: A History of Libertarian Exit, from the Era of Decolonization to the Digital Age* (PM Press, 2022); Douglas Rushkoff, *Survival of the Richest: Escape Fantasies of the Tech Billionaires* (W. W. Norton, 2022); Slobodian, *Crack-Up Capitalism.*

31. Krishan Kumar, *Prophecy and Progress: The Sociology of Industrial and Post-industrial Society* (Penguin, 1991), 13.

32. F. A. Hayek, "The Religion of the Engineers: Enfantin and the Saint Simonians," in *The Counter-Revolution of Science: Studies in the Abuse of Reason* (Free Press, 1955), 143–55.

33. William Easterly, *The White Man's Burden: Why the West's Efforts to Aid the Rest Have Done So Much Ill and So Little Good* (Penguin, 2006); Scott, *Seeing Like a State.*

34. Gueorgi Kossinets and Duncan Watts, "Empirical Analysis of an Evolving Social Network," *Science* 311, no. 5757 (2006): 88–90.

35. Elizabeth Popp Berman, *Creating the Market University: How Academic Science Became an Economic Engine* (Princeton University Press, 2011); Philip Mirowski, *Science-Mart: Privatizing American Science* (Harvard University Press, 2011). The dilemma of the Maussian bargain extends to conventional norms of science, too. For example, free and open-source tools for data analysis, together with open standards for reproducibility and data sharing, have never been more important in social science. But at the same time, the potential career returns to obtaining exclusive access to some private source of large-scale social data have never been greater.

36. Alexandra Heal and Philip Stafford, "How FTX Plans to Reshape the US Futures Market with Crypto Tech," *Financial Times,* July 20, 2022.

37. Emily M. Bender, Angelina McMillan-Major, Timnit Gebru, and Shmargaret Shmitchell [*sic*], "On the Dangers of Stochastic Parrots: Can Language Models Be Too Big?," in *FAccT '21: Proceedings of the 2021 ACM Conference on Fairness, Accountability, and Transparency* (Association for Computing Machinery, 2021), 610–23.

38. The fascination with out-of-control artificial intelligence is, unfortunately, not something we can treat in depth here. It is part of a mixture of concerns that have attracted the attention of the very wealthy, all of which involve seeking to avoid the end of the world, either personally (by finding a way to cheat death), in the medium term (by preparing to escape somewhere remote but well provisioned in the event of sudden civilizational collapse), or as a service to everyone (by making sure the robots do not take over). The insistence that this last problem is the most urgent and rational thing to spend time and money on is shared by many crypto celebrities, tech billionaires, internet autodidacts, and academic philosophers associated with the effective altruism movement. To its advocates this group represents the flower of contemporary, high-powered rational thought on the shape of the future. More skeptical observers have labeled it "IQ-Anon."

39. Karen Hao, "OpenAI Is Giving Microsoft Exclusive Access to Its GPT-3 Language Model," *MIT Technology Review,* September 23, 2022, https://www.technologyreview.com/2020/09/23/1008729/openai-is-giving-microsoft-exclusive-access-to-its-gpt-3-language-model/.

40. Todd McGowan, *Capitalism and Desire: The Psychic Cost of Free Markets* (Columbia University Press, 2016); Mosco, *The Digital Sublime,* 11. See also Carruthers, *The Economy of Promises.*

41. Fourcade and Johns, "Loops, Ladders and Links."

42. Wu, *The Master Switch.*

43. Julian Gruin, "The Epistemic Evolution of Market Authority: Big Data, Blockchain and China's Neostatist Challenge to Neoliberalism," *Competition and Change* 25, no. 5 (2020), https://doi.org/10.1177/1024529420965524.

44. Marion Fourcade and Kieran Healy, "Rationalized Stratification," in *Social Stratification,* 5th ed., ed. Nima Dahir, Claire Daviss, and David B. Grusky (Routledge, forthcoming).

45. E.g., the fields of fairness, accountability, and transparency in machine learning, critical artificial intelligence, and law and technology. In policy, see US Office of Science and Technology Policy, "Blueprint for an AI Bill of Rights," The White House, https://www.whitehouse.gov/

ostp/ai-bill-of-rights/. Meanwhile, critiques of the privatized internet are legion. See Cory Doctorow, *The Internet Con: How to Seize the Means of Computation* (Verso, 2023); Rebecca MacKinnon, *Consent of the Networked: The Worldwide Struggle For Internet Freedom* (Basic Books, 2013); Morozov, "Socialize the Data Centres!"; Ben Tarnoff, *Internet for the People: The Fight for Our Digital Future* (Verso, 2022).

46. Frank Pasquale, *New Laws of Robotics: Defending Human Expertise in the Age of AI* (Belknap Press, 2020).

47. Fabien Accominotti, "The Aesthetics of Hierarchy," *British Journal of Sociology* 72, no. 2 (2021): 196–202.

Acknowledgments

THIS BOOK WAS WRITTEN DURING THE COVID-19 PANDEMIC BY two people generally separated by the width of a continent but able to remotely meet and write thanks to tools that are at once technically remarkable and, by now, roundly disliked by millions. The ideas and arguments in it were developed over a longer period, so much so that it would be impossible to name everyone who contributed at one point or another. Our first thanks must go to the collaborators with whom our thinking on various parts of this project was formed: Alexander Barnard, Jenna Burrell, Henry Farrell, Jeffrey Gordon, Fleur Johns, Daniel Kluttz, and Alexander Roehrkasse. Patrick Chanezon, Henry Farrell, and William Janeway read the whole manuscript and provided generous, detailed, and insightful comments. Two anonymous reviewers for Harvard University Press also gave valuable feedback. For comments on particular parts of the manuscript, we thank Bart Bonikowski, Clayton Childress, Paul DiMaggio, Pierre-Olivier Gourinchas, Wang Jing, Jeanne Lazarus, Nicolas Lainez, Steven Lukes, Marek Mikuš, Liz Morgan, Horacio Ortiz, Federico Neiburg, Fareen Parvez, Erica Robles Anderson, Claire Sieffert, Sameer Srivastava, Iddo Tavory, and Ariel Wilkis. Elsewhere, we benefited from conversations with danah boyd, Jason

Ferguson, Greta Krippner, Jim Moody, Christopher Muller, Georg Rillinger, Sarah Quinn, Steve Vaisey, and Zeynep Tufekci. Special thanks are owed to Timothy Ahn, Thomas Haseloff, David Joseph-Goteiner, and Nataliya Nedzhvetskaya for their research assistance on this and related projects. None of them is responsible for any errors that remain in spite of their efforts.

At various times, audiences at the annual meetings of the American Sociological Association, the Society for the Advancement of Socio-Economics, and the Society for the Social Studies of Science provided helpful feedback. We also thank seminar audiences at the Center for Advanced Study in the Behavioral Sciences at Stanford University, Columbia University, the Hamburger Institut für Sozialforschung, the Harvard Kennedy School, Humboldt University, the Kellogg School of Management at Northwestern University, the Max Planck Institute for the Study of Societies, the New School for Social Research, New York University, Stanford University, the University of Arizona, the University of Bern, the University of Lucerne, the University of Notre Dame, and the University of Toronto.

Research supporting part of this project was funded by the National Science Foundation. We thank Michel Feher for planting the idea of a book after coming across some of our writing. At Harvard University Press we thank Ian Malcolm for his enthusiasm in initiating this project, Andrew Kinney and Grigory Tovbis for calmly but surely seeing it through to completion, and Brian Bendlin for his skilled and efficient copyediting.

MARION FOURCADE IS GRATEFUL for salutary inducements to get things done. Putting together a syllabus is a rarely acknowledged, but essential, source of intellectual nourishment, as is teaching. Much exploration and discovery has taken place through conversations with graduate students at the University of California–Berkeley and the University of Lucerne. Invitations to give the 2015 Lewis Coser Lecture of the Theory Section of the American Sociological Association, the 2019 lecture for the *British Journal of Sociology,* and the 2022 Siegfried Landshut Prize Lecture at the Hamburger Institut für Sozialforschung forced painful, but productive, moments of focused writing that ultimately benefited this manuscript. I also owe a great deal of gratitude to Didier Fassin for his invitation to bask in the tranquil atmosphere and intellectual energy of the Institute for Advanced Study during the 2019–2020 academic year. Much was learned from him, as well as from Alondra Nelson and visiting members in the School of Social Science. The self-organized working groups on "credit and debt" (Benjamin Braun, Arnaud Fossier, Isabelle Guérin, Lena Lavinas, Benjamin Lemoine, Susana Narotzky, Federico Neiburg, Horacio Ortiz, Fareen Parvez, Sarah Quinn, Chloe Thurston, and Frederick Wherry) and "digital society" (Ergin Bulut, Alexander Galloway, Fleur Johns, and Horacio Ortiz) were invaluable sources of knowledge, collegiality, and inspiration. Informal conversations with colleagues and friends at these institutions and elsewhere—too many to enumerate—have yielded countless insights that have made their way into the manuscript.

Kieran Healy has been a friend and a writing partner for almost two decades. For the better part of the last two years, we have met over Zoom several times a week. As I am writing these acknowledgments, this is where we are. It is difficult to imagine that these meetings are about to stop. They have been woven into my life to the point where they feel natural and expected, much like coffee in the morning. And yet they never were very natural to begin with. We often joke that our temperaments and intellectual dispositions differ on many dimensions. And so, it is a testament to the strength of our friendship and to the mutually generative nature of our collaboration that we were able to write this book in a way that does justice to our different inclinations. Hopefully the reader will feel that way, too.

I must close my portion of these acknowledgments with the essential backstage. My parents and my brothers in France, who know very little of the ordinalization of life, have kept me grounded and sane. My friends across the Atlantic, who know a bit more, have mercifully done the same. I am grateful that our pandemic bubble is still holding strong. Pierre-Olivier Gourinchas is the perennial source of strength and joy and complicity in my life. He is surely relieved that I have moved to another topic, though I am sorry to say that my slightly morbid fascination with the world of economics that he so elegantly inhabits still abides. It is very much present in this book.

KIERAN HEALY THANKS his colleagues and students at Duke University—in particular Chris Bail, Mark Chaves, Ashley

Harrell, Scott Lynch, Jim Moody, Craig Rawlings, Lynn Smith-Lovin, Steve Vaisey, and Chris Wildeman. In addition to being colleagues, in their role as department chairs Eduardo Bonilla-Silva, Jen'nan Read, and Martin Ruef were consistently supportive. Thanks also to Sam Anthony, Sarah Bagby, Dave Barber, Carin Calabrese, Steve Cook, Rose Curtin, Andrea Deeker, Greg Freed, Matt Harvey, Josh Kamensky, Ari Kelman, Matt Maguire, Ben Monreal, Eric Rauchway, Matt Reece, Marilee Scott, and Vera Tobin—the latter specifically for naming and making precise the Tobin Unit, which quantifies how much a manuscript must change for progress to have been made on any given day.

Marion Fourcade and I have been friends and coauthors for many years. She has spent most of that time patiently waiting for me to write the thing I promised her. I thank her for her forbearance as a research collaborator, and for her unfailing generosity as a friend. I thank my family, both in America and in Ireland, for their support and encouragement. My mother was of immense practical help at some key moments despite the fact that her son has the cheek to keep her grandchildren overseas. I am sad that my father did not live to see this book. I thank Liz Morgan for her singular wit, her unstinting heart, and her terrible cats.

WRITING ABOUT A FUTURE still being made in the present is a dangerous business, perhaps a foolish one. But it is the future we must face, and so it is there we turn for our dedication. Julie is almost as old as the World Wide Web, and Magda was born just before social media. Aoife and Finbarr lived long stretches of their teenage years through the seemingly endless screen time that COVID-19 imposed across the country. Their lives have given each of us insights about the rise of the ordinal society, and compelling reasons to think about it as clearly as we are able. This book is for them.

Index